THE MAN WHO BELIEVED HE
WAS KING OF FRANCE

TOMMASO DI CARPEGNA FALCONIERI
TRANSLATED BY WILLIAM McCUAIG

The Man Who Believed

He Was King of

𝕱rance

A True Medieval Tale

THE UNIVERSITY OF CHICAGO PRESS   *Chicago & London*

TOMMASO DI CARPEGNA FALCONIERI
is director of studies in medieval history at the University of Urbino and head of
courses in methodology of historical research and the history of the Middle Ages.
His publications include, most recently, *Il clero di Roma nel medioevo: Istituzioni e
politica cittadina (secoli VIII–XIII)* (2002) and *Cola di Rienzo* (2002).

WILLIAM MCCUAIG
has translated more than a dozen books from Italian and French, most recently *What's the
Use of Truth?* (2007) by Pascal Engel and Richard Rorty, and *A Day in a Medieval City* (2005),
by Chiara Frugoni, the latter published by the University of Chicago Press.

The University of Chicago Press, Chicago 60637
The University of Chicago Press, Ltd., London
© 2008 by The University of Chicago
All rights reserved. Published 2008
Printed in the United States of America

Originally published as *L'uomo che si credeva re di Francia: Una storia
medievale*. Copyright © 2005, Gius. Laterza & Figli. All rights reserved.

Illustration on p. i: reproduction of the coat of arms of "King" Giannino.

Map of Europe and genealogical charts prepared by Dick Gilbreath at the Gyula Pauer
Center for Cartography & GIS at the University of Kentucky, Lexington.

17 16 15 14 13 12 11 10 09 08   1 2 3 4 5

ISBN-13: 978-0-226-14525-9 (cloth)
ISBN-10: 0-226-14525-5 (cloth)

Library of Congress Cataloging-in-Publication Data

Di Carpegna Falconieri, Tommaso.
[Uomo che si credeva re di Francia. English]
The man who believed he was king of France : a true medieval tale / Tommaso di Carpegna
Falconieri ; translated by William McCuaig.
p. cm.
Includes bibliographical references and index.
ISBN-13: 978-0-226-14525-9 (cloth : alk. paper)
ISBN-10: 0-226-14525-5 (cloth : alk. paper) 1. Europe—Kings and rulers—History. 2. Europe—
History—476–1492. 3. Imposters and imposture—Europe. I. Title.
D107.D5213 2005
944'.024092—dc22
[B]
2008020061

⊗ The paper used in this publication meets the minimum requirements of the American National
Standard for Information Sciences—Permanence of Paper for Printed Library Materials, ANSI
Z39.48-1992.

To Father, dedicated to the study of language
To Mother, who loves history and fairytale

CONTENTS

·◁═▷·

PREFACE

(2005)

·◁▷·

I encountered Giannino (his name is actually a diminutive of Giovanni) for the first time in a codex in the Vatican Library while I was
trawling through works that had nothing to do with him. He then
turned up in a manuscript in the Bibliothèque Nationale in Paris,
while I was researching the life of the Roman tribune Cola di Rienzo.
Something drew me to Giannino, and I promised myself that one day
I would explore his story.

The merchant from Siena who believed that he was the king
of France was a man of the fourteenth century, a small man full of
intrigue and stubbornness, but also an ingenuous man, firmly convinced of the rightfulness of his claim, for which he abandoned a life
of ease and security and threw himself into a crazy adventure in various parts of Europe. He wandered among the courts of the princes
of Christendom, and sometimes got thrown into their prisons, and
everywhere he went—Italy, Hungary, France—he met lords and soldiers, innkeepers and merchants, clerics and confidence men of many
nationalities, with all of whom he entered into a complex web of relationships. This alone would have made him worth rediscovering.

Giannino's story is so absurd that it has been considered a literary
invention, like the *Novella del Grasso legnajuolo* (The Tale of Grasso
the Woodworker) or Pirandello's *Enrico IV.* Nevertheless, just as it
is certain that Giannino was *not* the king of France (because, apart
from anything else, he never succeeded in becoming so), it is likewise
certain that a Sienese merchant who claimed the Capetian crown for
himself really did exist.

The sources available to us for reconstructing his strange career
are atypical, and they have come down to us through complex channels of manuscript tradition and erudite interpretation. For this rea-

son, too, the challenge of trying to solve the puzzle of Giannino was worth taking up.

Actually, he is of interest for many other reasons as well. I think of him as an individual on the borderline, because his life unfolds along the frontier between two areas that are central to medieval studies: the sacrality of royal power and the commercial culture of the merchant—the frontier, so to speak, between the Île-de-France and Tuscany.

The merchant who tried to make himself into a king is not the only caprice of history which seems to have an endless capacity for leaving us stunned with amazement. But he is an apogee of sorts, because in Giannino's life truth and lies, essence and appearance are always interwoven, in a whirl of authentic, false, or nonexistent documents, of revelations, claims, inventions and intrigues, of factual record, memory, and literature. A medieval dreamer, Giannino inspires both fascination and melancholy.

PREFACE TO THE AMERICAN EDITION

(2008)

·〈══〉·

In the interval between the publication of the original Italian edition and this English version, I have had occasion to correct various minor errors (especially as regards the exact identification of a number of persons and places), and to do some further reading on the topic, all of which has been integrated into the notes and bibliography. One difference worth noting is the identification of the last place in which "King Giannino" was imprisoned: it was Castel dell'Ovo at Naples, and not Castel Nuovo (otherwise known as the Maschio Angioino), as I had written previously.

Who knows what the reaction of "King Giannino" would have been if he could have known that one day his story would cross the Atlantic Ocean and alight in a continent of whose existence he never even dreamed? I imagine him both astounded and delighted.

TRANSLATOR'S NOTE

·〈══〉·

I am greatly indebted to the author for all his help. My thanks go to the anonymous vettor as well for a careful review of the translation.

THE MAN WHO BELIEVED HE
WAS KING OF FRANCE

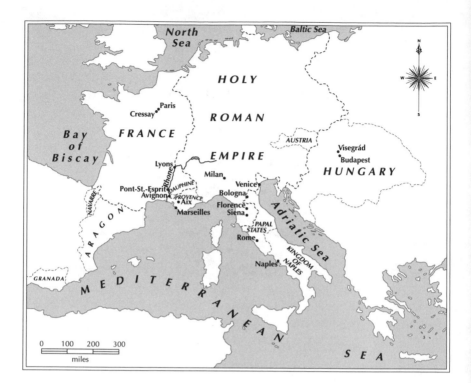

Europe in 1360

Chapter One

·⊏━━➤·

At Rome

Questo si è il modo, come fu scambiato lo re Giovanni, figliuolo che fu delo re Luigi, e dela reyna Clementia ragionevole re di' Francieschi, pochi dì doppo la natività sua.

This is the manner in which King Jean, the son of King Louis, and of Queen Clémence, who was rightful king of the French, was switched a few days after his birth.

—Istoria del Re Giannino

COLA DI RIENZO

When the messenger arrived at Siena requesting Giannino di Guccio to go to Rome immediately to confer with Cola di Rienzo, the merchant refused. The courier had not even brought a letter with him, only a message to be delivered orally, and the prudent merchant saw no good reason to trust him. He replied that he did not know Cola and had no business with him.

Everyone was well aware that Cola di Rienzo, who had returned to govern Rome after seven years of incredible adventures, was continually on the lookout for the money he needed to pay for his military campaign against the Colonna. Hadn't he had the condottiere Fra Moriale killed in order to seize his treasury? Wasn't it rumored that the senator, drunk with wine, was in the habit of locking people up in order to extort ransom payments? To go to Rome would be hazardous: at best Giannino would be exposing his purse and his life to the risk of highway robbery along the Via Cassia, and at worst he would be robbed by the very man who had summoned him.

It was early September 1354. Giannino di Guccio, a merchant aged thirty-eight with a wife and children, felt no compulsion to put his life and his wealth at risk through such a reckless act. But Cola di Rienzo wanted to meet with him at any cost. He had been conducting a search throughout Tuscany for some time, and now that he had found the one he was looking for, he had no intention of letting him go. On 22 September a second courier arrived at Siena, this time bearing an official letter dated 18 September in which the senator of the Romans requested Giannino to present himself in person without delay and as unobtrusively as possible.

This document from the Capitol convinced Giannino: he disguised himself as a soldier, complete with a fake beard, and set off for Rome. But his doubts persisted. Being a prudent man, he thought it wise to bring with him Ser Angelo d'Andrea Guidaregli, a notary and his *compare* (which could mean either the godfather of one of his children or the best man at his wedding), whom he trusted implicitly. If he were to find himself embroiled in some shady business, Ser Angelo would certainly know how to get him out of trouble.

He reached Rome on the evening of 2 October and found lodging in the Campo de' Fiori. When night had fallen, he had the innkeeper lead him to the Capitol, where he found Cola di Rienzo at supper. The senator was eating alone at an elevated table, with twelve to sixteen gentlemen seated at other tables. Giannino, still dressed as a soldier, advanced toward the tribune and, doffing his cap, kneeled and held out the letter. Cola di Rienzo immediately commanded him to rise and had the servants lead him to a private room. Shortly thereafter Cola ordered the trumpets to sound the signal that dinner was over and went to join Giannino. The first thing he did was invite him to take off his fake beard, saying "We know very well what you look like."[1]

It was barely two months since Cola di Rienzo had regained power. At the age of forty-one he had lived his life with great intensity, through periods so different from one another that they seemed like a jumble of different lives: the son of an innkeeper and a laundrywoman, he had succeeded in becoming a notary. He could speak and write so well that the people had sent him to Avignon as ambassador to the pope. There he had made friends with the poet Petrarch and had begun his meteoric rise. Seizing power in a bloodless coup, he had governed Rome from May to December 1347. In those glory days he dreamed of restoring the Roman people to their ancient grandeur: he tried to unite the cities of Italy in a league and had himself crowned "Tribunus Augustus," intending to assume the title of emperor the following year. This dream soon fell apart, and before long it had turned into a mirage even fuzzier in outline and ever more remote. Cola fled to the Maiella Mountains, and there he began to frequent a group of heterodox Franciscan friars who were living in seclusion. While reading certain prophetic texts they had in their possession, Cola became convinced that he was the instrument chosen by the Holy Spirit to save the world and guide it toward a new age of purity and perfection. So he went to Bohemia, to the court of Charles IV, the elected but as yet uncrowned Holy Roman Emperor, hoping to be sent to Rome as the emperor's emissary. What he got for his trouble, though, was years of imprisonment, first in a remote city on the Elbe and then, when the pope had succeeded in getting the emperor to hand him over, in a tower of the papal palace at Avignon. Accused of heresy, he might well have been burned at the stake if the sudden death of Pope Clement VI and the election of Innocent VI, who held him in high regard, had not turned the tables in his favor. The new pope was resolved to use Cola, whom the Roman people still adored, to bring the Eternal City back under papal control. So Cola left Avignon to join Cardinal Gil de Albornoz, the legate who was reconquering lost territories in Italy for the papacy. From 1 August 1354, Cola di Rienzo was once again in control of Rome's city government. The pompous and unusual title of Tribune Augustus was abandoned, formally at any rate, and, as regent in the name of the pope, Cola now took the traditional title of senator while the cardinal legate watched carefully from his headquarters at Montefiascone, 80 kilometers to the north.[2]

Cola was tall and corpulent, with a full red beard. Giannino, seated at his side, was a small man with a slender body. His growth had been stunted in his youth, he would say, because of the hard labor he had been forced to perform. Cola asked him to swear to tell the truth. He then questioned Giannino about his own name and that of his father, about his mother's name, and about his birth and his memories of childhood. And when this interrogation was over, the senator himself kneeled down before the merchant and kissed his right foot. When

Giannino protested at this honor, exclaiming "My lord, who am I that you should pay me this reverence?" Cola di Rienzo answered "Not just I but all of Christendom ought to do so, for you are not who you believe yourself to be and have told me you are. Rather, you are the proper and rightful king of France, for you were the son of King Louis and Queen Clémence, and were exchanged for another a few days after your birth."[3]

EPIPHANY

The senator, whom we can well imagine being pleased with the dramatic fashion in which he had revealed to Giannino that he was of royal descent and gratified by the Sienese merchant's surprised reaction, requested him to listen and began to tell his story.

He said that he had received a letter from a certain Friar Antonio, a member of the order of the Augustinian Hermits, which contained a stunning revelation about the king of France. The friar had set out for Rome in order to speak directly to the senator, of whose good reputation he had heard, but had fallen ill at Portovenere in Liguria. Fearing he might die there, he had decided to write Cola instead, in order to get the message entrusted to him by another friar named Giordano to its destination; he had also taken care to translate it from French into the Tuscan dialect.[4] So Cola was relaying the claims of a friar who was in turn passing on a message from another member of his order.

Near Paris, in a place called Cressay, there had lived a noblewoman by the name of Marie, the daughter of Sieur Piquart de Cressay and Dame Éliabel. Guccio di Mino, a Tuscan residing in a castle near Cressay called Neauphle-le-Vieux who was employed in the moneylending firm of his relative Spinello Tolomei, used to spend time with her brothers, who were his hunting companions. On one such hunt he spent several days in the Cressay household, and Marie de Cressay fell in love with the handsome youth. One day she had a servant bring him to her chambers, and there they were married without witnesses. Guccio gave her a ring, promising to keep the wedding a secret, and they consummated the marriage, causing her to become pregnant. When her brothers, who were acting as her guardians in the absence of her deceased father, realized this, they interrogated her.

Marie fearfully confessed everything. The brothers ordered Guccio to leave the area, threatening to kill him if he stayed, because they felt it was beneath them to have a Tuscan commoner for a brother-in-law. But Guccio, disguised as a pilgrim, managed to reveal himself to the servant and with her help to meet Marie to say goodbye. "I shall go back to my own land and remain there briefly before returning," he told her.[5] He urged her to entrust the baby—boy or girl, whichever it might be—to a wet nurse in secret, and to watch over it with care. He in the meantime would take steps to convince Marie's brothers that he would make an acceptable in-law.

But the brothers, who had already promised her to a nobleman of the vicinity and for that reason wanted to keep the matter from becoming public knowledge, sent the girl to give birth in a nunnery in Paris, where the abbess was a relative of theirs. They told her what had happened and asked her to keep Marie there until she gave birth; after that the abbess could dispose of the infant as she saw fit, as long as it disappeared without trace. In the nunnery a male child was duly born to Marie, whom she called Giannino. The abbess chose a wet nurse for him named Amaloth, who lived not far from Cressay and who was supposed to bring him up and pass him off as her nephew.

At just this time, before Amaloth had even left the nunnery with the baby, the queen of France also gave birth to a boy child. There was great rejoicing in Paris, and a search for a wet nurse to supply milk for the new-born prince was immediately launched. The royal bailiffs charged with this task knew that there was a young woman, noble and beautiful, who had just given birth in the nunnery. They went there attended by physicians and searched until they found her. They then forced the abbess to reveal, under oath, who she was. The abbess, greatly distressed, revealed Marie's identity and begged them to leave her alone, so as not to dishonor both her brothers and the nunnery. But the bailiffs needed to act fast, and after consulting the physicians they decided to entrust the king's son to Marie de Cressay to be nursed.

And so Marie became the prince's wet nurse. She and Amaloth shared the same room, one giving her breast to the royal offspring, the other to Giannino. No one else was present. But by chance little

Giannino died while lying in bed beside Amaloth. Marie then took her dead child into her own bed, and gave the king's son, who was alive and flourishing, to Amaloth to suckle. The wet nurse was compelled by threats and promises to go along with this exchange.

Marie then began to wail, expressing all her love for the child she had just lost. The royal bailiffs, the chevaliers, and the ladies in waiting all came running to see what had happened, and found Marie with the newborn baby dead in her arms. Believing that it was the prince (and Marie allowed them to think so), they too began to wail loudly. The deceased child was buried, and Marie left the prince to be wet-nursed by Amaloth, passing him off as her own. Marie had switched one baby for the other not out of special affection for the surviving infant, but on account of her love for Guccio, which was strong enough to make her reason thus: "If Guccio returns from his own land and finds his son dead, he will cease to love me, and I will have lost my honor, my son, and my husband."[6]

But six years passed before Guccio came back to her. Since Marie's brothers had been sent by the king to guard certain territories many days' journey from Paris, the merchant was able to meet his wife, who was living in her family home together with the son of the king of France, who had grown into a beautiful child. "Who is this boy?" Guccio asked, and Marie answered: "This is your son."

Guccio was delighted and spent several days in secret with her. When he left he said to Marie, "See that you send this boy to me in Paris."[7] Several days later Marie did so. But Guccio kept him in Paris for no more than a few days and then sent him to his own native city in Tuscany. Marie never saw either one of them again.

Many years passed, and in 1345 Marie's life was drawing to a close. At that point she summoned Friar Giordano, who was living as a hermit near Cressay. The narrative contained in the letter which Cola di Rienzo had received and was now summarizing for Giannino, shifted at this point from the third person to the first-person viewpoint of Giordano himself:

> And before she died she sent for me, Friar Giordano, a hermit living near Cressay, and made a general confession to me, and

told me the whole story. She imposed on me the task of looking for the child, and, should I find him alive, of immediately
informing the pope and the college of cardinals, and the current
king of France. I was then to reveal all to the man himself, so
that he might be restored to his royal dignity.[8]

After Marie's death, Friar Giordano began trying to trace Guccio. But upon discovering that Guccio was also dead, he gave up, and
remained trapped for several years in a kind of despair, on account
of the fact that he was quite unable to reveal what had happened to
the pope and the king in the absence of any proof. He had no idea
where to find the son of the king, and justified his inaction this way:
"I thought he must be dead, considering that more than half of the
people died in '48."[9]

But evidently the heir to the throne of France had not died in
the great plague of 1348. Friar Giordano, in fact, began to encounter
him in his dreams, kneeling before the king, his father, and begging,
"Father, give me your blessing, for I wish to go to liberate the sepulcher of Christ."[10] The prince began to appear to him every day in
this posture, as soon as the friar fell asleep. So Giordano started to
pray, asking the Lord Jesus Christ to reveal to him a way of finding
this blessed son of the king. After several days of prayers and fast-
ing, Giordano finally dozed off while kneeling before the altar. Then
it seemed to him that he beheld the king's son holding the standard
of the Church in his hands. The royal youth appeared to be saying,
"I will never rest until I have placed this ensign over the gates of
Jerusalem." And he continued, "the sepulcher of Christ must needs
be emancipated and free, and every faithful Christian must be able to
visit it safely."[11]

No sooner had Giordano awoken than he looked around for the
prince, believing that he must be near at hand. Not seeing him, he felt
great sorrow. Then he took counsel with some fellow religious, who
said to him:

You are old and no longer fit for travel. Dispatch someone to
visit all the places between here and Rome. Set down the confes-

sion of the woman in an orderly written document, and then the revelation you have had, so that he whom you send may be well informed when approaching the bishops and the lords of those places to find out if he is alive. And if he is found living, the bishop or lord of the place in which he resides should be urged to make the matter manifest to the pope and his cardinals, and to the king of France who now rules, and to his barons. And if he is not found, you are excused in God's eyes; and say nothing to them about it, for you might be punished for having kept the matter secret for so long.[12]

So this was the reason that Friar Giordano had written a letter to his fellow friar, Antonio, who had often traveled from France to Rome and was acquainted with all the territories that lay between, both entreating and commanding him to set off toward Rome to find out who Guccio di Mino and Spinello Tolomei had been, and to locate the son of the king, thanks to whom "general peace will prevail throughout Christendom, and the Holy Land be regained."[13] Once he had tracked down the prince, Antonio was supposed to alert the bishop or lord of the place in which he found him, so that he might inform the pope immediately. Not knowing the name of the royal offspring, which Marie had been unable to tell him, Giordano wrote to Antonio that the one he sought "will be named Giannino di Guccio, believing himself to be Guccio's son."[14]

Here matters came full circle. Friar Antonio, prevented from continuing his search because of a grave illness which he feared would soon carry him off, had written to Cola di Rienzo to ask him to complete it instead. He confirmed that the mission had been entrusted to him by Friar Giordano, whose disciple Antonio declared himself to be, describing his master as a holy man who had lived "as a hermit in the service of God, eighty years of age or more." Giordano had heard Marie's confession in 1345; at that time the king's son must have been twenty-six or twenty-eight years old.

Friar Antonio's letter was dated 25 August 1354: "That was the feast day of Saint Louis, who was king of France and made the passage [to the Holy Land] several times. And he for whom I am looking is descended from him, and will follow in his footsteps."[15]

Such a prophecy could not have failed to stir Cola di Rienzo, who had a strong faith in dreams, signs, and coinciding dates. When the senator received the letter on 6 September, he spotted the best clue to be found in the narrative: the fact that Guccio had worked for the Tolomei. Since they were a well-known family in Siena, he directed his men to look for Giannino there.

Cola, therefore, was telling Giannino a tale that a dying woman had confessed to a friar, who had written about it to a fellow friar, who in turn had written to him. Giannino hesitated to believe this reconstruction, declaring that he continued to regard himself as the son of Guccio and Monna Maria, just as he had always done; he requested the tribune not to trouble himself any further over the matter. But Cola urged him to overcome his astonishment. He showed him the letter of Friar Antonio, which contained Marie's confession, and "told him of numerous kings who had been switched at birth, being one who had all of ancient history at his fingertips . . . and so many things did the tribune tell him, that Giannino assented."[16]

IMPLICATIONS

In fact, Giannino already knew the story that the king's son had been switched for another baby in the cradle: he had heard it from a French knight whom he calls Francesco Guifredi of Paris, who had fallen ill at Siena while making the pilgrimage to Rome in the jubilee year of 1350 and whom the merchant had visited in hospital and treated with great courtesy. Now Cola di Rienzo was telling him that the prince who had been switched as a babe was none other than—himself. Giannino, who had shown the capacity to earn a lot of money and had held positions of prestige and responsibility, was no fool. But Cola's ability to persuade was exceptional. It was his best and most effective weapon, as he himself well knew. The senator, who had also heard the story previously from other sources when he was in Avignon, probably gave a fuller explanation of the position of King Jean I in the royal house of France, proving to Giannino that he was not only the son of a king, but the king himself, in person. Louis X the Quarrelsome, king of France and Navarre and eldest son of Philippe IV the Fair, had died on 5 June 1316, leaving his second wife, Clémence of Hungary, a member of the Anjou dynasty, pregnant. From the death of Hugues Capet in 996, it was the first time that a king of France had died without leaving a living male heir. A few months after the death of her husband, the queen brought a difficult pregnancy to term, giving birth on 15 November 1316 to a boy child to whom she gave the name Jean, on account of a vow she had made to John the Baptist. Little Jean, known to history as the Posthumous, was thus already king of France (the first to be called Jean) when he emerged from the womb; at that moment France was governed by a regent, his uncle Philippe, count of Poitiers, the brother of Louis X. But the infant only survived for four days, and so at his death the throne was inherited by the regent, who became Philippe V the Long.[17] Now, had Jean survived, he would, past all doubt, have been "the king of France in reason and in right," being the eldest male offspring of King Louis X, who had in turn been the eldest male offspring of Philippe IV the Fair, the heir and successor of Philippe III, the son of King (and Saint) Louis IX.

Giannino and Cola spent the whole night together in conversation. At dawn the senator summed up how they were to proceed. First, Giannino was to be escorted to safety inside the walls of Castel Sant'Angelo. Cola would then write letters to the pope, the emperor, all the kings of Christendom, and the communes and lords of Italy, inviting each of them to send two ambassadors to Rome. To these would be revealed "a great and excellent fact, which will be advantageous to all of Christendom."[18]

Upon the arrival of these representatives, Cola would dress Giannino in royal robes, surround him with Roman princes and barons, and finally reveal him for who he really was. He would request the pope and the other lords to treat with "him who improperly holds the crown of France"[19] and convince him to cede the kingdom to Giannino/Jean in peace and concord. Should the reigning king not agree to this, then the senator would order the commune of Rome with all its forces, together with the allied kings, lords, and communes to move against him and allow Jean to advance into the kingdom of France. Cola and the allies would swear an oath not to give up on their undertaking until the kingdom had been restored to its natural lord. In fact, the senator concluded, Rome is the head of the world and for that reason has the right to recognize who ought to rule in any kingdom, especially the kingdom of France "of which the first king was a Roman, from whom are descended all the kings and royals that there have been in France."[20]

The style in which this claim was couched was pure Cola di Rienzo, displaying his chronic taste for pomp and ceremony, rhetorical emphasis, and spectacular revelations. Political ideas bordering on the fantastic, and political machinations no less imaginary, aimed at planting those ideas in the shifting sands of reality, were not new to Cola either. The main features of his golden period, those few months in 1347 when Cola had believed he could become lord of the world, all returned. Back then he had repeatedly sent magniloquent letters to the leaders of Europe; had summoned two ambassadors from every power to which he wrote, many of whom had responded, initially at least, to his missives; had promised unheard-of revelations which he had gone on to actually pronounce; and had celebrated his own glory with ostentation and arrogance.

His intention now was much the same. He would prepare a solemn pageant, in which the central and decisive moment would be the revelation of the "rightful king of France." Having secretly revealed to Giannino his royal nature, Cola di Rienzo would now declare it publicly before the nations of the earth. The affair would reflect honor on him, as the new prophet who had brought the truth to light. And it would reflect honor on Rome, the city that ruled the world and the repository of imperial power, to which King Jean of France would certainly pay homage.

So in the mind of the man who was called "the last of the Roman tribunes," who was determined to restore to the Eternal City its ancient magnificence, the advantage to be derived from "revealing" the true sovereign of France was perfectly clear. As Cola saw it, France would revert to the status of a vassal kingdom.

But there was much more to it. Even in 1347 Cola di Rienzo, while enamored of Rome and its ancient culture, had already been filled with fiery religiosity and had based both his political program and his faith that he himself was called to hold power on signs from heaven. Now, in 1354, seven years later, even vaster horizons beckoned to him. For some time he had been convinced that he was a prophet, an emissary of the Holy Spirit, perhaps even the equal of such figures as John the Baptist and Francis of Assisi. His mission on earth, which he had discovered in a book entitled *Oraculum Cyrilli* (The Prophecy of Cirillo) composed by Franciscan spirituals under the spell of Joachim of Fiore, was essentially to announce the coming of the new era of perfection, the third age (or age of the Holy Spirit) of Joachimite thought, and to rouse Emperor Charles IV to action. If he saw Charles IV as a bearer of salvation, the role Cola saw for himself was to return to Rome and govern it in the emperor's name, paving the way for the imperial coronation there and compelling the emperor to strive for the reestablishment of universal order, primarily by launching an attack on the carnal church of Avignon. These projects, which he had set out with great oratorical ability and energy in 1350, had cost him a long period of imprisonment. It is highly likely that Cola di Rienzo had had to make a solemn and complete abjuration of any heresy and confess himself a faithful Christian, devoted to the keys of Saint Peter. But even if he had abandoned the beliefs of the followers of Joachim of Fiore, a few fundamental convictions must have remained, above all the notion that the world was in disorder and that it needed to be set right. Indeed, such convictions, far from being the exclusive prerogative of radical groups, were shared by large sectors of society at that time.[21]

For at midpoint in the fourteenth century, there were many who maintained that the world had plunged into chaos. Not that this way of thinking represented a novelty: mankind has often been convinced that those alive at a given moment are living at the worst time in history. But around 1350 such grim sentiments about life appeared to be confirmed by many unequivocal signs that went far beyond things like comets and babies born with two heads. Rich merchants were now going bankrupt after a century of splendor: the collapse of the Bardi and Peruzzi firms marked the end of an epoch. No less painful for Giannino must have been the failure of the Tolomei company, which left his relatives poverty-stricken. Along with financial crisis went demographic crisis. Cities that had expected to go on building walls of increasing diameter for their growing populations were now losing inhabitants. And the inhabitants they did have were restless and turbulent in their attempts to achieve popular governments, for even small artisans and manual laborers now wanted a voice in politics. Nor were the cities able to feed all their citizens, since the food supply was becoming increasingly precarious.

Shortage of bread and abundance of war were like the wings of a triptych, in which the central panel was the scourge of the century— the bubonic plague, which had reappeared in the West after an absence of eight centuries.[22] Arriving from the East in 1347, it spread throughout almost all of Europe in four years, laying low at least a third of the population and leaving behind a sense of despondency and permanent fear in the hearts of the people. From that time forward the plague was to remain endemic in the European population, surfacing periodically in epidemic form during the next four centuries. Even worse than the epidemic of 1348 was the one that would occur fifteen years later, because its main victims would be children and youths. "Free us, O Lord, from plague, famine, and war."

So the idea that there was a fourteenth-century crisis was one that people alive at that time already held. The negative Renaissance image of the Middle Ages sprang from their grim astonishment at what was happening to them, and the memories of it they passed on to their descendants. A question of economics and subsistence, of demography and culture it may have been, but in the eyes of contemporaries the crisis was particularly characterized—and explained—by a handful of situations that told them that the world was askew. The three main ones were that Jerusalem was again in Muslim rather than Christian hands, that the pope was residing at Avignon rather than at Rome, and that two pretenders, both laying claim to the kingdom of France, were waging a bloody contest for the crown.

The conflict that was tearing the kingdom of France apart would later be called the Hundred Years' War. It was caused, in dynastic terms, by the fact that the king of England and the king of France each regarded himself as the legitimate heir of the Capetian crown. This came about because the dynasty founded by Hugues Capet had become extinct in the direct male line when the last son of Philippe IV the Fair had died.[23] His three male offspring had acceded to the throne one after the other without sons who survived them and would have been able to succeed in their turn. In consequence, the crown had been allotted to a cousin, Philippe VI, who was the son of Charles of Valois, called the Landless, the brother of Philippe IV the Fair. Edward III, king of England, however, boasted a much closer blood relationship to the direct Capetian line, since he was the son of Isabelle, the daughter of Philippe the Fair. In France they invoked the Salic law, according to which females could not succeed to the throne of France, whereas the English for their part emphasized the direct line of descent, which from their point of view made Isabelle the heir and allowed her son to rule France as well as England. And so the two contenders, and subsequently their sons and grandsons, fought over the crown of France for over one hundred years (1337–1451). In the end it was kept by the Valois.

Actually, though, a third pretender appeared on the scene for a while: the merchant Giannino di Guccio. If he was really Jean I of France, in other words the firstborn male child of the eldest son of Philippe the Fair, then he ranked higher than either of the two main contenders for succession to the throne.

Returning to the widespread conviction in the fourteenth century that the world had fallen into a state of terrible disorder and that it was necessary to restore it to a condition of peace, we come to the heart of the matter, and we begin to see why Cola di Rienzo had decided to "recognize" Giannino. If we put ourselves for a moment into the world of metapolitical fantasy inside Cola's head, we realize that Giannino represented, in a certain sense, a real trump card, a panacea able to cure all ills.

Cola was utterly convinced that the one thing necessary to heal the world was a "man of destiny." Indeed, he had once been persuaded that he himself was the one who would lead mankind into a better future (and had been regarded as such by many others, Petrarch among them). Then he had transferred the mandate onto the person of Emperor Charles IV, keeping the role of herald and prophet for himself. And now it was the turn of the "king of France."

The fundamental reason that Giannino, alias King Jean, represented yet another man of destiny for Cola di Rienzo was that he would have been in a unique position to reverse the three major political calamities that were afflicting Christendom: the loss of the Holy Sepulcher in Jerusalem, the Avignonese captivity of the papacy, and the war in France. Why would he have been able to accomplish this? First of all because of his dynastic position, which would render the claims of the other pretenders completely unsustainable. The world would be set free from the catastrophe of war, something for which Cola had expressed a desire many years earlier when, on 1 August 1347, he had written to the kings of France and England urging them to peace and harmony.[24] Once recognized as king of France (and supplied with timely advice), Jean would certainly take steps to ensure that the pope should no longer reside at Avignon but rather return to Rome, just as Cola di Rienzo, his old friend Petrarch, and many others with them had been hoping for some time. Finally, the liberation of the Holy Sepulcher: Cola had once expressed his desire to construct an oratory in Jerusalem. On another occasion he had asked to be enrolled in the crusades. But it was Jean's destiny to succeed in the great enterprise by right of blood, inasmuch as he was a direct descendant, through an unbroken chain of consecrated sovereigns, of good king Saint Louis, who had set out on one last crusade and had died in the midst of it. The son of Louis X, Jean I (who bore the same name as one of the sons who had died in infancy of Saint Louis) was the one who would complete the mission of his ancestor. Friar Giordano, who saw things exactly the same way, had repeatedly seen the young man in his dreams in the act of requesting a blessing prior to departing for Jerusalem. And the letter that had reached Cola from Friar Antonio (himself convinced that the son of the king had a salvational role to play) happened to be dated on precisely the feast day of Saint Louis. The senator of Rome was convinced, and said so in writing, that that letter had come to him by the will of God.

Jean I of France, acknowledged in the person of the merchant Giannino di Guccio, would thus be the instrument through which

Christendom would attain peace, the pope would resume his mission at Rome, and the Holy Land would be reconquered from the infidels. And the merit of launching the process of restoration, by placing the true king of France on his throne, would be Cola di Rienzo's. In a world that, wisely governed by its legitimate sovereign, had finally recovered its proper, natural political order, those other sources of bitter distress that all could see, famine and pestilence, would be eliminated.

To what extent were Cola di Rienzo's plans capable of realization? How would those who were affected react? Would the pope heed him? Would the king of France regard Giannino as a noble rival, equal to the king of England, or merely as a clown? The senator of Rome may never even have asked himself these questions: an expert at contriving spectacular intrigues and uttering emphatic declarations, he had never been able to foresee what might follow from his own provocative actions.

SUBSTITUTIONS

Cola regarded Giannino as a successor of sorts in the mission he believed it was his own duty to fulfill, the one who might perhaps succeed where he himself had fallen short. The senator thought of himself not simply as an introductory figure, presenting the story and the main characters to a theater audience, but as the genuine creator of Giannino. In order to make this relationship between Cola di Rienzo and the king of France plain, Cola proposed, during that first night of revelation, when together they sketched their great plans for the future, that his protégé acquire an emblem of his own.

Since the coat of arms of the king of France bore golden lilies against a blue background, King Jean needed to create a standard for himself that derived from the traditional one, but that was also distinctive. Cola proposed that he should personalize it by adding "a *tondo* in the form of a star with twelve rays."[25] The sun's visage would occupy the center of the tondo, and at the tip of each of the twelve rays there would be a star. Each star would stand for one of the twelve peers of France. But what about the sun?

Solar symbolism was already part of Cola di Rienzo's own personal standard, which he displayed for the first time at Pentecost in 1347. On it the sun was shown surrounded by rays ending in stars, a telling device that referred to the tribune himself, who in battle had raised as his standard "his blue coat of arms with a golden sun and silver stars, and with the arms of Rome."[26] The lords of the Guelf party might feature the Angevin lilies on their coat of arms, and those of the Ghibellines the imperial eagle as a sign of their vassalage and devotion to the emperor: King Giannino would hoist aloft the sun of the tribune of Rome. Right at the center of the holy banner of France, the new lily-bearing banner to be carried into battle alongside the oriflamme, there would be an emblem very much like Cola di Rienzo's own. So much alike that Cola—according to what Giannino declared later—bestowed one of his own seals on the merchant from Siena, a seal considered unusable because of a design error (a lily where there should have been a star), so that Giannino could have it copied.

The close relationship that Cola saw between his own venture and that of Giannino was based on another aspect of the tribune's life, which the merchant seems not to have known about. If he had he might not have let himself be convinced so easily. In 1350, when Cola di Rienzo was in Bohemia trying to persuade Charles IV to send him to Rome and getting a cold response to his request, he had decided to play a wild card. Cola had written a long letter to the emperor in which he revealed that he was actually none other than the illegitimate son of Emperor Henry VII, conceived while the emperor was in Rome in 1312.[27] His account was intricate and detailed; the gist of it was that when Henry had come to Rome for his coronation he had stayed incognito for a few weeks in the tavern run by Cola's parents. While Rienzo, the husband, was standing guard at a barricade, his beautiful young wife Maddalena had supposedly given herself to the emperor. Just like Marie, the nurse of little King Jean, Maddalena, the mother of little Nicola, was supposed to have confessed the truth to a priest before dying.

Thus, emboldened by his tall stature and red hair, the typical somatic features of a northern European, Cola di Rienzo had unflinchingly presented himself to the reigning emperor as being of royal blood himself—indeed as being the emperor's own uncle.

No one knows, and probably no one will ever know, whether Cola di Rienzo really believed in his own imperial descent, or whether he simply proffered this revelation for tactical reasons, knowing it to be false. What counts as far as our story is concerned is that the tribune, long before launching the search for Giannino, had already showed himself markedly receptive to stories about members of royal houses not acknowledged by their relatives (stories which for that matter had always been frequent in literature), to the point of electing himself, like a new Saint Alexius, as the protagonist of one of them.[28] Since he was mentally inclined to believe in, or at any rate employ, this plot device (which students of drama call anagnorisis or recognition), it is not surprising that he sought out Giannino. Even the question that might seem most important of all, that is, whether or not Cola di Rienzo believed in Giannino's royal descent, really makes little difference since he would have followed the same course of action in either case. Suppose that the tribune really did believe that he himself was the bastard offspring of Emperor Henry VII, as revealed to him by a priest: that would have made him believe all the more readily that the king of France had been switched for his fellow nursling in the cradle, given that this tale had been related to him by men of God, hermit brothers of holy life, and that he himself had already heard about it when he was living in France. Suppose, on the other hand, that he had never actually believed that he himself was the son of Henry VII: the fact remains that he had uttered this colossal fib. Nothing would have changed in his dealings with Giannino: in either case, he would still have rolled the dice.

Jean of France, exactly like Nicholas of Luxembourg, as Cola would have been called if he really had been the emperor's son, thus had the task of restoring universal peace and order. There was nothing very novel about this idea of reform, of a return to a propitious earlier situation, whether it was ancient Rome, France united under a holy monarch, or the Church in its primitive form.

What was really novel, however, was the fact that the two men who had received this calling were simply a couple of good solid bourgeois. The one who had dreamed of being emperor was a notary, the one who now began to dream of being a king was a merchant. We might almost think we were reading one of those medieval *novelle* (tales) satirizing the bourgeois desire for ennoblement, or Molière's *Bourgeois Gentilhomme* with its burlesque protagonist, poor Monsieur Jourdain.[29] We're not, though: the author of the life of Giannino drops no hint of irony or sarcasm.[30]

Cola, with his ascent from humble beginnings to the status of notary, tribune, knight, and senator, and his longing to be acclaimed emperor, had "got somewhere," as we say. Giannino was born into the merchant class, and, compared to a king or an emperor, he too came from nowhere, a fact that did not, perhaps, displease Cola di Rienzo. Yet the two were very different. The tribune had won power because he had a strong dose of charisma. He could speak to a crowd and convey his ideas, which were attractive to many. Giannino, as a merchant, was more accustomed to managing money than to giving speeches. Yet the power he was meant to attain was that of the monarch of France, the individual who could cure scrofula with a simple touch of his hand.[31]

THE RETURN HOME

Giannino was brought back to the inn in the dead of night by Cola's servants, his fake beard once more in place. There he found Ser Angelo, the notary; they ate together and went to bed when it was already daylight. While he dozed, unable to fall into a deep sleep, two magnificent horses were brought for him, a gift from the senator. When Giannino did get up, he and his traveling companion went to Saint Peter's, where he made a contrite confession, heard mass, and took communion.

On 3 October Giannino spent the whole day as a pilgrim, visiting Santa Maria Maggiore, San Giovanni in Laterano, the abbey of Tre Fontane, and other holy places. In the afternoon he returned to the inn to eat. That evening Cola sent for him and invited him to dine at his own high table, while Ser Angelo ate with the gentlemen below. Giannino, still dressed as a soldier and wearing his fake beard, was served in lordly fashion with vessels of gold and silver, arousing wonder among those present, who asked the notary about him. The latter, though, told them that he could not reveal the identity of the gentleman from Tuscany because he was sworn to secrecy.

After the lavish meal Cola di Rienzo led Giannino to a private room, and they spoke together there for many hours. He told Giannino that he was certain the Colonna had ordered that Cola be killed and asked Giannino to leave next morning for Montefiascone, carrying letters addressed to Cardinal Albornoz asking for his protection.

That same night Cola di Rienzo ordered two copies to be made of Friar Antonio's letter containing Marie's confession, stamping them with his own pendant seal and adding a personal conclusion relating his hunt for, and discovery of, the merchant Giannino. At the end he declared:

> And truly he is the rightful king of France, as seems clear to us from the confession of the woman written down in the said letter, from the age he manifestly has, and from the words revealed to us when we were at Avignon on a visit to our lord the Pope. It certainly does seem clear that he is the son of King Louis, the firstborn son of King Philippe the Fair.[32]

Cola handed both copies over to Giannino, telling him to keep one on his person at all times and to conceal the other in a secure place. After further lengthy discussions, Cola dismissed him. Giannino returned to the inn with Ser Angelo. Next morning, Saturday 4 October, the merchant bid a final farewell to the senator and mounted his horse at around 9 AM.

He went to Saint Peter's and made a confession with the same priest as the day before. Once outside the city, he stopped at a tavern to drink some wine, and there he encountered an armed gang of Tuscans. Giannino was dressed as a soldier and was wearing his fake beard, but one of the gang, who was from Siena, recognized his voice and said to the notary, Ser Angelo:

> Tell Giovanni to get out of here as quickly as he can. If he doesn't leave he could get killed along with the tribune. There

are 200 of us, foot soldiers from Tuscany assigned by the Colonna family to kill the tribune. We have observed Giovanni
entering and leaving the Capitol repeatedly, and standing at the
window of the palazzo together with the tribune. So tell him to
leave if he doesn't want to get killed.[33]

Ser Angelo denied it, but the Sienese insisted he knew him and
urged him to get out of Rome immediately. Giannino then raced back
to Cola to warn him of the imminent danger, suggesting he leave
the Capitol and barricade himself somewhere safer. But the senator
refused and told him to leave. So on the evening of 4 October, Giannino departed from Rome.

He rode all night so that he reached Montefiascone during the
noontime meal next day, when he submitted Cola's request for help
to Cardinal Albornoz. The legate ordered one of his officials, Andrea
Salamoncelli of Lucca, to assemble a force of horsemen and foot soldiers. The next day the cardinal advanced to Orvieto, and Giannino
followed, but without revealing who he really was. Two days later, on
the evening of Wednesday 8 October, the news arrived that the senator had been killed during a street riot. "Wherefore the said Giovanni,
hearing of the death of the tribune, was saddened."[34]

He quickly took his leave of the cardinal and set off for Tuscany
together with the notary, whom he swore to silence concerning all
that had happened. At Arezzo he halted for a while before returning
to Siena. With him, as reminders of the incredible turn events had
taken, he brought a pair of magnificent horses, a defective seal, and
two letters patent from Cola di Rienzo.

Chapter Two

·◁══▷·

At Siena

*Imo si vera destituunt, simulata iungantur; non est mendacio
imputanda simulatio veri adiutrix; ut sis liber ut sis tuus ut sis sal-
vus ut sis bonus, omni ingenio enitendum est.*

Indeed, if real things are missing, let simulated ones be added;
simulation that heightens truth is not to be imputed to mendac-
ity; what you must do is strive with all your might to be free, to
be yourself, to be saved, to be good.

—Francesco Petrarca, *Familiar Letters* 22.5

THE BABE OF FRANCE
AND THE MERCHANT OF SIENA

Giannino son of Guccio son of Mino son of Geri Baglioni: this is how
a conscientious notary would have written out his name, following
the custom, widespread in Italy, of including in a person's own name
those of his father, grandfather, and great-grandfather. Giannino
had never doubted that he belonged to a family of wool merchants
founded by an ancestor, Baglione, whose own name had become the
surname of the lineage. Now all that had changed. His new, extended
genealogical heritage would have made him Jean son of Louis son
of Philippe son of Philippe of France, of the "race" of Saint Louis
and, distantly, of Hugues Capet. But in truth his memories were few:
they needed to be confirmed and fleshed out with memories supplied
by others.

He recalled a fatherless childhood lived, until age nine and a half,
in the village of Cressay with the woman whom he had always naturally believed to be his mother and who perhaps truly had married
the young Guccio in complete secrecy.[1] In 1326 his father Guccio had

had him brought to Paris, promising to send him back to his mother within three days. Marie had let him go reluctantly, fearing she would never see him again. And she was right: the Sienese merchant had equipped a horse with wicker panniers, seeing that the boy was not yet capable of mounting a horse, and had entrusted him to a courier named Giannottino to be carried to Italy. Years later the merchant well remembered the long trip in a pannier, the name of the man who had brought him to what was supposed to be his homeland, the day in early May when he had finally arrived in Siena.

He was taken into the house of his grandfather Mino, who directed him into the calling for which all assumed he was born. The little French boy went to school, where a few months spent in the company of boys his age were enough to make him forget his mother tongue and start to speak Tuscan. He learned to read and write the mercantile script used by all who made their living from commerce.[2] He did not study Latin, for which he had no need, but he did learn arithmetic. After two years of schooling his grandfather put him to work in the wool guild, as an apprentice. Giannino remembered three years of hard labor carrying heavy bales of wool on his back. The work was so crushing that it stunted the boy's growth, leaving him with a slender physique. That was why he was always called Giannino, a little Giovanni who had failed to grow to full stature. Mino subsequently sent him to work for dealers in iron and steel, where the boy spent three more years carrying heavy loads. At age eighteen he enrolled in a merchant company and for five years earned a meager salary, enough to put clothes on his back and shoes on his feet. His grandfather had lost all his clout in the city after the collapse of the Tolomei company, in which he held a share, and could no longer help his grandson get ahead.[3]

But Giannino got a break: a relative, Bonaventura Ugolini, who was rector of the Casa di Santa Maria della Misericordia, chose him for his chamberlain, meaning the treasurer responsible for all the income and expenditure of that rich charitable institution, one of the main ones in the city. So by around 1340 Giannino had attained a decent position and was finally able to start earning well. Indeed he soon accumulated the sum of 12,000 florins by investing the money citizens had deposited with the Casa. Giannino grew wealthy along with Siena, as the city prospered during the time of its greatest splendor, with the cathedral and the Torre del Mangia both rising from busy construction sites.

Bonaventura Ugolini, who was looking out for the young man, chose a wife for him: Giovanna di Nicolò Vivoli, a girl of fifteen or sixteen who was the niece of one of the friars of the Misericordia. Giannino married her on 13 June 1342. Three male children survived infancy: Guccio, Nicolò, and Gabriello. Then the great plague carried Giovanna off on 23 June 1348, and Giannino buried her at San Domenico.

Meanwhile Bonaventura had died, and Giannino, still the chamberlain of the Misericordia, was accused of misappropriating the charity's funds. But a commission consisting of three examiners appointed by the commune and six friars of the Casa pronounced him innocent. Now a fairly rich merchant, Giannino remarried in January 1349, seven months after the death of his first wife. Necca was sixteen, the daughter of Vanni di Giello degli Agazzari. They had six children, three boys and three girls. The oldest boy was called Giovanni, the second Luigi, and the third Francesco. The oldest girl was called Bartolomea, the second Clemenza, and the third Isabella. So four children of the merchant's second marriage were baptized with the names of French royals (Giovanni/Jean, Luigi/Louis, Clemenza/Clémence, and Isabella/Isabelle), and a fifth, Francesco, clearly bore a propitious name (in medieval Italian it literally means "French"). Apart from Bartolomea, whom I imagine was the oldest, the children must have been born after the revelation of 1354. Giannino, while believing himself a king, still kept a precise record, like any merchant, of the vital data, concerning his family members, as though he were compiling a *libro di ricordanʒe*, a "record book."[4] Thus we know that three of his children died young and were buried in the church of S. Pietro alla Magione, known locally as the Magione del Tempio.

Giannino maintains in his memoirs that he put his business dealings on hold throughout 1350, out of devotion to the jubilee year proclaimed by Pope Clement VI. Instead he engaged in service to the poor at the Hospital of Saints Andrea and Onofrio and traveled to

Rome to obtain pardon for his sins. Now a capable businessman, he left the Casa della Misericordia and went into partnership with Gherardino di Cenni, a wool merchant. In June 1351 he himself enrolled in the wool merchants' guild; he was earning a lot of money for himself and others. He then partnered with another Sienese, Pietro Landi, building a profitable wholesale trade in cloth, wool, woad, and wine. He bought several cellars, in which he sold wine at retail. Growing ever richer, he joined Pietro di Messer Tancredi of Siena to open a bank. Giannino changed money, continued to trade cloth and wool wholesale, and even dealt in pearls and precious stones.[5]

He remained in partnership with Pietro di Messer Tancredi until March 1355, when the government of the commune of Siena changed. The popular Guelf regime *di gente mezzana* (meaning, roughly, wealthy merchants, the bourgeoisie or middle class of the time), which had governed since 1286, fell the day after Emperor Charles IV entered the city, on his way to Rome for his official coronation. An uprising of the "little people" (*popolo minuto*), organized and supported by the leading noble families of Siena with the emperor's approval, drove the "Nine," the governing body of the Sienese republic, from the palazzo of the commune on 26 March to shouts of "Long live the emperor, death to the Nine and their taxes." The insurgents threw the chest containing the names of those entitled to be eligible to public office out the window of the palazzo, and offered the city to Charles IV. The emperor remained in Siena for several days. He was crowned in Rome on 5 April and was back in Siena two weeks later where he promoted many citizens of limited means to the status of *cavalieri* (knights). When he departed he left his brother behind as lord of Siena, but on 18 May another uprising led to the formation of a new regime headed by twelve magistrates, some from humble trades and others with varied family backgrounds, called the "Twelve Governors of the city and territory of Siena."[6]

The replacement of the regime of the Nine with that of the Twelve must have given a boost to Giannino di Guccio, who used the political storm to enhance his status. His own position, as well as that of his extended family during the period of transition, is unclear. His grandfather Mino had in fact been a member of the magistracy of the

Nine some time previously, and right in the midst of the upheaval one of the four officials in charge of the tax office was a certain Vannino di Guccio di Baglione, whom I take to have been a "cousin" and virtual namesake of Giannino.[7] Hence we would assume that the Baglioni belonged to the group of families that were, in part, shouldered aside by the change of regime. Instead we find that not long after the revolution Giannino was elected chamberlain of the Biccherna, the city treasury, for the semester January–June 1356.[8] Further research may shed fresh light; we might even find out that Vannino and Giannino were actually one and the same person. In that case, we would be dealing with a man capable of rising to the top of both the old regime and the new—not so surprising since the change of regime did not cause too much harm among the ruling class, and the system of government survived largely intact. Let us focus for now on the fact that the merchant managed not only to avoid disaster but even to hold an important charge, for the chamberlain of the Biccherna, also known as the major chamberlain of the commune, was the most powerful magistrate in the city. Many years later he referred to this with satisfaction, stating that "all the money flowing into this city passed through his hands, and all the outlays, and he was much honored and loved by all the citizens."[9]

A FORGERY FOR A GOOD CAUSE

While Giannino was becoming a wealthy merchant, a businessman at the top level of city government, he grew increasingly convinced that he was a king as well. Cola di Rienzo had opened up a new world to him, but with the tribune's death a few days later that vista had suddenly been slammed shut, leaving Giannino deeply disappointed. From then on he must often have thought about what to do next, without reaching a decision. He had sought counsel from a Dominican friar, Bartolomeo Mini, with whom he spoke in confession. The priest, who already knew about the legend of the switched babies, having heard it twenty years earlier in Paris as a university student, suggested he keep silent, await developments, and content himself with the solid position he had attained in the city. Should he declare himself, people might think he was out of his mind and turn him into a laughingstock. So Giannino let all of 1355, and a good part of 1356, go by without saying anything to anyone except for a few of his closest friends.

But during that period of silent waiting he was probably finding out more about events at the court of France around the time of his birth. Cola di Rienzo's letter describing what had taken place and declaring him a king, although crucial in his eyes, was very skimpy with details, leaving the door open to endless questions. For example, in Cola's account the members of the royal family were not identified by name, not even the son of the king who had been switched in the cradle (the ignorance of the wet nurse Marie being blamed, nonsensically, for this). Moreover, the letter showed ignorance of the dynastic position of the poor child, who was not just the offspring of royalty but himself the king in person, having been born when his father was already dead. Despite that, Friar Giordano claimed to have had a vision of the prince asking for the blessing of his own father, whom the friar evidently believed to be still alive. Thus on the face of it the whole story could not refer to the little King Jean I the Posthumous. For another thing, Giannino knew perfectly well that he had lived in France until the age of nine, for he could remember the year and the month of his arrival in Siena, whereas the letter stated that he had been taken away at age six.

There was more. Responsibility for the switch was attributed to the wet nurse Marie, who had supposedly decided to claim that the son of the king had died in order to have a baby to show her husband. But according to widespread rumor, probably disseminated by the enemies of Philippe V, the baby had been the victim of a conspiracy at court. Giannino had heard it from various persons, and each version contained different, although equally chilling, details. These would not have seemed like tall tales, for the French royals had more than once committed atrocious crimes in order to shift the crown from one head to another. Queen Marguerite of Burgundy had been strangled to allow Louis X to marry Clémence of Hungary—Giannino's own mother.

Then there was the problem of the wet nurses, which needed to be sorted out. In the original version, the queen had availed herself of

Marie to nurse her child, and Marie in turn had brought along Amaloth to act as wet nurse to hers. Three women in descending order, none of whom had given her breast to her natural child: the queen alone in her own bed, the lady with the king's son, the wet nurse with the son of the lady. It was all too complicated, not to mention the fact that if Amaloth had milk to give, she too must have had a baby, though luckily there was no mention of this third infant. This wet nurse, Amaloth, was certainly a convenient character though, being the one who had accidentally smothered the newborn child while sleeping beside him (something that did often happen); her presence in the story freed Marie of any suspicion of being responsible for the death herself. In a court conspiracy, though, her participation in the sequence of events was more difficult to account for.

Worst of all, there was a serious problem with the setting that threatened to bring the whole house of cards down, for according to the version authenticated by Cola di Rienzo it appeared that the little prince had been sent to the monastery where Marie was staying so he could be nursed: the heir to the throne of France had supposedly been taken out of the royal palace within a few days of his birth, at considerable risk, to be lodged with a wet nurse. Such a procedure would have been normal in a bourgeois Tuscan family: people of that class did normally send their children out to be wet-nursed; but it certainly didn't fit with usage in a royal household.[10] Those who had retailed this version of the story probably did not have a clear idea of how things were done at court. For that matter, the idea conveyed by the Tuscan folktales of what it meant to be a sovereign was so far-fetched that, as Italo Calvino once observed, in some of them "you find a king whose next-door neighbor is another king, and they catch sight of one another through their windows, and pay each other visits like a couple of solid local bourgeois citizens."[11]

So Cola di Rienzo's letter was a good point of departure, no doubt, especially since it was authentic and emanated from a head of government in office, but it had the defect of relating events without clearly defining times, places, protagonists, and motives. Reality can always be improved upon, though, especially when you have the right resources. And Giannino had plenty: he was convinced of his own good claim, and he could count on a network of connections who were in a position to supply him with information about France (indeed, in April 1356 he had requested one of his correspondents in France to investigate Friar Giordano). His close friend, the notary Angelo d'Andrea Guidaregli, had shared the marvel of the royal revelation with him. Finally, he possessed an authentic seal of Cola di Rienzo, although it was slightly defective. Why not try to put all these assets to use, and tidy his own story up a bit? The resulting document would be a fake, but it would certify something that Giannino considered authentic: his own royal descent. The procedure was not new, and many forgeries have come about, and still do, for the purpose of supplying the missing proof of something regarded as true. In the Middle Ages it was done all the time.[12]

Thus, using the bare bones of the story we already know, which narrates in Tuscan dialect the events revealed by Marie to Friar Giordano, by Friar Giordano to Friar Antonio, and finally by Friar Antonio to Cola di Rienzo, a new version was constructed, the sole version that Giannino, many years later, would transmit to posterity. In short, how he came into the world had to be entirely rewritten.[13]

THE NEW VERSION
This new version was embodied in a letter composed in Latin and attributed to the chancellery of Cola di Rienzo. It had its roots in the story transmitted from Marie to Giordano to Antonio, but it was a different narrative, and not just because of the different language.[14] Read with care, it reveals new and different plot twists and information.

The letter begins with a detailed review of the recent generations of the royal house of France. It then recounts how, at the death of Louis X, it became known that his wife, Queen Clémence, daughter of Charles Martel of Anjou, the titular king of Hungary, was expecting his posthumous child. So it was decided that Philippe the Long, the brother of the dead king and uncle of the expected child, would occupy the throne until the queen had given birth, and that, if she produced a boy, the kingdom would be held for him until he was able to rule. If she produced a girl, however, then Philippe the Long would be crowned legitimate king of France, "since a female must not inherit." At this time Philippe the Long was married to the daughter of the countess of Artois, who was "the greatest lady then to be found in the whole kingdom of France."

In order to keep the pregnancy under surveillance and make sure no fraud was committed, such as substituting somebody else's baby boy if the queen should give birth to a girl and then passing him off as the new king or claiming that a live baby had been born when it was really a stillbirth, or vice versa, the regent, his brother Charles, and other great lords chose two elderly barons, wise and honest men faithful to the crown of France, to watch over the queen.

While Clémence was waiting to deliver, she made a vow to John (in French, Jean) the Baptist, swearing that if she had a boy she would call him Jean. A boy it was, and Countess Mahaut of Artois held him at his baptism. This great lady was jealous of the child though and wanted him dead, for if the little king should die, her son-in-law, Philippe the Long, would be crowned legitimate king of France, and her daughter Jeanne would become queen.

Mahaut of Artois spread a rumor that the baby was sickly and would not last more than a few days. She did so with the intention of murdering him in secret, since it would be difficult to charge her with causing his death if it was already being bruited about that the infant was weak and unlikely to survive.

The two barons who were guarding the baby and the queen sought a woman of the nobility to suckle him. Among those they found was a woman named Marie, whose father was a nobleman, Piquart de Cressay, and who was residing in a monastery where she had given birth to a boy at the same time as the queen. The father, a youth aged almost twenty named Guccio di Mino, came from Tuscany but was engaged in money-changing as well as money-lending on behalf of a relative, Spinello Tolomei, at a castle called Neauphle-le-Vieux not far from Cressay. Guccio was a friend of two other young men, Marie's brothers Pierre and Jeannot. They often went out hunting and snaring birds together, and had so much trust in him that they didn't keep a close eye on him, regarding him as a brother. And while enjoying this level of trust from Pierre and Jeannot, Guccio fell in love with their sister, who was fifteen. Unbeknownst to the brothers and their mother Élia-bel (the father was deceased), Guccio contrived to wed her, gave her a ring, and lay with her, which led to her becoming pregnant. When the pregnancy could no longer be concealed, the mother and brothers demanded to know how it had happened. The young woman, fearful and greatly ashamed, told them everything. Her relatives, furious with Guccio, sent a message to him telling him to leave the kingdom and in order to conceal their dishonor sent Marie to Paris, to a monastery for noblewomen where the abbess was a relative of theirs, asking her to shelter the young woman until she gave birth and then to do as she saw fit with the baby. Their motive was the fact that they had promised Marie's hand to a local noble.

Marie was lodged in the monastery and gave birth to a boy, whom she named Giannino. After his birth, the barons entrusted with custody of Queen Clémence's son ordered Marie to be brought at night to the queen's chamber in the royal palace with her son. While Marie was there nursing the little king, the barons and knights of France were staging elaborate festivities to celebrate the birth of their new lord, and it was decided that the baby would be displayed to them after ten or twelve days so that they could show him the honor and reverence a sovereign deserves.

The countess of Artois then asked the queen for the special favor of being the one to hold the baby in her own arms and exhibit him to the throng, and this was granted. The two barons charged with watching over the newborn were afraid, however, that the countess might find a way of murdering him and gave orders that on the day the baby was to be shown, the son of Guccio and Marie should be wrapped in royal robes with a crown on his tiny head and displayed in place of the real king. They reasoned that if some misdeed were attempted, the victim would be the substitute, not the genuine son of Louis X. And their orders were followed.

On the night after he had been publicly exhibited, Guccio's son died. There were some who said that the countess had squeezed him too tightly as she held him, and others who said she had smeared poison on his tongue. In any case, the baby died. The barons in charge of surveillance, seeing what had happened, said to themselves: "We see clearly and manifestly the ill will of the countess of Artois and Prince Philippe, who doubtless believe that they have murdered our lord. But thanks to God they have not accomplished their end. Let us think of a way to get the royal baby out of here."

They went to Marie and informed her that her baby was dead, explaining how and why this had occurred. Hearing that her son was dead, Marie began to wail and cry loudly, and the barons comforted her, saying:

> You are young, lady, and can still have many children. We wish you to declare that the son of the king, not your own, has died, so that our lord and yours may escape the threat of death. We then wish you to raise the boy as your own, in the greatest possible secrecy, until we tell you to declare him. From that you can become the greatest lady of the realm and will be able to set your family and all your relatives up in great state. But if it should happen that this our lord should die as your son did, then you would lose both your son and your lord and ours, and all of us would be in peril of our lives.

Hearing their words and not knowing what else to do, Marie consented to follow their wishes, tearfully claiming that the son of the king had died. The court and the barons were greatly distressed, but none dared to ask questions about the cause of death, because those conducting the investigation were the very people who had wanted the baby out of the way, Philippe the Long and the countess of Artois. Queen Clémence, exhausted by childbirth and confined to bed, knew only what she was told and genuinely believed that her son had died.

The queen subsequently continued her life amid the trappings of royalty, but Marie and the barons, who knew what had really happened, never revealed the substitution to her or anyone else, out of fear of those who ruled the kingdom at that time and later. The dead child was buried with full honors, and a statue of him, suitable for a king, was erected. The barons, for the good of the king's offspring and the preservation of his life, had Marie brought back to the monastery in secret with the baby, treating it as hers. In due course Marie left the monastery and returned with the child to Cressay, where she continued to live with her brothers.

From then on Marie never had another man, and Guccio never took another wife. When the boy was nine or ten years old, Guccio, who resided in Paris, requested that little Jean (or Giovanni, as his father would have called the boy he believed to be his son) be sent to visit him for a few days. Marie, not suspecting he might be abducted, agreed. But Guccio sent Giovanni to his own native city in Italy. Marie never saw him again but was very fearful about what might become of him. She was so afraid of the French royals that she never revealed anything to anyone until she was on the point of dying, fearing that the boy would be killed or carried off someplace where he could never be found.

Just like the earlier version, the account now proceeds in the first person: the speaker is Friar Giordano "of Spain," an Augustinian, who states that he resided in a convent with the friars of his order near the castle of Cressay and that he had heard the whole story in confession from Marie in the month of June 1345. Marie died in the same month and was buried in his convent. The lady had begged the friar to find out, after her death, what had become of Jean, who would then have been between twenty-six and twenty-eight. If Giordano did find him alive, he was supposed to tell him who he really was and how he was entitled to the crown of France. Friar Giordano decided to find out what had become of Guccio, reasoning that if he found him, he would also be able to find the man known as his son. He discovered that Guccio had died at Châlons-sur-Marne in Champagne in 1340. Fearful of Philippe VI of Valois, the reigning king, Friar Giordano spent several years gloomily pondering what he ought to do. His conscience bothered him, because he was not looking for the young man, but his fear of those in power was so strong that he let the time pass. Caring little about himself, for he was convinced that he had only a short time left to live, Giordano feared provoking a scandal or causing harm to his order more than anything else.

Eventually he decided that it was better to put his own person, and his whole order, at risk rather than allow the legitimate lord of France to perish and the royal house to remain perpetually enslaved, robbed of its natural king. For, declared the friar, those who had acted thus had done so with good intentions, and anyway, apart from anything else, "this prince is indigent and without means, and externally is stripped of all nobility." Since the kingdom of France had never been free of great pestilence or internal conflict, contested as it was among its inhabitants, ever since that substitution, the friar set about finding the true and natural king of France so that God would put an end to his personal poverty and misfortune and to the many grave afflictions of the French people, and so that the world would be set right and guided in the way of God. For, said the friar, it was certain that God would not have kept him hidden for so long unless it was to reveal him at the right time, so that he might bring universal order and peace to the world, and conquer the holy land of Jerusalem across the sea. And Giordano trusted that it would be so.

But since the friar was getting old and it was difficult for him to walk, he had entrusted the hunt to Friar Antonio of the kingdom of France, a member of his own order, whom he identified as a man of great saintliness who had been to Rome a number of times. Friar Giordano had given Friar Antonio a copy of the part of Marie's last testament that dealt with this affair. His fellow friar had undertaken the task with great devotion, and had promised to do all that he could. He left the convent at Cressay in July 1354; proceeding with his inquiries as wisely and as tactfully as possible, he reached the town of Porto-venere in Italy, where he fell so ill he believed he would die. This pained him greatly because he had not yet accomplished his mission. Learning that Nicola, the tribune of the Romans, had regained power and having heard that he was a man of great sensitivity and courage, Friar Antonio decided to tell him all about the matter and to set it down in writing in orderly fashion. Which he did.

The letter ends with a long recognition by Cola di Rienzo declaring that he considers it authentic and that he is convinced that the great war and the other plagues that have long afflicted the kingdom of France have been permitted by God on account of the fraud committed toward, and against, King Jean. Cola tells how he had conducted a secret search for the latter and had located him in Siena living under the name of Giannino di Guccio and believing sincerely that he was Guccio's son. Giannino had entered his presence on 2 October 1354, a Thursday. Before telling him anything, Cola had examined and interrogated him and had then revealed all to him, with every sign of reverence. But well aware of the conspiracy afoot in Rome and fearing he might die before he could do anything to help Giannino recover his kingdom, Cola had had the letter copied and handed it over to him on Saturday 4 October 1354, stamped with his own seal, which he describes as a large star surrounded by eight smaller stars, with a roundel in the middle in which were portrayed the coat of arms of the holy Church and the Roman people. Cola di Rienzo ends the letter with a prayer to the Lord Jesus Christ to grant him the grace to live long enough to see such great justice restored to the world.

SENTIMENT AND POLITICS

Now Giannino had a new story to exhibit, corroborated, like the first, by the seal of Cola di Rienzo. It was a made-up story, of course, as we can tell from various clues. For one thing, in its conclusion it describes the same seal that was also to be found physically attached to the end of the document. This was a very unusual thing to do, revealing excessive zeal on the part of someone who did not trust the credibility of his own creation and was trying to enhance its authenticity. It was, as the Latin has it, an *excusatio non petita,* a justification offered without having been asked for, and so amounting to an *accusatio manifesta,* a manifest self-accusation.[15]

This new version was much more useful to Giannino. He had ironed out almost all the problems, taking the trouble to find out what rumors were in circulation and making sure his story matched them, highlighting the fact that the little king and the little son of the merchant bore the same name, and establishing the death dates of Guccio and Marie. A few things remained from the earlier version: the love story between the French noblewoman and the Tuscan merchant, and the secret switching of a secret baby.

But the main plot dynamic regarding the switched infants and the death of one of them was completely different. The characters, the place, and the motive had all been altered. The only characters left unchanged were Marie and her baby, and even they had different roles now. In the first version, Marie's baby had died in bed beside its nurse, and she had secretly replaced it because of her passion for her husband, whom she feared losing if he learned that their baby was dead. This version was sentimental, whereas the second was political, frankly accusing those who occupied the French throne of murdering a rival. Marie was no more than a pawn in a much bigger game, in which the barons, the regent, and the countess of Artois were the main players. The struggle for power that had taken place around the cradle now had a cast of characters with distinct motives.

We do in fact know that little Jean I the Posthumous had been an inconvenient heir for many, above all for the house of the dukes of Burgundy, which had a baby candidate of its own for the throne: Jeanne, a daughter of Marguerite of Burgundy, the first wife of Louis X, and thus a half-sister of little Jean. The latter, as a male, would have a prior claim to the throne, and besides, the little girl was strongly suspected of being illegitimate. But there were other princes of the blood who would also have been glad to have little Jean out of the way. With him gone, the regent, Philippe of Poitiers, could become king, his mother-in-law, Mahaut of Artois would see her daughter crowned queen, and she could hope to see her grandson on the throne eventually: little Louis, born just a few months before but destined to die in infancy as well. For that matter, Mahaut had a reputation for being adept with poison: in June 1317 she had been accused by Isabelle and Jean de Fériennes of having poisoned Louis X in order to get her son-in-law onto the throne, in other words for the same reason that she was supposed to have poisoned Louis X's son. Since those who brought the charge were "vile persons," Mahaut, a peer of France, needn't have answered it. But Philippe the Long, her son-in-law, decided to order an inquest, which was conducted in the presence of the widowed queen, Clémence, and ended on 9 October 1317 by pronouncing Mahaut entirely innocent.[16]

Many years later Giannino once again revisited the story of the switch in the cradle, the thought of which must have haunted him every day. In his memoirs he tweaked the facts a little bit more, to make them fit better with what he had felt and, perhaps, with some faint memories. These were not dramatic changes, just little touches assigning gestures of affection to those who had been (or whom he remembered as having been) close to him in childhood. Thus, the first time he mentioned himself, he used the name "Giannotto" rather than Giannino, probably because he remembered being called "Jeannot" in France. Once again he named the nurse Amaloth, who may really have existed, but without giving her any role in the plot. He wrote that Guccio, the man whom he had believed for years to be his father, had been pardoned by Marie's brothers, who had themselves been knighted by Philippe of Valois at the battle of Crécy. Above all, he wrote that Marie, the woman who had raised him as his mother, "was beautiful, young, and gentle, and . . . her milk was good and tender, better than that of any woman then to be found in Paris."[17] This woman, whom he had loved as a mother and from whom he had been separated while still a boy, had not simply abandoned him to fate by handing him over to Guccio without hesitation; on the contrary, for a long time she had refused to do so, declaring her great love for the child, and had only given in at last "with tears, and great reluctance."[18]

One more thing was needed to make the story credible: the names of the two faithful old barons who had switched the babies but then dropped out of sight. Giannino must have tried for years to put names to them, with no luck. He wound up writing in his memoirs that these great lords had written testaments before dying in which they revealed to a bishop and an abbot what had happened. These documents were supposedly preserved in the bishopric of Paris and the abbey of Saint-Denis, respectively. But the device of the deathbed revelation had an all-too-familiar ring.

MAIN DIFFERENCES BETWEEN
SENTIMENTAL AND POLITICAL VERSIONS

SENTIMENTAL VERSION	POLITICAL VERSION
Marie's age when she marries Guccio is not stated.	Marie is said to be 15 when she knew Guccio.
Guccio's age when he marries Marie is not stated.	Guccio is said to be almost 20 when he knew Marie.

The names of Marie's brothers are not stated.	Marie's brothers are identified as Pierre and Jeannot (Pietro and Giannotto).
The names of the French royals are not stated.	The French royals are identified. The genealogy of recent generations is fairly accurate.
The name of the king's son is not stated. It is even said that the nurse Marie did not recall it.	The king's son is named Jean (Giovanni).
The protagonist is simply "the king's son." Nothing is said about his posthumous birth.	The protagonist is "the king." His posthumous birth is part of the story.
The switch appears to take place in the monastery, to which the king's son is supposedly brought.	The babies are switched in a royal palace.
The death of Marie's baby Jean is caused by his wet nurse Amaloth. Members of the court do not appear in the story, except as the king's "bailiffs and doctors."	The death of Marie's baby Jean is caused by the countess of Artois. The wet nurse Amaloth does not appear in the story.
The switch is made by Marie, the king's wet nurse, after her own baby's death, so she can keep the surviving baby as her own and not lose her husband's love.	The switch is made by two barons who are keeping watch over the little king before his presentation in public, so as to shield him from possible danger.
The dead baby is buried.	The dead baby is buried and a statue to him is erected [at Saint-Denis].
When Marie returns to Cressay, the child is entrusted to the wet	When Marie returns to Cressay, she brings the child with her by

nurse Amaloth, who lives in the vicinity.	order of the barons who had ordered the switch.
The child is abducted by Guccio at age six.	The child is abducted by Guccio at age nine or ten.
Marie's confession is dated 1345.	Marie's confession is dated June 1345. She is said to be buried in the convent of Friar Giordano at Cressay.
Guccio is merely said to be deceased.	Guccio's death is placed at Châlons-sur-Marne in 1340.
Friar Giordano despairs because he cannot inform the king of France without adducing any proof of the existence of the prince. Thus he is unaware of the dynastic position of the prince in question.	Friar Giordano fears the king of France, because he knows that the one he is seeking is the legitimate king.
Friar Giordano often dreams of the king's son asking for his father's blessing and wishing to liberate the Holy Sepulcher. He also dreams of him wearing the emblem of the Church.	Friar Giordano's visions are not reported.

THE PROCLAMATION

Early in the morning of Monday 19 September 1356, around seven thousand soldiers, including English and Gascon archers, heavy cavalry and light horse, routed the army of the king of France, who had sent many more troops into battle. The Anglo-Gascons, entrenched on elevations bristling with hedges and brambles that could only be reached by a narrow and completely exposed path, picked off the French cavalry, who were fighting on foot and suffered very heavy casualties. An impromptu counterattack led by Edward, the Black Prince, the son of the king of England, drove so far into the ranks of the retreating enemy that it came up against the squadron commanded personally by the king of France, Jean II, called the Good. The king dismounted and threw himself into the fray armed with a battle-ax, but when he saw that all was lost he surrendered to an enemy knight by offering him his right-hand gauntlet.[19]

News of the great battle of Poitiers and the king's capture reached Siena on 9 October, a Sunday. Friar Bartolomeo Mini, the priest who had learned Giannino's secret in confession, gave the citizens of Siena his own take on what had occurred, pointing out the setbacks suffered by the French royal house, which had been in decline for some time and was plunging toward its ruin. The friar thanked God and proclaimed, "Now the reason and the truth of Giovanni will be evident."[20] He told everyone the tale of the switched babies and displayed a copy of the revelation of Marie that he had had made. So it was that by next day, 10 October 1356, the whole city of Siena knew Giannino's story, without his having decided to reveal it. On the contrary, Giannino was very displeased with Friar Bartolomeo and denied everything. But news travels fast, especially when carried by the rapid letters of merchants. Within a few days it was known in Palermo, where, Giannino claims in his memoirs, Friar Giordano and Friar Antonio were staying en route to the Holy Sepulcher. The two holy men had fled France in fear of the king, he maintains, and had confirmed everything in a series of letters sent to the commune of Siena, the local bishop, and Giannino himself, which had convinced him to declare himself and to exhibit all the written material and *chiarezze* (literally, clarities, meaning certificates or proofs) in his possession. It is certainly hard to believe that Friar Giordano, who could barely walk, had set out for Jerusalem: once again, Giannino can't be taken at face value, especially since we know from a letter of a merchant writing in December 1356 that Friar Giordano had been missing from Cressay since the previous Lent and that the king of France was suspected of having had him killed, precisely on account of a "certain confession."[21] It might well be that Friar Giordano had fled, but that he had got as far as Palermo seems unlikely.

Giannino claimed that the two friars had not been idle in any case, having brought their tale to Rome in the year of the Jubilee, even before making contact with Cola di Rienzo; at Rome they had met with some French knights, with the senators, and with Giacomo, the preceptor or head of the house (*magione*) of the Knights of San Giacomo of Altopascio, near Lucca, an order known as the Knights of the Tau because of the form of the cross emblazoned on their coat of arms. Over the years Giannino had tried to get the preceptor on his side, with what success we do not know, just as we are ignorant of exactly what his role, and that of his order, was in this affair, except that he was supposed to act as intermediary between Giannino and the princes of the House of Navarre. In 1330 the Knights of the Tau had been arrested in France and had had their property confiscated, on the grounds that they had been granting indulgences more extensive than their papal warrant allowed: there might be some sort of linkage between this event and Giannino and the opposition he represented.[22] Moreover the preceptor of Altopascio, identified as Giacomo Chelli, belonged to the Augustinian order too, just like Friars Giordano and Antonio. This tangle of clues and hints is not easy to unravel.[23] At any rate the newly declared sovereign was able to produce in public the letters of the tribune, which we already know, as well as ones from the preceptor of Altopascio.

Giannino claims in his memoirs that the commune of Siena believed him so completely that six noblemen were chosen to form his council, with authority to send letters and embassies on his behalf and spend the required sums. The king-merchant, attentive to details, records the names of these councilors, all of them prominent personalities: Spinello Tolomei (his relative, a member of the family in whose firm his father and grandfather had worked), Vanni Malavolti, Brandoligi Piccolomini, Giovanni d'Agnolo Bottoni de' Salimbeni, Agnolo di Pietro Fortiguerra, and Giovanni di Mino of Percenna, who was currently captain of the people and *gonfaloniere* (standard-bearer) of justice. Giannino was also given a notary, one Michele di Ser Monaldo.

It challenges belief, however, that the commune of Siena was so easily persuaded to back Giannino's claim, even if its relations with

France were not good at this juncture. No matter how emphatically his memoirs record the honors heaped on him, we may doubt that such an unlikely event took place because, for one thing, the Sienese archival sources, which are well preserved for this period, are silent about it and because, for another, perhaps even more telling, the Florentine chronicles don't mention it either—and they would have snapped at such a glorious chance to make fun of their rival city. What we probably ought to read into Giannino's words is simply the formation of an influential group of backers. They might well have been driven by the conviction that the facts claimed were true, having assessed the documents presented by Giannino as genuine, and they might have been struck by the appearance of King Jean I at the very moment at which King Jean II (a remarkable coincidence of names) had been defeated in battle and taken prisoner, his illegitimacy exposed by divine judgment. Above all, during the weeks in October 1356, when they made their decision, the French government was in deep trouble: formally the lieutenancy of the realm had been assumed by the Dauphin, Charles, duke of Normandy, but the Estates of the Langue d'Oïl, meeting in Paris, were loudly demanding direct administration, the formation of what we would call a parliamentary monarchy, the firing of the principal members of the royal council, and the release from jail of Charles II the Bad, king of Navarre, held prisoner by the king of France since 5 April 1356. Paris was gathering itself for the revolt that would explode within a year under the leadership of Étienne Marcel; the prevailing atmosphere was one of enormous confusion and anarchy. France was in real danger with its king in enemy hands: the presence of a free claimant became a strong vehicle of opposition, delegitimizing a king who could do nothing to oppose him and offering an alternative choice. Politically, it was an opportune moment. So there was certainly some plotting going on around Giannino, and, as we shall see in due course, the followers of the jailed king of Navarre were keeping track of developments.[24]

The six councilors of King Giannino decided to send an embassy to the Roman senators, so that they in turn would write letters to the pope, the emperor, the kings of Naples, Hungary, and England, the king of Navarre and his brothers, and the representatives of the

Estates General of France. Therefore, they sent Friar Bartolomeo to Rome, where, in late April 1357, he spoke with senators Pietro di Giordano Colonna and Nicolò di Riccardo Annibaldi and with Pons de Péret, bishop of Orvieto and papal vicar for the city of Rome. Giannino claims that the Romans believed the ambassador, that the city council was convened, and that it ordered seven letters to be written on behalf of the senators, and seven on behalf of the vicar.

The truth was certainly different; Giannino was reshaping it in his usual way. Now that he was no longer alone, pondering his adventure, but had a group of influential backers behind him, he needed to take rapid and decisive action to try to get as many leaders of Christendom involved as possible. For this purpose, the best thing would be to have a constituted authority on his side who would reveal him to the world, as Cola di Rienzo had already tried to do. And this was the line Giannino followed, seeking the help, in ascending order, of the preceptor of Altopascio, then of the commune of Siena, and finally of the commune of Rome. Authority was manifested, in the medieval world and today, through officially documented public proceedings. Having been rebuffed by those he had approached, his only recourse was to produce the necessary documents himself.

So Giannino and his friends, chief among them the notary Angelo d'Andrea Guidaregli, simply carried on as before, but on a much bigger scale, creating numerous forgeries so as to put together a complete dossier. As a first step, Giannino had his notary authenticate the letters of Cola di Rienzo en bloc. On 24 January 1357 Ser Angelo and another notary transcribed onto one parchment the tribune's letter of summons, the one containing the first version of the switch in the cradle, and a third letter supposedly written to him by Cola the day before dying.[25] In this way Giannino set himself up to be able to exhibit originals, genuine and fake (we recall that he possessed Cola's seal, and we begin to wonder how he got it), and a copy that, having been authenticated by the *publica fides* (public faith, conferring legal validity) of a college of notaries, put even the false papers into a setting of truthfulness. The result was the opposite of what happens with mushrooms: the poisonous one, placed in the same basket as the edible ones, became edible itself instead of poisoning the rest.

But naturally Giannino did not stop there. At some undetermined point he also created seven letters from the preceptor of Altopascio and, early in 1357, fabricated seven letters from the senators of Rome. Giannino, ably assisted, practically set up his own workshop of forgeries, to prove to the world who he really was. The reason I state the matter so bluntly is that it actually highlights his utter candor. When, after many years and many dramatic turns of fortune, he asked the archbishop of Naples to return his letters patent, Giannino listed them one after another. He did indeed possess a letter of Cola di Rienzo, addressed to him, but he also had seven letters from the senators of Rome addressed to European sovereigns, seven letters from the preceptor of Altopascio, as well as a number from the king of Hungary.[26] The very fact that Giannino retained all these originals in his own possession is not just circumstantial evidence, but proof, that they were forgeries. Giannino was not the recipient of those letters but the head of the very chancellery that had produced them.

Chapter Three

·◅══▻·

In the East

Hodie pecunie / custos diligitur / pauper homo spernitur. / Regis curia /nil sine pecunia / prodest morum copia

Today the keeper of money is cherished, the poor man is spurned. At the king's court, abundant morality without money is ineffectual.

—Ernoul le Viel, *Crescens incredulitas/go.*

IN SEARCH OF AN ARMY

In May 1357 Giannino was abandoned by most of his followers, a strategic move on their part when the Dauphin, having been unable to govern for several months, regained a solid grip on power and forbade any further meetings of the Estates General. On 23 March 1357, at Bordeaux, he and the English agreed to a truce to last from Easter of that year, 9 April, until Easter of 1359, 21 April. The king of France, Jean II the Good, was taken to England by the Black Prince, which meant that the Dauphin could rule the kingdom without the awkward presence on French soil of his captive father and the heir to the English throne.

The magistrates of the commune of Siena, who until then had taken a hands-off approach, began to worry about the reprisals that Sienese merchants in France might suffer if it became known that back home the self-proclaimed sovereign of that kingdom was being harbored and honored.[1] Giannino, isolated and risking heavy fines for passing himself off as someone else but quite unable to revert to his previous status, wrote again to the leaders hostile to France, that is, the kings of England and Navarre and to the king of Hungary and the pope as well, sending each of them his "clarities." He received, so he tells us, a reply from the king of Hungary, who, nonetheless, declared that he could not help him. He also received, and this we can more readily believe, a reply from Philippe of Navarre, count of Longueville, the brother of Charles the Bad, king of Navarre, at that moment a prisoner of the French. The count, who did not regard himself as bound by the truce between France and England, sent him word by way of the preceptor of Altopascio that he would not write him directly, the reason being that if he did he would have to address him as a sovereign, which he couldn't do as long as his brother's life was at risk in prison. Despite that, Philippe of Navarre assured Giannino of his full support. There was intrigue afoot, and Giannino di Guccio was a pawn, only half aware that he was being used by the Navarrist opposition to the crown of France.[2]

But Giannino was rich. Having sworn to himself to "spend whatever he had, and die in this enterprise," he decided to try his luck with an approach different from the diplomatic one he had been pursuing.[3] So he sought meetings with the captains of the mercenary companies that were then ranging throughout Italy and set out one day in secret with two squires and the notary Ser Paolo of Castiglione Aretino, headed for Cesena.

Here, according to plan, he was supposed to meet two redoubtable German condottieri, the celebrated Konrad von Landau, known in Italy as Count Lando, and Hartmann von Wartstein, whom the merchant-king calls Count Antimanno.[4] They were known to him by reputation if nothing else, for in that very year, 1357, Siena had hired the mercenary companies to wage war on Perugia. Count Lando had repeatedly traversed Sienese territory, taking sizeable payoffs not to sack the countryside or assault the city. These violent bands of armed men, whom Matteo Villani calls "the damned companies," were one of the worst problems of the later fourteenth century, especially in the Midi and in Italy. But they were armies for hire, and Giannino urgently needed an army.[5]

The difficulty arose when, having reached the Romagna, Giannino discovered that his mercenaries were not there. So he sent his notary and a squire to Bologna to look for them, remaining in Cesena himself. The two condottieri sent him word that "they were at his service freely, at no cost and with all their forces, which amounted to six thousand horsemen and as many well-armed foot soldiers."[6] But, they added courteously, they were unable to help him just then, since they had taken other contracts from the marchese of Monferrato and Giovanni Visconti of Oleggio, lord of Bologna. Giannino, not knowing what else to do and failing to realize that he was being mocked, went back to Siena to ruminate. For now the raising of his army had to be postponed.

AT VENICE

But what could he accomplish back in Siena? Short of armed men but not short of money, Giannino decided to try yet another tack, going in person where his missives had already gone. He resolved to set out for Hungary, then ruled by Louis I the Great, son of Charles Robert of Anjou and therefore nephew of the woman whom Giannino considered his own mother, Clémence of Anjou. The uncrowned king was sure that his first cousin would help him in every way. Only a few years before, the king of Hungary had advanced into southern Italy to avenge the assassination of his brother Andrea and defend his claim to the succession to the throne of Naples; what might he do now for a close relative, practically half Hungarian himself, who needed his help? He would certainly assemble an army of formidable cavalrymen of the sort Giannino was familiar with, having seen so many of them employed as mercenaries in Italy, and come to his aid. Accompanied by a companion, Baldo degli Albizzeschi, and four squires and with the notable sum of 2600 ducats sewn into his doublet and 250 florins in his purse, Giannino set out on Monday 2 October 1357. The florins would pay his travel costs, and the ducats, Venetian coins equivalent in value to the florin, would come out of his close-fitting jacket when the time came to pay for the expedition. Naturally he brought along his whole dossier of documents.

He reached Bologna, where he was received by Giovanni of Oleggio, and continued on to Venice, where he encountered some Sienese and Florentine merchants. They advised him not to speak

with Count Lando, who happened to be in the city, to avoid arousing the suspicions of the Venetians, who happened just then to be at
war with the king of Hungary for control of the Adriatic and the
Dalmatian cities. At mass in San Marco, Giannino recognized an old
acquaintance, a Jew recently converted to Christianity named Daniello with whom he had done business in the past. As described by
Giannino, Daniello was 45 years old; born at Buda, he had fled to
Austria when the king of Hungary had expelled his people. He was
knowledgeable about precious stones and spoke many languages,
including German, Slavic, Latin, even Tartar and Turkish, for he had
been raised at the Tartar and Turkish courts, taken there by his father,
a trader in jewels who had also shipped silk and gold cloth back to
Venice. Daniello and Giannino had a long talk in the chapel of Pope
Alexander. The Jewish merchant, whom Giannino quickly came to
regard as a great friend and confidant, revealed that he knew about
Giannino's situation and promised him all kinds of help, asserting
that he was ready to discuss his case with the Tartar and Turkish
lords, the king of Serbia, and all the Jewish-Hungarian exiles scattered throughout the duchy of Austria. With the latter, said Daniello,
he would negotiate a large loan in Giannino's name, as long as Giannino promised that, once he was king, he would receive the Jews
back into the kingdom of France and guarantee their franchises and
freedoms. Giannino agreed to this, provided it was not "against our
Christian faith, nor against the custom of the ancient and holy kings
that have been in France."[7]

Who was this Daniello? The individual who directed Giannino's
eyes toward eastern horizons was to play an important part in his
story, and Giannino always presents him as a faithful servant. Yves-
Marie Bercé, who has studied this and similar cases of self-proclaimed
sovereigns, notes that quite often such claimants were aided by Jewish merchants because of the social marginalization of merchants and
the dispersion of the Jewish people and also, perhaps even especially,
because of their propensity to believe in utopian political schemes for
the restoration of order, so closely akin to messianism. That the Jews
had been expelled from the kingdom of France is in fact true: practically every time there was a change of sovereign, they were either

driven out or brought back in, until the expulsion of 1394, which lasted for several centuries.[8]

As Giannino tells it, Daniello offered to act as interpreter on his behalf with certain Tartar and Turkish merchants then in Venice, suggesting that he negotiate his rights to the French crown with their sovereigns: King Jean would cede these rights to them, in exchange for lands in their territories, for, Daniello claimed, the pagan lords were very angry about the fact that the French royals, that is, the Angevins of Naples, had acquired sovereign rights over Jerusalem. Hence, continued Daniello, "I believe I can work on them, to get them to purchase your rights willingly, at a better price than any Christian lord, and you will have greater security."[9]

The proposal was embarrassing, and a bit wide of the mark. Giannino said that he would prefer to find another way and that the earlier idea of taking out a loan with the Jewish merchants struck him as more appropriate. Still, he didn't want to miss the chance to make the acquaintance of the Turkish and Tartar merchants. The next day he did so, together with his interpreter, and naturally he showed them his documents. We know little of these merchants, who may have arrived recently from the East or may have been permanently stationed at the commercial headquarters (*fondaco*) of their nation in Venice. They did—in this account—request a copy of his attestations, and Giannino gladly gave it to them, stamping it with his own seal. But, to avoid misunderstanding, he wanted to make a note on these transcripts that they were merely copies. And for even greater security, he added an ample power of attorney in his own hand, giving Daniello the capacity to treat with distant sovereigns but not to conclude anything without his own explicit consent.

Well pleased to have a Jewish representative at the court of Sultan Orkhan, Giannino left Venice with his attendants and traveled about for some time, waiting for news. He went to Padua, Ferrara, and Verona, traversed the March of Treviso, and headed for Austria, where, according to him, he was received with full honors by the duke in person. From there he resumed course for Hungary once more, arriving in the capital of that kingdom (which was much larger than modern Hungary) on 3 December 1357.

Giannino stayed in Buda incognito for several days.[10] Then, unable to keep his secret to himself any longer, he revealed who he was to the innkeeper, Alessandro Bisdomini of Siena, and right after that to a certain master Saracino of Padua, coiner to the Hungarian crown. These two urged him to make his arrival known to the king, and so Giannino wrote to the sovereign, who was in Dalmatia, entrusting the letter to a courier, a certain Giovanni Berti of San Casciano, the associate and factor of the Florentine Niccolò di Taldo Valori:[11] both were refiners of gold and silver by trade. The courier accomplished this task with some difficulty, the king having left Zagreb for Zara, and returned to Buda bringing along Tollio degli Albizzeschi, the brother of Baldo, who had left Siena with Giannino. Tollio, who proposed to enter Giannino's service, had recently been in France, England, and Navarre. Prince Philippe of Navarre had honored him and kept him for almost two months at his table, presenting him with a horse, clothing, and money. So the representatives of the crown of Navarre, of whom we have already caught a glimpse, were continuing to keep tabs on our Sienese merchant.

Here it is not necessary to follow all the twists and turns of the *Istoria,* which abounds in minute details, especially about names and dates. The gist of it is Giannino's attempt to have himself received, and acknowledged, by Louis the Great. Right away a fly appeared in the ointment, in the shape of another self-proclaimed sovereign, a Bohemian shoemaker passing himself off as "King Andrea," in other words as the brother of the king of Hungary and husband of Giovanna, queen of Naples, who was known to have been strangled, perhaps at the instigation of Giovanna, in 1345. Louis I had this putative Andrea arrested as soon as he returned to Buda on 3 March 1358. Once the shoemaker had confessed, his ears, nose, hair, and beard were cut off, and he was exposed in public bound to a column for three days and then expelled from Hungary. Giannino was convinced that this impostor was a creature of his French enemies, conjured up to spoil his own plans. In voicing such thoughts the merchant-king reveals that he himself was well aware that self-proclaimed sovereigns could have a role in political intrigues. In "King Andrea" he detected a phony created on purpose so as to cast a ridiculous light on the position of an authentic king: himself.[12]

Despite this incident, it would seem that King Louis wished to find out more about Giannino, and on 24 March 1358 he sent several high dignitaries of the court to the house of master Saracino at Visegrád, on the banks of the Danube. Among them were Nicholas Konth, palatine of the kingdom of Hungary, and Thomas, archbishop of Kalocsa.[13] These men listened to Giannino and inspected his attestations. Giannino himself—as he tells it—was admitted to see the king the next day.[14]

A few days later King Louis let him know, through the two dignitaries, that he did not believe a word of what had been revealed to him, adding a warning that ecclesiastics acting on behalf of the enemies of France ("all the evil in the world comes from the tonsured ones") were maneuvering against him.[15] The king's analysis captured a facet of political reality, but it agitated Giannino, who replied that he was not in the least professing himself a king and that what he wanted was for King Louis to enquire more closely and carefully into the matter, or at any rate to supply him with a safe conduct to visit the pope, who would conduct the necessary investigation. In the meantime he would not budge from Buda. The king then sent to ask Giannino if he had received letters from any baron of France. Louis of Hungary was obviously going straight to the heart of the matter, which was to find out whether the legend of the babies switched in the cradle had ever been confirmed by any great lord of France, especially by those two famous barons who had supposedly carried it out. Giannino then sent him the letter that Philippe of Navarre had written to the preceptor of Altopascio, which must have convinced the king once and for all that the merchant was being manipulated.

Giannino passed four months in Buda without any news from the king or about his letter, which was not returned to him. During this time he apparently met with Count Lando, but above all he lost most of his servants, who, observing what had happened to "King Andrea" and fearing that Giannino's stubbornness would put them all at risk, left for home. The merchant, almost totally isolated, was approached by another interesting character, the Minorite friar Francesco di Mino di Buonconte dal Cotone (a castle in the Sienese countryside, near Scansano), who claimed to be a bishop and listed among his credentials a position as chaplain of the sovereigns of Naples and Hungary. Friar Francesco, alias "the Bishop," offered to act as Giannino's counselor, chaplain, and secretary, and Giannino immediately nominated him, issuing a fine privilege to this effect "with his seal of his face hanging from it."[16]

Using his entrée at court, the new secretary would be able to make fresh contact with the king and convince many Hungarian nobles to take up arms and join in the enterprise of conquering France. And lo and behold, in the following months Friar Francesco conferred with numerous counts, archbishops, and great lords, showing them Giannino's documents and succeeding in assembling on paper an army of fifty-six nobles with the capacity to equip and supply a thousand horsemen and four thousand archers at their own expense. When the plan had assumed this firm contour, which greatly pleased Giannino, "the Bishop" executed the sting, telling him: "If you expect to receive help and favor from the king of Hungary, you have to present yourself in the manner expected at court." When Giannino legitimately asked what this manner was, "the Bishop" revealed it: "In every court I have ever frequented, or heard of, those who hope for grace from a king or a pope or any other lord, always want to have an intermediary who is a confidant and secretary of the lord from whom they expect to receive benefits; and that you cannot have without some gift of money or other present."[17]

He suggested the names of three men close to the king: Count Nicholas and the archbishop of Kalocsa, already known to Giannino, and a man identified only as "master William from Germany." Giannino responded promptly: "I don't know what finer and better gift I could give, or more confidential, than money."[18]

He extracted the money he had sewed into his doublet, put it into three purses of white silk, each containing five hundred florins, and handed all three over to "the Bishop," adding another two hundred golden ducats as a gift.

Thus Giannino put himself into the hands of a man who, pretending to believe in and share his dream, succeeded in relieving him of a considerable sum. Friar Francesco had made Giannino see the world through rose-colored glasses, managing relations on his behalf with the court, to which Giannino was naturally never summoned. But the story Francesco spun was so seductive, and matched Giannino's desires so closely, that the merchant king continued to trust him and never showed any sign of realizing that he was being duped.

Another six months passed without fresh developments, when Daniello suddenly turned up in February 1359 with big news. He had been in Tartary with the merchants, had been received by the king of the Tartars and Turks, and had written to the sultan of Babylon and the caliph of Baghdad, "who is the pope of the Saracens."[19] The great lords of Tartary and Turkey, and "all of Saracenia," had assembled to deliberate, and had decided to offer Giannino all the cities, castles, and money he wanted, in exchange for his rights to the crown of France. This had all been set down in documents stamped with their seals, which Daniello showed to Giannino. The Jewish merchant had also been in Germany and Carinthia, and had conferred with the leading Jews there, who, having seen the copies of Giannino's documents, had decided to donate the enormous sum of 50,000 gold florins to him, and loan him the truly stupendous sum of 200,000 florins. The 50,000 were already in Daniello's hands, and he was ready to spend them in the service of King Jean.

Giannino, faced with what looked like a fork in the road, had a hard choice to make. He, a Christian king, refused to cede his rights to the Tartars, keeping this as a fallback option. Even if he should barter his kingdom for land inside Islam, he said, he would build churches and sacred places and install bishops there, just as in France. But it was much better to opt for the loan instead. Thus the merchant Daniello, with a slick move, became the banker of a man whom he knew to be as rich as he was eccentric, offering him unlimited credit.

Word must have got out, since other colorful characters began to show up at Giannino's door. One was a certain Andrea di Mastro Isopo of Perugia, who appeared in April claiming to have been a member of Cola di Rienzo's council and thus to be well acquainted with Giannino's good claim. Andrea, who was destined to accompany Giannino on his peregrinations for some time, also said that he was on a mission from the commune of Perugia, which had decided to offer Giannino the lordship of the city.

Meanwhile, "the Bishop" had not been idle. After making Giannino wait several months, he informed him that the king had finally been convinced that his claim was good and had declared himself ready to follow him in the holy undertaking of conquering France in his name. But there was a problem: being at war with Serbia, King Louis could not abandon his own kingdom, nor allow military forces needed for his own defense to leave Hungary. One minute Giannino is being assured by Friar Francesco of the king's support and an army of five thousand men, the next he finds himself left holding a handful of nothing. The merchant-king was devastated and requested Francesco, who was his only conduit to the court, to ask that the king of Hungary at least furnish him with credentials he could present to the pope and the other leaders of Christendom. "The Bishop" promised to call on the king and the barons whom he had sweetened up with the purses of florins. Upon his return he told Giannino that he had had letters sent to the pope, the king of Navarre, the "twenty-seven regents of France," all the lords and communes of Italy, King Luigi of Naples, the grand seneschal of the kingdom of Naples, Niccolò Acciaiuoli, and all the other royal princes. Not only that, he had had letters sent to all the Hungarian mercenaries then present in Italy, with orders to obey King Jean and follow him as though he were the king of Hungary in person. With this master stroke, "the Bishop" directed Giannino's gaze toward the distant mirage of an army already formed and awaiting his command beyond the frontiers of Hungary.[20]

Nor was that all Friar Francesco had accomplished. Alleging that the king did indeed wish to write to all the lords whose support was being sought but did not know all their names and could not afford to get their titles wrong, the three courtiers who had become friendly thanks to those purses had decided it would be a good idea for Giannino to acquire a brass seal just like the king's, so that he could write—on the king's behalf, of course—to the lords from whom he required any service. So "the Bishop" had obtained for Giannino a faithful copy of the secret seal, meaning the one used primarily (but not exclusively) for authenticating the secret correspondence of a public authority, leaving it up to him to create all the letters he wanted.

We do not know whether Francesco di Mino had really, as Giannino obviously believed, succeeded in bribing those high courtiers, or whether, which is just as likely, he had made it all up. But the outcome was the same, because in either case it came down to getting hold of a false object in order to create forged documents. Nor should we imagine that Giannino was unaware of the nature of the seal—a copy of a very precious original which the sovereign probably kept on his own person. In his account of the affair, in fact, the merchant appears well aware of the fact that this object was counterfeit, calling it "a seal of brass made just like . . . the secret seal."[21]

Although Giannino was to some degree letting himself be conned by "the Bishop," it is clear that he knew perfectly well what he was doing. If we pause for a moment and review the collection of characters surrounding him in Hungary, darker suspicions come to mind. Two of Giannino's friends were Florentines expert at melting gold and silver; and the man he had chosen to reside with, Saracino, was "coiner to the crown."[22] These were persons with skills, professional stamp-and-die men perfectly able to copy the design of a seal and make a new matrix. The suspicion, far from groundless, is that the merchant had surrounded himself with counterfeiters and that they had served him well.

And there is more. At the same period (we are now in spring 1359), the king of Hungary had also been robbed of his great seal, the one used for public documents. He had sent Nicholas Konth and his chancellor, Nicholas, archbishop of Esztergom, with other barons and a large army, against some Bosnian rebels. They had laid siege to the castle of Zrenk, and one night the king's authentic two-sided seal was stolen from the chancellor's tent. Some time later the thieves had sold it to a goldsmith, and it had finally been broken up. Unfazed by this incident, the king had immediately had another authentic seal made, which was assigned to the chancellor so he could confirm letters already sent under the lost seal. And indeed the privileges of the Hungarian crown from this period allude repeatedly to these duplicate authentications.[23]

In sum, just at the time when Giannino was receiving his counterfeit copy of the secret seal, the Hungarian chancellery was living through months of travail, having had its great seal stolen as well. There might be some connection, but we are in the dark about that, and whether it was significant. The fact remains that Giannino and his associates were operating in a murky atmosphere.[24]

Giannino now had his own personal seal, made of silver, on which his own visage was portrayed, the seal of Cola di Rienzo with the large star, and the seal—unquestionably counterfeit—of the king of Hungary. There was nothing to fear from Cola di Rienzo, who was dead, but the merchant knew he risked being arrested by the king of Hungary and charged with forging documents in his name. And the penalty for crimes of that kind, which were seen as subverting the natural order of things, was burning at the stake. On top of that, ambassadors from the Dauphin arrived in Hungary at this time, with a recommendation from the pope, to discuss certain matters with the king in person.[25] It would seem that the queen mother Elizabeth of Poland, having also received letters from the Dauphin and the emperor, showed open hostility to the Sienese merchant.

Whatever the reason, as soon as Giannino had the seal in his possession, he hastened to get out of Hungary. The earliest of his letters attributed to the king was dated Buda, 15 May 1359. The following day, Giannino departed for Italy.

THE KING'S LETTER

Giannino returned to his homeland with Andrea of Perugia, a German chaplain, a Sienese priest, and twelve Hungarian and German servants; "the Bishop," on the other hand, had been careful to cut loose. Giannino had with him the numerous credentials he had set out with, plus a supply of letters from his own phantom Hungarian chancellery to which he could add as necessary. We know that toward the end of his life he claimed possession of six letters patent written by the king of Hungary "to the universal [i.e., collective] and individual kings and princes of the world"; of six letters from the same monarch to Hungarians resident in Italy; and an unknown number of other letters stamped with the secret seal testifying that his claims had an authentic foundation.[26] So the workshop of forgeries had been humming.

Out of all these attestations to Giannino's royal dignity, there survives a copy transcribed into a register of the commune of Siena, which is worth paraphrasing and commenting on.[27] The epistle, which imitates the tenor of one of the king's safe-conducts, was addressed "to the universal kings, prelates, princes, dukes and counts, barons, cities, and the universal rectors of the same, constituted in the name of Christ." There followed a salutation from the king of Hungary, who proffered to all the recipients his wish for their well-being and his sincere affection for them. Then the reason that had finally decided King Louis, after initial hesitation, to act in favor of Giannino, was explained: "Since the sun, previously clouded over, shone in us, and a fire was lit of marvelous clarity, of truth and clarity, it must be regarded as worthy and be considered governed by reason, that, where we know we can succeed, we should bestir ourselves to bring effective help."

What the king actually states is that he has been enlightened by new information received subsequently. The use of the metaphor of the sun is arresting: the text derives from a passage in 2 Maccabees,[28] and it also appears to refer directly to the coat of arms adopted by Giannino di Guccio, who had been urged by Cola di Rienzo to furnish himself with an emblem similar to his own, including a large star with a face at its center "such that that visage appears to be a sun."[29] The sun, obscured at first but then resplendent, of which the pseudo-king of Hungary speaks was an allegory of Giannino himself, the hidden king who had finally been revealed. Cola di Rienzo had likewise written of himself once as a sun that, "having been obscured by clouds, blazes more welcome now."[30]

The letter of pseudo–King Louis continued with a narrative of the facts of which he had become aware. It told how Giovannino, called the son of Guccio and raised in the city of Siena, a noble man descended from the royal line of the progenitors of the sovereign of Hungary, the son of Louis, king of the French, and of Clémence the queen, both of blessed memory, having with due consideration directed his steps to the kingdom of Hungary, had demonstrated in an evident manner, through many authentic instruments and other documents, that the crown of France was owed to him by right. In these documents—the king is made to say—one saw clearly that the countess of Artois had had the intention of provoking the death of Jean a few days after his birth, in order that her son-in-law, Philippe the Long, paternal uncle of Jean, could reign more freely in the kingdom of France. But this had not happened, because Divine Providence, with the aid and help of the wet nurse, had switched the baby and caused another to be displayed in his place. The little king had been taken away in secret and concealed, just as the Baby Jesus had been by the Virgin Mary when she fled into Egypt. The substitute baby having been carried off by the will of the Most High, Providence had been careful to save the life of him in whose place the other had been murdered.

The account, which to this point rehearsed details already possessed by Giannino, was now enriched with fresh particulars:

> The nobles too, we read in the letter, including the oldest and highest-ranking nobles, the barons and baronesses of our kingdom, who years ago, after the death of the aforesaid lord Louis, king of France, had been sent by the most serene lord Charles [Charles Robert] of pious memory, our father, to visit the aforesaid lady, Queen Clémence, his sister, supply testimony of truth to all of this.

The barons added other elements that served the purposes of Giannino's reconstruction: they affirmed that they had learned that Jean, after having been switched in the kingdom of France, had been transferred to Tuscany, to the city of Siena to be precise.

"To investigate his case with greater security," continues pseudo-Louis, "while the aforesaid lord Jean was present in our kingdom, I secretly sent some discreet and prudent men as envoys into the kingdom of France." Questioned upon their return, they had recounted exactly those things asserted by Giannino. Therefore, all who received the letter were requested to consider Giannino as "recommended" in the affairs that he had to undertake, with the assurance that whatever they might do in his favor would be regarded as a favor to the crown of Hungary.

All in all, Giannino did not add much that was new. The word brought back by elderly Hungarian dignitaries sent to offer condolences to Queen Clémence was a fresh invention, as was the convergence of detail between Giannino's account and that of the envoys sent secretly to France. The testimony of the elderly barons and the envoys supplied Giannino with one more guarantee. But in reality this kind of evidence (if we can call it that) had been tried out before, and its flaws were familiar. Once again, probative value was attributed to the assertion of great barons informed of the facts, like the ones who had carried out the switch in the first place and therefore knew all about it. But just as the names of those French barons were never given, neither were those of the Hungarian lords and envoys. Without these names, the familiar, indeed formulaic, story was still not anchored in any reality outside itself. Giannino and others could have objected that the king's own word was enough, its authority rendering the citation of any other witness superfluous. This was formally true, but not at all conclusive: it simply demonstrates that in Hungary Giannino had got nowhere.

The seal of Louis the Great, a solidly established monarch, was worth a lot more than that of Cola di Rienzo, and his letter, circulated in who knows how many copies, might really have made a difference. But the grammatical errors, the repetitions, the Italianisms, which unsophisticated readers might not notice, would represent a serious risk if the letter were assessed carefully. Moreover, to introduce Hungarian dignitaries sent to Paris in 1316 to extend condolences to the queen risked overburdening the whole house of cards, since it implied that Queen Clémence herself was aware of the switch in the cradle. If so, why had she kept silent? Why live on for another twelve long years without revealing anything?[31]

GIANNINO, QUASI-CONDOTTIERE

Setting out from Hungary with his baggage of letters and dreams, Giannino traveled for eight days with an ambassador of Giangaleazzo Visconti, lord of Milan, who was headed the same way. Upon reaching Italy the two split up, and the Sienese merchant went to Mestre and from there to Venice in secret to confer with Daniello. Since he was now ready to raise an army, Giannino wanted to order some new clothes, "honorable and royal attire," to match his status.[32] His first suit was scarlet, with a mantle of the finest ermine, gold trimming, and strips of pearls and precious stones. On it were embroidered narratives of Hercules and of Jason departing in search of the golden fleece (an appropriate choice) and carrying off Medea. Altogether it cost 2600 florins. His second suit was blood-red, lined with ermine, and trimmed with gold in a herring-bone pattern, for the price of 120 florins; and the third deep violet, lined with grey vair and costing 60 florins. He arranged with Daniello, his all-purpose supplier as well as banker, to acquire the pearls and jewels needed to fabricate his crown, belt, sword, outer garment, and everything else he would need. Daniello made a note of all these requirements, and Giannino departed, short of funds and without his sumptuous suits.

Once again he passed through Treviso, Padua, and Ferrara, finally arriving at Bologna on 3 June 1359, where he arranged to be received by Giovanni of Oleggio and set about assembling his army.

Gil de Albornoz, the cardinal legate of Italy, who was reconquering the Papal State piece by piece for the papacy, was also in the vicinity. Learning of Giannino's presence, his twelve-man armed guard, and his intention to recruit other armed Hungarians and join Count Lando in Tuscany and discovering, moreover, that Giannino was negotiating to hire a company of 300 German horsemen, Albornoz became convinced that Giannino and his soldiery intended to join up with the Great Company of Count Lando, then hostile to the Florentine republic, which the Church supported. To prevent that, the cardinal arranged for the lord of Bologna not to allow either Giannino or the Germans he was busy signing up to leave the city.

So on the point of raising his standard, Giannino found himself blocked in Bologna. He wrote to Count Lando and to his friends in Siena, announcing his early arrival. But he was not allowed to cross the Apennines before Count Lando had left Tuscany for Piedmont to join the marchese of Monferrato. Giannino had perhaps had the secret intention of using Count Lando to seize control of either Siena or Perugia, as his follower Andrea of Perugia had once urged; now he was at a loss. Meanwhile expenses were mounting and his ready cash—an amount certainly much smaller than his credit of 250,000 florins, which would have been enough to buy the whole city of Bologna—was used up. To pay his innkeeper, the Florentine Felice Ammannati, Giannino was forced to sell his own horses and those of his retinue.

This predicament was not so unusual, since mercenaries, which at this point is how we may regard Giannino, often found themselves short of cash and forced to pledge all they possessed. But the Hungarians, deprived of their horses, grew restless, convinced that they had been tricked by their employer. The merchant-king had money sent from Siena so he could pay the innkeeper and pay off some members of his retinue. But he did not have enough to pay the Hungarians too, so he stole away in secret with Andrea of Perugia and two German squires, leaving them in the lurch. His eastern adventure was at an end.

He traversed the Apennines with hired horses, crossing the mountains near Mangona. Finally, on 6 August 1359, he entered Siena. Two years had passed since he had left, and he was back where he had started.

Chapter Four

·◁═▷·

In the West

Ohimè! Sarei io mai Calandrino,
ch'io sia sì tosto diventato un altro
senza essermene avveduto?

Alas! Am I Calandrino,
that I have so rapidly turned into someone else
without noticing?

—*La Novella del Grasso legnajuolo*

KING GIANNINO AND HIS FELLOW CITIZENS
While he had been in Hungary, our Sienese merchant had not lost
his eligibility for public office back home, as a citizen enrolled in the
wool guild and a resident of the ward of Terzo di Camollìa. And in
April 1358 Giannino di Guccio had in fact been selected for the highest magistracy of all, the Twelve Governors of the Commune and
People of the City of Siena. But as he was notoriously absent, someone else took his place.[1]

Two months after his return, the General Council of Siena,
known as the Council of the Bell, drew lots to choose the Twelve for
the period November–December 1359.[2] On 18 October one of the
names read out by the notary for the Riformagioni was that of Giannino di Guccio, wool man. But during the meeting many objected
that he ought to be prevented from holding this office, since the word
was out that he was in line to succeed to the French throne, being of
royal blood. This was seemingly confirmed by declarations contained
in several parchment letters bearing a round pendant seal the size of
a florin, with white wax outside and red wax inside. On the red part
the shield of the king of Hungary was visible, with lilies, bands, and

crest, and a Latin script reading "Secret Seal of King Louis." These letters had been presented at the offices of the Twelve, the captain of the people, and the gonfaloniere of justice of the commune of Siena and appeared to originate with the king of Hungary.

So on that 18 October 1359 Giannino was not confirmed in office. Instead his name was placed in the container of the *sciolti* (those released), meaning those who had been chosen but could not assume office, normally because at the moment of election they were not present in Siena or because they were already holding another office or because too little time had passed since their last turn in a magistracy. The sciolti were a reserve pool, available to replace, if necessary, those who did take office.

A few days later, on 27 October, the General Council of the Bell, regularly convoked with a quorum of 207 and with the *podestà*, the Twelve, the captain of the people, and the gonfaloniere of justice presiding, met to deliberate on this strange case. One of the Twelve, speaking for his colleagues, stated that after the election of 18 October, the same Giannino—referred to on this occasion as "signore Giovanni"—had asserted and affirmed before the Twelve and the captain of the people that, although in the past he had gone by the name of Giannino di Guccio of Siena, he was in truth signore Giovanni, "son of the most serene prince and lord, Lord Louis, once king of the French, and the most excellent Queen Clémence of Hungary." He had further affirmed that, as the letter narrated, he was of royal descent and entitled by right to succeed in the kingdom of France, since he had been switched at birth and brought to Tuscany.

Since, the magistrate went on, the said Giannino, "now called signore Giovanni," no longer wished to be called Giannino di Guccio, wool man of Siena, and did not wish to take office under the name Giannino di Guccio, although he had in the past borne that name, and since he was now declaring himself the son of the late king of France, and thus of royal blood, successor by right in the kingdom, a knight, and foreign by his own and his paternal origin: according to the tenor of the Sienese statutes, he could not be a member of the Twelve. The podestà took the slip with the name Giannino di Guccio out of the container of the sciolti for Terzo di Camollìa, and ripped it up. He then drew another, which bore the name Grifo di Lotto. To the official transcript of the proceedings of this meeting was appended the transcript of the letter from the king of Hungary in its entirety.

Poor Giannino, now "signore Giovanni" for the record, but probably already being called King Giannino in the street, as he was known forever after in Siena, hadn't given too much thought to the trouble that his forgeries and his stubbornness might get him into.[3] The merchant-king had never imagined that the letters he had showered on the magistrates of the commune might provoke such a reaction. The decision of the Council of the Bell must have exasperated him so much that he never even mentions it in his memoirs. On the other hand, it was a perfectly logical and legitimate provision. If Giannino were really, or even only claimed to be, a member of the royal house of France, that made him a noble and a foreigner, and thus ineligible to be a magistrate in the popular regime. Nor could his status be considered temporary, which would have allowed his name to remain among the sciolti. By calling himself king of France, Giannino was saying that he was not and never had been Sienese. Thus, by becoming a king, Giannino lost his Sienese citizenship: his name, removed from the container had been, in a highly symbolic gesture, ripped up. It was as though Giannino di Guccio were dead. As king, he was barred from government.

But what were the Sienese magistrates thinking anyway? Did they believe him? Did they perhaps intend to pay him homage by officially accepting his declaration? I have my doubts. Between the lines of this document, registered with all due care, I perceive a double attitude: on one hand the prudence of those in receipt of what appear to be letters patent from a sovereign and on the other gusts of Sienese laughter. The city's leaders have before them letters they suspect may be false (not just because of what they state, but also because they have not been delivered by official messengers from the king); yet they do present the external characteristics of letters from the king of Hungary. The Sienese drafted their public record cleverly so as to cover all bets. It says nothing about the authenticity of the letter, merely reporting its contents, carefully describing the seal and appending a transcription of the text. It states that Giannino's claim *appears* valid, and that the letter in question *appears* to come from King Louis. Like-wise the Sienese are careful not to recognize formally that Giannino is of royal descent: they simply take note of his affirmations, pointing out that it is Giannino himself who is claiming to be the heir to the French throne.

The whole business has the air of what Italians call a *beffa*, a mock-ing practical joke, here played by the city government on a reckless individual. In effect they were saying to him: You want to be king? Fine, but here's the downside.

Tales of this kind are a typical theme of the medieval and Renais-sance Italian novella: Boccaccio dedicates two whole days to the motif, the seventh and eighth in his ten-day marathon of storytell-ing, the *Decameron*. In the collective beffa a fictitious parallel world involving many accomplices is created around the victim; often he is made to believe that he is someone other than who he really is. Famous examples include the stories of Calandrino and the *Novella del Grasso legnajuolo* (The Tale of Grasso the Woodworker). The fifteenth-century novella, *Mattano da Siena*, by the Sienese writer Gentile Sermini, bears some resemblance to the adventure of Gian-nino: twelve well-born young Sienese convince a citizen named Mat-tano, the son of country folk, that he has been elected to the highest magistracy, the *magnifici signori*. The beffa involves the whole city: the guards at the gate doff their caps, his neighbors show him rever-ence. Even the captain of the people, the outgoing signori, the notary of the Riformagioni, and the prior get involved, welcoming him to city hall. There the prior reveals that his election has been quashed, because he was believed to be not in Tuscany but in "Trebizond." Mattano is told that his name has been put into the container of the sciolti, and at this point the notary makes a remark dripping with sar-casm to the effect that he really belongs in the container of the *legati* (the bound, as opposed to the released, which to Italian ears suggests *matti da legare*, those so crazy they ought to be tied down). The beffa continues, with the jesters getting Mattano to pay for one dinner after another. In the end the foolish, but above all presumptuous, Mattano is elected *priore dei Mugghioni e papa dei Bartali*, the prior of a group of revelers or lunatics of some sort.[4]

Mattano was mocked by the whole commune of Siena. In Giannino's case the prank was even more ferocious, since it took the form of accepting into the real world the parallel world in which the victim was already living and making him pay a heavy price.[5] Like the Florentine woodworker Grasso, the target of a terrible beffa on the part of his friends, who make him believe that he has become someone else and drive him to the brink of insanity, Giannino must have feared that his life in Siena was turning into a nightmare: "I am certainly not Grasso anymore, and have become Matteo; damned be my luck and my disgrace, for, if this fact becomes known, I shall be scorned and regarded as mad; gangs of youth will pursue me, and I will incur a thousand dangers."[6]

For all we know, gangs of youth were already pursuing the poor merchant, scoffing at the "King Giannino" residing in Terzo di Camollìa.

A derisory king, excluded forever from city government, and probably from the capacity to do business, resume his former life, or regain credibility, Giannino might also have run into serious difficulty with the fisc, since the moment he declared that he was not the son of Guccio and grandson of Mino, and thus by law not their heir, he was no longer entitled to possess the family property, which became liable to confiscation. For all these reasons, Giannino was already thinking of leaving Siena soon after he got back. In December he met Niccolò Acciaiuoli, grand seneschal of the kingdom of Naples, who passed through Siena on his way to Avignon as ambassador to the pope, on a mission to plead the case of the kingdom, over which the pope was trying to regain sovereignty. Giannino showed Acciaiuoli the king of Hungary's letters and inquired whether it might not be a good idea for him to head off to the kingdom of Naples himself and speak there with the king and the other princes whose relative he was claiming to be. But the grand seneschal advised him to go north to the pope at Avignon rather than south to Naples.

As well as the advice of Niccolò Acciaiuoli, Giannino had another good reason to proceed toward the kingdom he was claiming as his own. From spring of the previous year, as soon as the truce of Bordeaux ended, the king of England had resumed warfare in France, conducting an effective military campaign that was putting pressure on the Dauphin. In October 1359, while Giannino was in Siena, complicated negotiations between emissaries of the two warring kingdoms had begun in order to reach a new truce, the liberation of Jean II the Good, and ultimately a lasting peace. So it was not unlikely that Jean II would soon be freed, leaving the merchant no more room for maneuver.

Giannino therefore put his affairs in order, probably made a will, arranged the terms on which his wife and children would remain in Siena, and on 31 March 1360 set out for Avignon. He traveled with his customary faithful companion, Andrea of Perugia (who had dropped the idea of Giannino's seizing power in Perugia), and with a brother-in-law, a certain Neri d'Andrea Beccarini. He took ship at Livorno, and after a stop at Genoa disembarked at Nice, and set out from there for Avignon, where he arrived on 21 April clad as a pilgrim.

AT AVIGNON

Giannino now needed to get a meeting with the pope, but this was easier said than done. As soon as he arrived, Giannino spoke with Tommaso of Montella, procurator general of the order of friars minor, to find out how he could arrange a meeting with Innocent VI. The friar suggested that he be received, still dressed as a pilgrim, by the head of the Apostolic Penitentiary, Cardinal Francesco degli Atti of Todi, the bishop of Florence and cardinal protector of the kingdom of Naples. This was good advice, since the court of the Penitentiary also had jurisdiction over problems of legitimate and illegitimate filiation, an area pertinent to Giannino's obsession.[7]

Wearing white jackets, gray cloaks lined with white, high boots, and spurs, Giannino and his two companions crossed the Rhône and entered the kingdom of France at Villeneuve, where the cardinal resided. Giannino had passed through Provence, which belonged to the queen of Naples, and through the Comtat Venaissin and Avignon, which belonged to the papacy. Now for the first time he set foot in the kingdom of France proper—the kingdom he claimed as his own.

He had himself announced to the cardinal penitentiary as a pilgrim on the road to Santiago, who wished to discuss a confidential matter with the cardinal alone. Upon entering the cardinal's reception room, he revealed his true status, stated that all he wanted was the cardinal's advice, and begged him to bring the matter before the pope so that there could be an inquiry. Should the pope discover that Giannino was in the right, then Giannino requested that the pope intervene between him and the French, so that he could be received peacefully in the kingdom; if on the contrary the pope should decide that Giannino was in the wrong and had been deceived, then Giannino would immediately abandon the enterprise, having no intention of claiming what did not belong to him.

The cardinal was amazed that Giannino had been foolhardy enough to leave Avignon and cross the Rhône into the kingdom of France, where he risked capture and death. He advised him to pursue his project with care and secrecy. The cardinal dismissed him, but not before assigning a chaplain to him, a fellow citizen, Girolamo Piccolomini of Siena, whose job was to hear all he had to say, review his documents, and report back to the cardinal.

Giannino made a full confession to Girolamo and gave him the letters in his possession. Girolamo brought them to the cardinal, and the cardinal brought them to the pope. If the matter was ever discussed in consistory, the decision taken was that the Roman Catholic Church should not get involved in it. Eight days later, the cardinal sent him back his documents.

Giannino's position in Avignon, so close to France and so openly exposed, was now becoming quite dangerous. Perhaps this was why his faithful companion, Andrea of Perugia, who had joined up with him in Hungary, suddenly betrayed him, stealing all his documents. Giannino paid thirty florins to get them back, and Andrea vanished for good.

The merchant followed his usual practice when abroad, lodging with a fellow Sienese, Benvenuto,[8] who ran the inn "at the sign of the Saracen." With this as his base, Giannino began knocking at the doors of the cardinals' palaces. He did not behave at all surreptitiously, as he had been advised to do. He met with Guglielmo della Pusterla, then Latin patriarch of Constantinople (named archbishop of Milan in the following summer), who gave him a little money. He then wrote to a dozen cardinals, prudently pretending to be in Genoa instead of Avignon, addressing them as though they were intimate friends and requesting each to obtain the papal audience that Innocent VI continued to refuse him. Making the rounds of the cardinals' palaces, he managed to speak with the cardinal bishop of Palestrina, Pierre Després, and with the cardinal of Aragon. Exploiting the entrée he had with merchants, he made contact with the chamberlain of the Roman cardinal Nicola Capocci, a Sienese named Luca Tolomei, and with other prelates and lords. A few encouraged him, suggesting he begin by conquering some territory, after which he would certainly receive help, openly or secretly, from the Church.

THOSE PULLING THE STRINGS

Who were these people spurring him to take action, and in any case keeping a close watch on him? I am prepared to advance a political hypothesis at this point. From roughly 1354 to 1364, the Hundred Years' War was fought between not two crowned heads claiming the throne of France, but three. Naturally there was the king of France, Jean II the Good, still a prisoner of the English but expected to be released soon. His son Charles, duke of Normandy and dauphin of Viennois, governed in his name, first with the title of lieutenant, then as regent. Father and son belonged to the line of the counts of Valois, who had succeeded to the direct Capetian line upon the death of the last male son of Philippe IV the Fair.

Then there was the king of England, Edward III, who proclaimed himself king of France and refused to recognize the legitimacy of the dynastic succession in the Valois line. His mother, Isabelle of France, had indeed been a daughter of Philippe the Fair. With the extinction of the male line—the English claimed—the crown ought to have passed not to the counts of Valois, a collateral branch descended from Charles the Landless, the brother of Philippe IV, but to the latter's direct descendants, who, albeit through the female line, were fully entitled to reign in France.

The third crowned head with ambitions to reign in France, and the one relevant to my hypothesis, was the king of Navarre, Charles II the Bad.[9] Sovereign of the diminutive kingdom of Navarre in the Pyrenees, Charles was also a prince of the royal house of France, being the son of Philippe III, count of Évreux and Jeanne, queen of Navarre, a daughter of Louis X. She, a half-sister of King Jean I the Posthumous (from Giannino's point of view, his half-sister), had been refused the right to succeed her father and brother by an assembly of great nobles that had met in Paris in 1317 and ratified the legitimate succession of her uncle, Philippe V, declaring after the fact that female members of the royal family could never inherit the throne. On that occasion a celebrated dictum, based on a saying from the gospels (Matthew 6:29), had been coined: "the lilies don't spin wool" (the lilies are the emblem of France; wool-spinning is the emblematic activity of women). The precedent cited was the Salic law of the ancient Franks, in fact a code of private law that had been opportunely elevated to the status of public law and used to resolve the succession controversy.

In consequence the king of Navarre regarded himself as the legitimate heir of the Capetian crown, both through his mother and through his maternal uncle, Jean I. His rights as he saw it were superior to those of the king of England, whom he preceded by a generation in a direct line that, starting from Philippe IV, passed to his eldest son Louis X, then to Jean I the Posthumous, then to Jean's sister Jeanne, Charles's mother, and from her to him. From this perspective, moreover, the reigns of his grandfather's brothers, Philippe V and Charles IV, were illegitimate. That was not all. Charles of Navarre, who possessed extensive landholdings in Normandy (including the county of Évreux, close enough to Paris to constitute a security threat, and the entire Cotentin Peninsula), also claimed the county of Champagne and the palatine county of Brie, and he did so precisely as heir of the rights that had passed from little Jean I to his half-sister Jeanne. Indeed, whether the Salic law was seen as valid or not, there was no doubt that, for these counties, succession in the maternal line was considered legitimate, since the uncle of Charles of Navarre, Louis X, had received them from his own mother. So for the king of Navarre, unlike the kings of England and France, the position of Jean I was of paramount importance, since it constituted one of the links in the chain of succession leading to him.

Overtly hostile to the king of France, who was nonetheless his father-in-law, and responsible for the assassination of the constable Charles of Spain, the close friend of Jean II, Charles of Navarre had been imprisoned on 5 April 1356, and several great lords from his following had been executed. But his partisans, led by his younger brother, remained active; indeed, the first contact between their emissaries and Giannino took place around then. The intrigues and the secret diplomatic maneuvers at which the princes of Navarre were so adept were entering a heightened phase at this time.

Charles of Navarre remained a prisoner of the king and then of the regent until the night of 7–8 November 1358, when he escaped through a trick. According to one version of the story, his jailer was kidnapped a few days previously, and his seal stolen. This was used to authenticate letters ordering the release of Charles of Navarre and opening the gates of the nearby cities to him—a colossal example of a kind of counterfeiting with which we are already familiar.[10]

As soon as he was free, Charles of Navarre had resumed his war against the regent, proclaiming himself the legitimate king of France. He had allied himself with the commune of Paris and the bishop of Laon and had even delivered speeches to the people of Paris in a direct challenge to the Dauphin, who was present in Paris at the time. He had maintained a close alliance with Étienne Marcel, the "provost of the merchants" of Paris, as the mayor of the city was called, and in June 1358 was actually named captain and governor of Paris himself. After Étienne Marcel met his end in July 1358 there was a short truce, and then Charles of Navarre resumed open warfare against Jean II the Good and his son Charles. Only during the brief interval of the Jacqueries, May–June 1358, during which the peasants, generically called Jacques, had revolted against their masters, had the sovereigns of France and Navarre seen eye to eye on the need to deal with this emergency, moving together to massacre the rebels.

In sum, in the period that interests us, 1357–1360, Charles the Bad of Navarre was at war with the regent of France, and even after that, the troops of lawless soldiers that ravaged the countryside were largely composed of Navarrists. We begin to grasp the reasons why Charles of Navarre had an interest in keeping the memory of Jean I alive: it reminded everyone of the illegitimate assumption of power by Philippe V, to the detriment of Jeanne of Navarre, and so of the house of Évreux. We likewise begin to grasp the motives Giannino might have had to seek support from the man he considered his nephew, the son of his half-sister.

Having kept an eye on Giannino for some time, the house of Navarre, which was closely monitoring the outcome of the peace between France and England, was keeping him ready in case they needed to put him into play. A clause of the peace of Brétigny stated that the king of France would pardon Philippe of Navarre, restoring to him and his followers their cities and castles if they went back to being loyal vassals. But not a word was said about his elder brother, King Charles the Bad, who remained a fugitive and a felon in the eyes of King Jean the Good, who apparently detested him.[11] Consequently the position of Navarre during the phase of Anglo-French reconciliation was far from unambiguous.

It is not conceivable that Charles of Navarre really intended to set Giannino up as Jean I; indeed he and his followers took care never to recognize him or even write to him. Apart from anything else, as direct heir of Louis X the merchant prince would, in strict logic, have been not only king of France but also king of Navarre. So his role as far as the Navarrists were concerned was mainly to stir up trouble. Even without any concrete prospect of success, Giannino might seize the chance to raise his standard in some localities in southern France, exploiting the power vacuum and the general state of confusion, and undermining French morale. Naturally he would never be anything more than a half-aware pawn, a momentary ally to be supported for as long as he was useful. In similar fashion, the English and the Navarrists, both grasping for the same crown, had often found themselves temporarily allied against their common foe. Giannino would therefore receive help from a party skilled at intrigue and hostile to the French crown, along with support from competing princes, and thus would play his part in an aristocratic plot, just as many other self-proclaimed sovereigns and claimants had done and would do in European history.[12]

So much for the general background. Let us now examine the evidence leading me to think that this political alignment between Giannino and Navarre existed in fact. A few clues have already been noted: there was the way the preceptor of Altopascio made contact with Giannino, letting him know off the record that he had the support of Philippe, count of Longueville and brother of Charles of Navarre, who recognized him as legitimate king. We have seen Giannino writing from Siena to the king of Navarre and an emissary from the king subsequently putting himself at Giannino's disposal in Hungary. What hasn't been mentioned so far is that the very origin of the process by which the merchant king was recognized may have been launched from the court of Navarre.

In April 1356, before he decided to reveal himself, Giannino had had inquiries made in France about the circumstances of his birth, receiving a reply on 15 December from a merchant resident in Paris, Giovanni di Bartalo Martelli of Florence. Martelli's letter, the authenticity of which is not unimpeachable, since it was copied by our friend the notary Angelo d'Andrea, an intimate of Giannino, may contain information that, if true, would be very suggestive.[13] The Florentine merchant had made inquiries about Friar Giordano, the man to whom Marie de Cressay had told all, elsewhere referred to as Giordano "of Spain," and had found out that during the previous Lent the friar had been seized by the king of France. According to Martelli, there was a connection between that and the capture of the king of Navarre, which followed shortly after. Giovanni di Bartalo did not know what had become of the friar, but he reported that his fellow friars had the impression that the king had had him killed in secret "on account of a certain confession which he had to reveal, said to be detrimental to the king."[14] Suppose that the letter was just one more forgery by Giannino and his notary: it would demonstrate in any case that Giannino himself considered his situation as being linked to that of the king of Navarre.

We now return to Avignon, to the cardinals and great lords with whom Giannino had established contact. Though he could not get a hearing from the pope, who favored the king of France, doors had been opened to Giannino in the retinue of Cardinal Capocci, who was bishop of Urgel, in the archdiocese of Tarragona. In 1359 this cardinal had managed the peace treaty between the Dauphin and Charles of Navarre, showing himself more inclined to the latter. Giannino also got a meeting with Cardinal Nicholas Rossell of Tarragona, known as the Cardinal of Aragon, and with the cardinal bishop of Tusculum, Guillaume Court, called the White Cardinal because he was a Cistercian, a native of the county of Foix. None of these cardinals was pro-French, and all were close to the interests of Navarre and Aragon, kingdoms that were allied on account of the marriage between Marie of Navarre, the sister of Charles the Bad, and Pedro IV, king of Aragon, known as the Ceremonious.

As princes of the Church, the cardinals were in a position to pursue policies of their own, ones not always in conformity with those of the pope. Not long before, at the end of 1354, Cardinals Gui de Boulogne and Pierre Bertrand de Colombiers had collaborated on a project to dismember the kingdom of France by facilitating meetings in their own residences between the duke of Lancaster and the king of Navarre.[15]

All this does not mean that these cardinals and prelates did plot against France and did support Giannino, which is the impression he conveys in his memoirs. But his choice of which cardinals to approach does reveal that Giannino (or whoever was behind him) was following a genuine strategy, trying to win over high-ranking ecclesiastics who did not have close links to the king of France but did have them with other foreign powers.

Among the secular lords with whom Giannino made contact, there was the count of Foix and Béarn, both extensive territories; Gaston was his name but he was also known as Phoebus because of his blond hair and his good looks. Like the king of Aragon, he too was a brother-in-law of the king of Navarre, whose sister Agnès he had married in 1348. So the count of Foix was also a nephew of Giannino, in a manner of speaking. The political grouping from which the Sienese merchant-king sought backing, and to some extent found it, constituted what we may regard as a southern front vis-à-vis France.

The only piece missing was the support of the counts of Provence, in other words the Angevin royals of Naples, and in fact Giannino was maneuvering in their direction as well.[16]

Like his relatives, Gaston de Foix was careful not to reply in writing to Giannino's letters, but he sent word that as soon as Giannino had raised his own standard and won some territory, he would follow him immediately with all his forces and induce others to do the same. This set Giannino off on a fresh round of letter-writing to various lords, who all responded in the same terms.

He had decided not to stay put in Avignon and had taken to changing locations for greater security. As in the past, an individual was assigned to accompany him and keep a close eye on his doings. This was Pierre de La Courneuve, whom Giannino himself identifies as "a substantial merchant and draper, a leading bourgeois of Paris, who was a very faithful servant of the king of Navarre and one of the companions of the provost of the merchants."[17] Indeed he was: Pierre de La Courneuve had played a leading role at the time of Étienne Marcel's rebellion, had fled Paris after Marcel's death, and, having been banished from the kingdom of France, took refuge at Avignon, where he maintained contact with the king of Navarre, the principal backer of the regime of the Parisian bourgeois. The draper fell to his knees before Giannino, swore loyalty to him, and promised to live and die in his service. So frequent and fervid were his displays of love and loyalty that Giannino named him his secretary and counselor.

At around the same time another character joined the little court of King Giannino, composed mostly of Tuscans. This was a certain Federico degli Ubaldini, a monk of Vallombrosa, who passed himself off as the abbot of the famous monastery (we know that the abbot at this time was actually Michele Flammini). Much like Francesco dal Cotone, alias "the Bishop," the grey monk immediately became Giannino's chaplain and counselor, and "drafted all his letters and privileges."[18]

THE PEACE OF BRÉTIGNY

The events already narrated, and some of those that follow, took place between spring and autumn 1360, more precisely between the initial accord reached at Brétigny on 8 May and the final draft, dated at Calais on 24 October. In virtue of this treaty, the king of France ceded a large part of the kingdom, including complete sovereignty over Calais, Poitou, Périgord, Limousin, and Aquitaine, in exchange for the English king's renunciation of all claims to the French crown, and his withdrawal from his strongholds. Jean II the Good was to be released immediately following ratification, in exchange for the enormous ransom of three million gold écus, to be paid in instalments.

Giannino in the meantime, realizing how the restoration of peace and the return of the king would harm his interests, prepared for war. Even before arriving at Avignon and calling on cardinals, he had sent for Daniello, who was still in Venice and had not been seen for months. Daniello got to Avignon in May, a few days after Giannino himself, bringing money and jewels.

Time was passing quickly, and although Giannino had been given vague assurances by various prelates, the pope resolutely refused to receive him and he was at an impasse. The return of his namesake Jean II to French soil would ruin everything. Over the summer Giannino came to the conclusion that Avignon was a dead end, and began once more, as he had already done in Siena, to consider going to the kingdom of Naples, gaining audience with the royal house there, his close relatives, and asking them about the best way to establish himself peacefully in France. The voyage was dangerous—one could be captured or killed at sea—and Giannino decided to protect his succession: he made Daniello his procurator, with the power to sell his rights to the caliph of Baghdad, the sultan of Babylon, and the lord of the Tartars, so that his sons would not be left entirely unprovided for. This extraordinary (and for us, barely comprehensible) act of solemn renunciation, sealed with the pendant seal bearing Giannino's face, was made subject to two conditions: before trading these rights, Daniello should wait eighteen months from the date of Giannino's capture, and the Saracens who acquired them were to take revenge on whoever had captured or killed him.

But at this point something unexpected occurred, which convinced him to remain in Avignon and gave him fresh hope. The commander of a mercenary company named Nicolò Buglietti of Florence offered to put himself and his men at Giannino's disposal. The historical context for this is that, right after the signing of the peace of Brétigny, the kings of France and England began to demobilize their troops in France and evacuate their fortresses. The soldiers left unemployed did not, however, disband; instead they regrouped into new military formations to make war on their own account, or to hire themselves out to any prince or lord who could use them. These soldiers were of all nationalities: Giannino himself enumerates "English, Germans, French, Bretons, Gascons, Burgundians, and speakers of other languages."[19]

The majority were English and Navarrists, members of companies of demobilized soldiers already formed after the arrest of King Charles of Navarre in 1356, whose ranks were now swelling rapidly. These violent mercenaries were commonly known as *routiers* (*route* or *rote* being an old French word for "band") and also as *tard-venus* or "late-comers," because they had arrived after the peace. If they were employed by a lord then they could be seen as regular troops; if not they were considered outright criminals. "In the agreement reached by the two kings of France and England, from which a good peace was confidently expected, with the king of England returning to his island with his sons and his host, many English horsemen and archers accustomed to predation and robbery remained in the country."[20]

Almost all of these bands formed in the north of France, specifically in Champagne and Brie, the territories claimed by the king of Navarre. In the months following the Anglo-French peace they assembled into larger units and headed south, killing, burning, and looting as they went. The first and biggest of these new military formations called itself simply la Grande Compagnie. At Lent 1362, two years subsequent to the point we have reached, it contained 15,000 fighting men.

Matteo Villani records no less than five such companies operating in the Midi between the end of 1360 and the spring of 1362. They maintained cohesion for a fairly long period in Provence and the lower valley of the Rhône, and soon appeared at the gates of Avignon, proposing that the pope and cardinals hire them, or failing that, pay them off to keep Avignon and the Comtat Venaissin from the certain prospect of being sacked.

With the wars over and peace made between the two kings of England and France, and King Jean back in France with the intention of gently reordering the kingdom, he proclaimed throughout the kingdom that all evil people must leave and get out of his kingdom under grave penalty. For this reason various companies assembled, and one after the other set off for Avignon.[21]

Nicolò Buglietti was at Avignon during the month of August 1360. He went to the pope to propose that he and his men be hired for the war against Milan. After being told that the Church did not currently need armed men and being thanked for taking the trouble, Buglietti remained for a time at Avignon, making the acquaintance of another Florentine captain, Agnolo Banchi. Banchi proposed that he take service with the legitimate king of France, known to us as Giannino di Guccio.

The soldier and the merchant king met, and Giannino as usual showed him all his certificates. Buglietti then requested copies to show to his soldiers, and Giannino immediately complied, adding that he had no intention of seizing cities, castles and villages, or even the money that might be captured, and that he would gladly hand everything over to the army that chose to follow him: as far as he was concerned, the title of king was enough.

With the promise of retaining all the booty, the certainty that there were no other offers at the moment, and the presumption of fighting for a just cause, Buglietti left Avignon on 24 August 1360, accompanied by Giannino's brother-in-law, Neri d'Andrea Beccarini, who acted as ambassador. Buglietti explained to his mercenaries that the Church did not need men, but that they could accomplish another meritorious deed by helping King Jean I to recover his throne. His men decided to try this adventure, and set about recruiting more soldiers. Letters were written to many barons in France and magistrates of city governments; the merchants of Paris were contacted as well. The bulk of those who joined, so Giannino himself informs us, were "all those who had been on the side of the king of Navarre and the provost of the merchants."[22]

So the troops offering themselves to Giannino in late summer of 1360 were essentially followers of the crown of Navarre, mostly demobilized and unpaid. Their plan was to take Toulouse, Lyon, Nîmes, Béziers, Carcassonne, Montpellier, Roquemaure, Villeneuve, and Pont-Saint-Esprit on the Rhône—in other words, many of the cities of modern southeastern France.

The captain of these troops was a young English lord from a great family, Andrew de Beaumont, who must have been a younger brother of Isabel, wife of the duke of Lancaster, one of the principal English commanders. This meant that Andrew de Beaumont was closely related to the English royal house.[23] But—so Giannino maintains—the captain general of his force was too young, being less than twenty, and since—so I would add—it can't have suited Beaumont very well to campaign on behalf of a flimsy "king of France" when his own sovereign, Edward III, was at peace with the legitimate king, Jean II the Good, the soldiers themselves chose a proven soldier as their deputy commander, an English gentleman with plenty of combat experience who had distinguished himself in the Anglo-French wars.

This was not so much the appointment of a deputy commander, I suspect, as an irregular substitution. What probably happened is that the soldiers commanded by Andrew de Beaumont, having been ordered to disperse, stayed together instead and picked one of their officers as their new commander themselves. Giannino calls him "Giovanni Vernee"; what his true name was in English we do not know. He was a robust captain of forty, to whom the soldiers were devoted.[24] Having been placed in command by the troops with the mission of fighting for King Jean, Giovanni Vernee chose his own captains, councilors, standard-bearers, smiths, and other officials, and selected the city of Lyon as his first target.

While this war planning was going on, Giannino resumed his own personal preparations. He summoned Daniello once more and ordered him to prepare banners with the royal emblem, and shields and armor, sending him to Milan to purchase these supplies. Daniello brought back with him three sets of armor for the king and three for his horses: the first was made of overlapping steel scales, the second of mail, and the third of marine turtle shells.

Giannino had three suits made to wear over his armor, each a different color, and a sword-belt studded with jewels and pearls. He also had a crown made, a gold circlet with lilies and equipped with hooks so that it could be worn over a helmet, a hood, or a silk bonnet. It was meant to be encrusted with precious stones, which were not yet mounted: four large rubies, four balas rubies, four diamonds, four sapphires, four emeralds, 100 large pearls and 100 smaller ones, for a total value of 10,000 florins. The almost-crowned king sewed all these pearls and jewels into a garment, along with 4500 ducats; another 500 were sewn into a pair of pants. The last item he prepared was two small protective vests, to be worn at all times under his clothing. As soon as he had conquered some territory and raised his standard, Giannino planned to mount the jewels in his crown and send money to his wife and children so they could join him.

Everything necessary for fielding an army and making war was got ready: Giannino procured boilers, pots, ladles, tripods, chests and valises, and ten large war tents called *trabacche*, complete with ropes and other gear. He also had a royal pavilion made, waterproof and lined with blue cotton fabric patterned with lilies and gold stars.

By around November 1360, therefore, with Jean II having just left English territory at Calais headed for Paris, Jean I was ready to go to war. It was a moment of great excitement; even today we can sense Giannino's nervousness in his memoirs, which at this period are full of interruptions, asides, and reprises. Trying to remember and recount events, he continually loses his train of thought.

Waiting for news and fearing for his own safety, the merchant left Avignon repeatedly, residing for two weeks at Orgon, a city in the county of Provence, where he encountered other soldiers and fellow Tuscans, all of whom were regaled with his story. Among them was one Luchetto of Pistoia, and a certain Bartolomeo di Pagno of Siena, whom he made his servant. Giannino then went to Saint-Rémy and succeeded in making contact with Gaston de Foix through the archdeacon of Saint-Paul-Trois-Châteaux; the White Cardinal had a hand in this as well. With the probable approval of Gaston and the help of the archdeacon, secret discussions were held with the chatelain of Roquemaure, a formidable stronghold on the Rhône a little north of Avignon on the road to Lyon. It was arranged that, as soon as Jean I had raised his standard, Roquemaure would immediately be handed over to him without resistance. The reconquest of France would start there.

Finally, on 21 November 1360, the two condottieri, Buglietti and Vernee, went to Avignon to inform Giannino that all was ready. They conferred for two days and made their plans. The merchant king then nominated Vernee "his lieutenant in act of war throughout the realm of France . . . by a privilege stamped with his seal bearing his face."[25] And he wrote to the twelve peers of France commanding them to present themselves before him forthwith, and to prepare for his reception as legitimate king and lord, and to organize everything so that he would be welcomed in peace and concord in the kingdom. And he wrote as well to the king of England, the king of Navarre, and various other lords.

His captains—Giannino claims—had the approval of friendly prelates, meaning the patriarch of Constantinople and the cardinals of Palestrina, Aragon, and Florence. As soon as hostilities commenced, these ecclesiastical dignitaries would secretly advance his cause with money and soldiers and would win over the pope and the other cardinals. Although the latter were not actively helping, they still guaranteed their neutrality. Encouraged by these assurances, the two captains left Avignon on 27 November to rejoin their army of routiers. Everything was ready for Giannino's war, which would begin with the seizure of Roquemaure and continue with the conquest of Lyon. They had the weaponry, and above all they had the men.

But with France and England making peace, Navarre could not afford to be left out. As early as 26 October, two days after the signing of the treaty of Calais, Philippe of Navarre, the king's brother, dined with Jean II and ratified the clauses of the peace between the two kingdoms. Ambassadors of France and Navarre met with the aim of reconciling Jean the Good and Charles the Bad as rapidly as possible. The two sovereigns met on 12 December 1360 at Saint-Denis and swore reciprocal oaths. Next day Jean II entered Paris. Naturally a few pending matters had to be cleared up to make this reconciliation last. One of these was the amnesty to be granted to the principal followers of Navarre and the participants in the revolt of Étienne Marcel. Charles of Navarre drew up and handed over to the king of France a scroll containing the names of 260 persons to whom he wished letters of remission to be granted, reserving the right to nominate another forty before Easter. The deal was done: a few months later Jean II in turn drew up a scroll containing the 300 names of those he was pardoning for all the misdeeds they had committed in their lives down to the cutoff date of 12 December 1360. Among the names of those pardoned on both scrolls—they included the principal and most authoritative supporters of the king of Navarre—we find that of a character we have already met: Pierre de La Courneuve.[26]

So by November Giannino di Guccio, who until then had been receiving the secret backing of Navarre, was already becoming an inconvenience. Having helped him acquire arms and troops, the princes of Navarre now had no intention of playing the card of insurrection or, for the moment, prosecuting the war: the pawn had to be sacrificed.[27] Their man Pierre de La Courneuve, who had not left the side of the king from Siena, must have been assigned to deal with the matter. Giannino sorrowfully records his betrayal, attributing it to lust for money and the wish to be resettled in Paris. That is not impossible, but there is good reason in my view to suppose that Pierre de La Courneuve was following precise instructions. It must have been early in December that the Parisian merchant went to see the powerful Cardinal Élias de Talleyrand, of the family of the counts of Périgord, who was the mediator for the peace between France and England and had negotiated the release of Jean II the Good and who indeed had tried in the past to reconcile the Dauphin and the king of Navarre, showing decided partiality to the former. The cardinal, who—what a surprise—held the city of Roquemaure, the intended launching pad for Giannino's conquest, welcomed the French draper (who had got away from Giannino by claiming he was going on pilgrimage) and learned the whole war plan of the Sienese merchant from him.

Giannino at this point had to be got rid of, either with poison or by handing him over to the justice system, represented by the seneschal of Beaucaire. But our merchant-king, who was evidently keeping a close and watchful eye on developments, must have been alerted in time, and did the only thing he could do: flee into Provence. He left Avignon around 6 December escorted by a single squire, Giannino (or Giannuzzo) de' Bardi of Florence. Crown and armor were entrusted to Daniello, but Giannino held onto his money and jewels. He took refuge in Seillons, and shortly after in the nearby castle of Saint-Estève, the domain of Raymond of Montauban. There was a woman 50 years old living there named Tora, who had the advantage of being Sienese, a relative of his, and a lady-in-waiting of Queen Giovanna of Naples.

It was time to start plotting afresh. With no more hope of support from Navarre, and knowing that he risked death if he set foot in Avignon again, but with an army of mercenaries who had sworn fidelity to him, Giannino tried his luck with the Provençal nobility, who were proud of their political and cultural identity and had good reason to hate the Dauphin, who had recently supported the revolt of the lords of Baux and who aimed to restore, to his own advantage, the ancient kingdom of Arles. Giannino wrote out in his own hand a list of Provençal lords and cities, intending to send a letter to each of them requesting reinforcements. But while he was sheltering in Provence, his mercenaries were not sitting idly by.

THE SHORT WAR OF KING GIANNINO

It was almost Christmas, 1360. Around two weeks before, King Jean II had reentered Paris, pacing in a triumphant procession beneath a golden canopy while King Jean I was holed up in a castle in Provence. His mercenaries, commanded by Giovanni Vernee, must have wondered about their situation as well. No longer tied to either Navarre or England, this body of unemployed soldiers, whose size we don't know (but it must have been considerable) may have joined forces at this time with an even larger force that had assembled shortly before in Champagne and was heading for Avignon.[28]

On 27 December a few bands, very likely including Giannino's, were in the vicinity of Roquemaure, fifteen kilometers downstream from Pont-Saint-Esprit. But Roquemaure had been alerted, as we know, and was stoutly defended. On that day the routiers sacked and burned the village of Chusclan, situated between Roquemaure and Pont-Saint-Esprit. On 28 December they took the village and fortress of Codolet, a few kilometers further south, toward Roquemaure, at the confluence of the Rhône and the Cèze. The companies that devastated the two villages were almost certainly the same ones that, at dawn on 29 December 1360, overran Pont-Saint-Esprit itself. Froissart and Villani both state that the assault was carried out by a strong contingent, apparently composed of English, Gascons, and "renegade French," that had approached during the night by a forced march, catching the inhabitants off guard.

Pont-Saint-Esprit (Holy Spirit Bridge) is a small city on the west bank of the Rhône, which enters Provence at this point, around forty kilometers upstream from Avignon. It had long been strategically important, for it sat next to one of the few bridges spanning the Rhône. In the fourteenth century, in fact, there were only four. So to hold Pont-Saint-Esprit was to control both banks of the great river: France on one side and the Dauphiné on the other, a vassal territory of the Holy Roman Empire. Froissart states: "From there they could carry out raids at their ease and without risk, at one hour in the kingdom of France and the next in the Empire."[29]

The routiers who had captured the bridge represented a serious threat to the papal court, since they could easily reach Avignon from the left bank and Villeneuve from the right bank. They could extort a toll from merchants, travelers, and above all ecclesiastics on their way to the papal court. Worse than that, they were in a position to intercept the convoys of foodstuffs and merchandise whose highway was the Rhône Valley and so starve Avignon. Froissart again: "They would be masters and lords of the Rhône and the keys of Avignon."[30]

Despite its strategic importance as a nodal juncture between three states and chokepoint along a vital route, the city of Pont-Saint-Esprit was not well defended; indeed, it was not even completely girded with walls, lacking any protection along the riverbank. The walls that were standing had been rebuilt in 1231 and were in bad shape. For lack of funds, they had been patched up here and there with simple palisades. The only strong defense was the central tower, erected in 1202. The bridge for its part was defended by two towers, one at either end. The city and its bridge were guarded by a citizen militia, reinforced shortly before the attack by a small garrison under the command of a man from Lucca, a sergeant of the king of France who acted as provost. If resistance proved unavailing, three barred gates giving access to the river would provide a means of escape into the swamp on the east bank.

The chronicles give varying accounts of how the battle unfolded, but it is likely that several *routes* made a combined attack and that they met little resistance. The Lucchese commander was captured and quickly released but was soon placed under arrest in Avignon on suspicion of having sold out Pont-Saint-Esprit. Some inhabitants sought refuge in the church, which was fortified, carrying their valuables and hoping for the arrival of a relief force. This did not appear, and after six days they made a deal with the mercenaries, paying a ransom of 6000 florins to salvage their lives and property. Villani adds that although the sum was paid, the mercenaries did not keep their side of the bargain, robbing the victims and seizing some girls. According to Froissart, a number of men were killed and women raped.

What was the mercenaries' purpose in taking the city? Apart from its strategic value, which they certainly knew, their aim was to seize the money gathered by the seneschals of Toulouse, Carcassonne, and Nîmes to pay the first installment of the ransom of Jean II. The money, 46.4 kilograms of gold in various coinages, had been brought to Avignon on 26 December and was meant to be transported to Paris under armed guard. During the night of the twenty-seventh, or the next day, the seneschal of Beaucaire, who was charged with taking delivery of the gold, had passed through Pont-Saint-Esprit. In theory he was supposed to make the return trip immediately, passing back through the town with that huge fortune. But, learning that it had been captured, he had the treasure brought to Nîmes, where it remained until March. The routiers had evidently found out that it was to be moved and had decided to get into position with a lightning maneuver (the forced march by night) so as to gain control of an obligatory passage. But they had moved too soon, when the money was still safely in Avignon.

That may be the primary reason several bands got together to take Pont-Saint-Esprit, but we may suspect that many of those soldiers took part for a different motive: to conquer the kingdom of France in the name of Jean I. At any rate that is how Giannino tells it in his memoirs:

And the said Giovanni being at the castle of Saint-Estève, the above-mentioned Messer Giovanni Vernee with four thousand horsemen of high caliber, learning that the plan to take Lyon-sur-Rhône had been revealed and laid bare through the treachery of the said Pierre de La Courneuve, then took Pont-Saint-Esprit, and its territory and everything; this bridge is on the Rhône and belongs to the kingdom of France. He took it at night on Friday, 25 December 1360.[31]

Giannino exaggerates the size of his force, attributing all the glory of this feat of arms, which caused a great stir at the time, to his own men. He also mistakes the day, placing the battle, either for symbolic reasons or perhaps through simple error, on Christmas day, whereas we know it was fought at dawn on the 29th. Yet he is credible, for the taking of Pont-Saint-Esprit is evidently linked to the strategy he had planned with his commanders, based on the surrender of Roquemaure and a march on Lyon. So it is possible, even probable, that Giovanni Vernee, unable to seize Roquemaure, had joined other mercenaries instead and taken part in the battle of Pont-Saint-Esprit. Or perhaps, as we learn from other sources we shall examine below, Vernee did no more than sack the nearby village of Codolet; but Giannino decided to attach his name to the bigger event anyway. Above all, the prudent merchant-king was far away while his men were fighting, concealed in a Provençal castle, and probably did not have good first-hand information. A complete antihero, a sovereign but no chevalier, Giannino di Guccio did not even take part in person in his first and only battle.

But it is pleasing to think that, for a moment at least, the banner of King Giannino did flutter from the flagpole of the highest tower of Pont-Saint-Esprit. While half of France was colored with lilies on a field of blue and the other half obeyed the lilies and lions of England, a strange flag fabricated in Milan by Daniello waved from the tower of a small town in the south. A blue flag adorned with golden lilies, and with a large sun planted in the middle.

Chapter Five

·◁===▷·

In Prison

*Dans ma ville de Sienne, chaque citoyen peut être roi à son tour. Et
qui veut prendre en gire Guccio Baglioni n'a qu'à le dire!*

In my city of Siena, each citizen can be king in turn. And anyone who wishes to deride Guccio Baglioni has only to say so.

—Maurice Druon, *Le rois maudits*

FROM BUFFOON TO BRIGAND

Matteo Villani writes that the capture of Pont-Saint-Esprit sparked a
wave of panic:

> And the noble bridge over the Rhône was presently occupied
> by the men of the company, which gave them free access to the
> Comtat Venaissin, and meant they could gallop right to Avi-
> gnon if they pleased. For this reason the pope and cardinals took
> great fright; the shops were closed and the city took up arms.
> Everyone flung himself into the task of erecting stockades and
> drawbridges around the city and the great palace of the pope,
> and laying in stocks of victuals. With the soldiers they mounted
> good guard by day and by night. And in addition to these mea-
> sures, the pope proclaimed a crusade against the company.[1]

The members of the Sacred College remembered all too well
what had happened just two years earlier, when the notorious mercenary commander Arnaud de Cervole, known as l'Archiprêtre, had
visited havoc on Provence, with his troops, who were unemployed
following the truce of Bordeaux.

To keep him away from Avignon, the pope had repeatedly invited l'Archiprêtre to dine in the papal palace, absolving him of his sins and receiving him "as though he were the son of the king of France."[2] To top it off, he had made him a gift of 40,000 gold écus.

Now, two years later, the city saw itself virtually under siege once more, and traffic in and out slowed to a trickle. Between January and March 1361 other mercenary companies, attracted by the capture of the key stronghold on the river, entered Provence from Gascony, threatening the papal city at close range: "and they reinforced the bridge such that ships coming from Burgundy toward Avignon with foodstuffs could not pass, whence the court suffered serious dearth."[3]

At the end of 1360 the pope had already ordered the routiers to withdraw and abandon the region, but had waited in vain for an answer. So it was resolved to proclaim a crusade, and the Cardinal of Ostia was made captain general. Early in January Innocent VI wrote to the principal lords of the region, requesting them to take the cross. On 10 January he wrote to Philippe, duke of Burgundy, to the governor of the Dauphiné, and to Amedeo, count of Savoie. On 17 January he wrote to King Jean of France urging him to take action "like a pugilist and athlete," and guaranteeing him spiritual indulgences.[4] He also sent letters to many bishops and cities in France, inviting them to "break the horns of the pride of those wicked ones." The pope wrote likewise to Emperor Charles IV, to whom he related the savage acts perpetrated against virgins and nuns. Missives were also sent to Rudolph, duke of Austria, the duke of Normandy, the count of Armagnac, many other French nobles, and Giovanni Boccanegra, doge of Genoa. This was a large-scale effort, filling the first pages of the pontifical register for year nine of Innocent's papacy with around 100 letters in this vein.[5] Few, however, heeded the urgent request of the pontiff, who was guaranteeing eternal salvation but not offering to pay for a military campaign.

In this emergency Giannino and his followers, separated as they were from their mercenary troops, did not even have the time to reflect on what was occurring. On 2 January 1361, just four days after the capture of Pont-Saint-Esprit, the entire household of the merchant-king, including Neri d'Andrea Beccarini and the monk Federigo degli Ubaldini, was arrested in the palace of the cardinal of Florence. Bartolomeo di Pagno managed to escape to Orgon in Provence, but was captured some time later. Daniello also escaped: sensing that support was ebbing away, he had planned to save Giannino's money, chattels, and arms by loading them all on a ship and sailing down the Rhône to the sea, and then heading for Venice. But he was unable to depart in sufficient secrecy to prevent word getting out. Pursued on land and water by a papal marshal, Daniello was caught near Arles. He put up a fight and was wounded, two of his squires were killed, and everything was seized: money, chattels, the documents "he had brought back from Saracenia," and the power of attorney assigned him by Giannino.[6] Taken to Avignon and imprisoned, he died shortly after from his wounds. This, at any rate, is the story Giannino read, a year after the fact, in a letter he received at Naples sent by "certain friends of Daniello" in Venice.[7]

Although it was independent of the kingdom of France and the papal domain, not even the county of Provence was secure. The pope sent word to Matteo (or Mattia) di Gesualdo, seneschal of Provence, urging the capture of those sheltering in his territory. In consequence, on Thursday, 7 January 1361, at around ten in the morning, the vicar of Marseille, Giovanni di Caramanico, together with the vicar of Saint-Maximin-la-Sainte-Baume and Luchetto of Pistoia, who knew Giannino by sight, presented themselves at the castle of Saint-Estève with an escort of twelve well-armed men. Caramanico compelled the lord of Montauban to hand Giannino over and took him to Aix-en-Provence, capital of the county and headquarters of the seneschal.

Giannino declares that, under an agreement reached between the cardinals in consistory and the seneschal of Provence, Matteo di Gesualdo was to receive no less than 100,000 florins if he brought the prisoner to Aigues-Mortes and delivered him to the seneschal of Beaucaire, governor for the king of France, so Giannino could be taken to Paris. But if Matteo executed the prisoner, he would receive just 500 florins; and if he decided to keep him in prison in Provence, he would get 50,000. There is no way of knowing how real these figures are, but we do know that Matteo di Gesualdo chose the third option, holding Giannino prisoner in Aix-en-Provence.

The bizarre king of France, who until then had been regarded perhaps with suspicion and perhaps also with amusement by those who met him, had now become an outlaw.

IN PRISON IN AIX-EN-PROVINCE

When Giovanni di Caramanico took custody of Giannino, he treated him with courtesy and comforted him, saying that the seneschal would do him no harm, indeed that he had already gathered 500 horsemen and 1500 infantry to put at his disposal. Matteo was supposedly going to assist him in getting all of Provence to join his venture, guarantee supplies, and allow his army free passage. The seneschal was going to do all this—Caramanico claimed—to avenge the shame and the damage inflicted by the Dauphin on the Provençals when the latter had aided the lords of Baux, and also to earn a proper reward on the day when Jean I had conquered the kingdom of France.

On the morning of the next day, Giannino met the seneschal in person, and Matteo di Gesualdo gave him similar assurances. This filled the merchant, who must have been bewildered when the Provençals captured him, with relief and delight. He was housed with every consideration in a tower in Aix-en-Provence, in the custody of Monna Tora, dressed in the garments secretly lined with money and jewels, and wore a sword and a dagger. But he was not allowed to leave.

This courteous treatment must have been intended to soothe Giannino and get him to talk as freely as possible. But he was able to receive a visit from the attendant who had been with him at Saint-Estève, Giannino de' Bardi, who informed him that his captors were still weighing their options about what to do with him. Giannino also received letters from citizens of Aix and learned in this way that he might soon be bundled off into the kingdom of France.

He decided to play along, to keep his jailers from becoming suspicious. With the help of Giannino de' Bardi, his contact with the outside world, he arranged to have an innkeeper he trusted write letters for him and send messengers to all his potential allies: to Pont-Saint-Esprit, where his army was lodged; to Avignon, where he knew he had friends; and to Lombardy, Tuscany, and the royal family of Naples. He and his attendant also set about getting the leading citizens of Aix, and the leaders of the local government, to speak to the seneschal.

A delegation of citizens did pay a visit to the seneschal, who denied that he was holding "the king of France" but did admit that he was holding a foreigner for other reasons. But the inhabitants of Aix were loyal to the memory of Queen Clémence, a daughter of the house of Anjou who had arranged in her will to leave her heart in the nearby monastery of Sainte-Marie-de-Nazareth, where she had resided for several years during her widowhood: they wanted to know more about this putative son of hers. Giannino had succeeded in creating enough of a stir to make some people come to his aid, or at least make them curious enough to demand a full explanation of what was going on.

We don't really know to what extent Giannino's memoirs, here and elsewhere, reflect the genuine attitudes of those who took an interest in his case, because for one thing we have no way of assessing how widespread and influential his network of contacts was. What is evident, though, is the tactic of deception and subterfuge in which the merchant (who still thought he could prevail) and the seneschal were both engaged, the former to try to galvanize support, the latter to gather intelligence while keeping things under control and preventing any outbreak of disorder.

On that basis, the seneschal evidently concluded that it would be counterproductive to deny local representatives permission to meet with the prisoner, but he suggested to Giannino that he not declare his true status (in which he himself was thus pretending to believe). It would only make the situation worse, he said, since the citizens had no way to help him. To which Giannino replied: "If those who come to speak with me are respectable persons, I will not conceal it in the least; but if they are base folk of low condition, do not summon them, because I do not wish to make myself the object of derision, or scatter my words in vain."[8]

He feared being treated as a laughingstock —as he probably had been more than once already—and wished to speak only with office-holders and leading citizens. The idea of a popular insurrection never crossed his mind. Naturally Giovanni di Caramanico, the seneschal's emissary, seized on this sign of weakness, promptly affirming that those seeking an interview "were not respectable at all, but rather the sort more likely to turn the whole thing into a farce than anything else."[9]

A few influential Tuscans living in Provence, including Giovanni Bisdomini of Arezzo, described as high judge for the king, and Alamanno of Florence, high treasurer of Provence, and others, wrote to him to suggest that he not declare himself because if he did, he risked being handed over to the French. The purpose of this advice was to keep him from the gallows, perhaps out of compassion, perhaps out of fear of reprisals against other Tuscan merchants.

Finally on 12 January a delegation of forty citizens of Aix-en-Provence arrived to visit the prisoner: the syndics, the captain, the chatelain, the master bookkeepers, and other officials and merchants, who treated Jean I with reverence, saying:

> Lord, the citizens of this town have learned that you are the son of King Louis and Queen Clémence and that the crown of France belongs to you by right. Hence these whom you see here represent the whole city, and all Provençals, in the wish to know from you, if you are who you are said to be. May it please you to reveal yourself, for our intention, and that of all Provençals, is that you not be held prisoner, rather that you receive the honor due you as king, inasmuch as your mother had singular love and devotion in Provence, especially in the city of Aix. And thus we wish to beg, that it please you to state the truth.[10]

Giannino summarily confirmed his identity, and as he tells it, the citizens went to the seneschal to ask that he be released forthwith. But the seneschal asked for time to write to the king and queen for instructions. The citizens asked for Giannino to be released into their custody, saying they would detain him "honorably, as a king" while awaiting the reply from Naples, but the seneschal refused. The citizens then requested assurance that Giannino's treatment would be dignified, and the seneschal gave it.

At this time Monna Tora, who had kept all her copies of Giannino's attestations, showed them to many citizens of Aix, who had them read out in public and voiced their demand for Giannino to be set free and given rich presents. The situation as depicted by Giannino is that of an entire city persuaded of his good right, much the same way he portrays Siena in October 1356, at the time of his public revelation. But this time Giannino was held prisoner by men who would not let him do as he pleased. The seneschal refused to take any action without precise orders from the sovereigns in Naples and, when he learned about the attestations, convinced the merchant (who still trusted him) to show them to him. Naturally Giannino's "clarities" were all sequestered, and the little king never saw them again.

No more than a week had passed since his capture, when on 16 January the seneschal, who until then had allowed Giannino a certain freedom of maneuver, probably in order to gain intelligence on his network of connections, departed from Aix with a contingent of armed men to aid the pope in driving out the routiers who were infesting the region. The prison regime changed immediately: Giannino was fettered with two rings on his legs and a heavy iron cross-bar. For 23 days he wore these chains day and night, but after that only at night. This lasted until 16 July.

The time for treating Giannino blandly and milking him for intelligence had passed, and he was no longer allowed contact with anyone outside. For the rest of his time in Provence he was unable to dispatch messengers, read or write letters, or have visitors. Two of the seneschal's squires, Martuccio and Martino, who were guarding him, robbed him of everything he had with him: clothing, breastplates, arms, money and precious stones, for a total value of 15,000 florins.

Luckily, in the days before his regime of confinement grew strict, Giannino had succeeded in having his seals and a few rings delivered to a trusted innkeeper of Aix, Messer Francesco of Montefioralle, a man from Florentine territory who managed the hotel delle Mazze.

While in jail, Giannino learned that his lieutenant, Giovanni Vernee, had been captured. According to one version of events, he was taken by troopers of the king of France even before Giannino's arrest. According to Giannino, on the other hand, Vernee's arrest took place subsequent to his own, on the orders of the pope, who dispatched an armed gang pretending to be bandits and enemies of the pope to Pont-Saint-Esprit, where they were received without suspicion. Waiting until Giovanni Vernee went out one day, they wounded him in an ambush and brought him to Avignon. The pope later handed him over to the French, who killed him with poison. The cost of the whole operation was 10,000 florins.

The capture of Vernee alarmed his subordinates, who wrote to the pope to inform him that they were not acting against the Church, but were only "in the service of the said G[iovanni], to acquire the kingdom of France for him, as the rightful and natural king of France."[11] They also requested the release of all those whom the pope had seized in Avignon. To the seneschal of Provence and the city council of Aix they wrote asking that Giannino be released and allowed to proceed to Pont-Saint-Esprit, threatening to invade and sack Provence if he were not. But whereas the city council (going by Giannino's account) favored releasing him, the seneschal adamantly refused and even threw the bearer of the letter into jail. With the king in prison and his commander dead, no one else came forward to offer support.

THE POPE'S LETTER

In spring 1361, the constable of France, Jacques de Bourbon, accompanied by a contingent of troops, visited the pope at Avignon for a few days to discuss various problems, principally the ongoing occupation of Pont-Saint-Esprit. I believe that the affair of King Giannino must have been on the agenda too. On 16 April 1361, Innocent VI wrote to the king and queen of Naples; his letter, clearly dictated by pressure from the French court, attempted to convince them to accede to the demands of Jean II the Good. Here it is in full:

> To our dear and illustrious son and daughter in Jesus Christ, Luigi king and Giovanna queen of Sicily, salvation and apostolic benediction.
>
> Insatiable for every evil, the Enemy of the human race, of the tranquility and peace of mankind, who is above all the tireless persecutor of the faithful of Christ, does not cease to search every day for the ways and means to arouse scandal among the

peoples and oppose the public good. You will have received notice some time ago that a rash idea has entered the head of a certain *Johannes,* surnamed *Guga,* a citizen of Siena, which is a madness of a new kind, and lodged so deeply in his mind that, inventing novel and ridiculous arguments, he has dared and still dares to proclaim himself king of the French and preach, with shameless discourse and rash deed, that the kingdom of France belongs to him. And although a fantasy so extraordinary, invented, we have no doubt, through the suggestion of the malign spirit, can arouse nothing but derision in men of sound judgment, he has nonetheless found not a few accomplices, confederates, and supporters of such fantastic rashness. Among them was a certain English knight named *Johannes de Vernayo,* exiled and banished from England (as we have learned) for a multitude of enormous crimes. He, not blushing to define himself, in favor of the said Johannes Guga and under the mantle of this madness, "lieutenant of the king of France," had gathered a company of soldiers and wickedly carried out pillage and rapine, homicide and burning, in the kingdom of France.

Finally, having taken with a major assault, under the false title he had assumed, a fortress situated near Avignon called *Codelectum,* he has been taken prisoner there during an encounter by the forces of our dear son in Jesus Christ, Jean, the illustrious king of the French, and is currently in prison. Shortly after, the said Johannes Guga was arrested by the forces of our dear son, the noble Mattia di Gesualdo, knight and seneschal of your county of Provence, and, captured by the same seneschal, is now in prison as well.

Since it is dignified for your excellence to further, with the zeal of fraternal charity and full desire, the honor and state of the king—to whom you are linked by a not insignificant bond of consanguinity—and of his kingdom of France, and agree, to the extent fitting under God, to his requests, and satisfy him in his licit and honest petitions, we ask your serenity, and exhort you insistently, to accept the requests with which he will present you, as honesty will not fail to convince you to do: ordering the aforesaid seneschal to take all measures relative to the aforesaid Johannes, with precautions such that your noble conduct may be commended to us, and the king have reason to be satisfied. Given at Avignon on 16 April, in year nine of our pontificate.[12]

Pope Innocent VI's letter relays a version of the facts that diverges in part from that given by Giannino, who maintained, among other things, that the town of Pont-Saint-Esprit rather than the nearby town of Codolet, had been in his power. But it is a particularly important historical source for our purposes, inasmuch as it proves that the Sienese merchant did constitute a diplomatic problem at this time.[13]

The claims of the madman (as the pope considers him) had already caused serious difficulties, and might give rise to more: note the apprehension that Giannino, albeit in prison, could provoke further "scandals," in other words win more followers, especially the citizens of Aix-en-Provence, who were particularly restive, as we have seen. And since Pont-Saint-Esprit was still in the hands of the bandits, there was a risk that if Giannino were liberated he would make his way there, gain strength, and take the offensive. What if people then started to recognize him? What if the mercenary bands flocked to him? What if the king of Navarre decided to exploit the situation for his own advantage? These risks were real.

The pope, acceding to a request from Jean II the Good, presented himself as a mediator and lent his authority to a delegation that was headed for Naples. To convince Luigi and Giovanna, he reminded them of their blood relationship with the French sovereign: a ploy worth noting, since it carried the implication that any concession made to the pretender would shame them as well, inasmuch as the house of Anjou was a branch of the reigning house of France. What might the "licit and honest petitions" advanced by the king of France have been? Perhaps an exemplary sentence or, more probably, delivery of the prisoner into the hands of French justice.

It is certain that neither the king of France nor the pope regarded the prison of Aix-en-Provence as a secure place of detention for Giannino, since it was exempt from their control. So the focus shifts to the attitude adopted by the sovereigns of Naples, who as we have seen did not have a very clear notion of how to deal with the case. Giannino remained in jail with no formal accusation against him and, as far as we know, no trial in the offing. But it is highly probable that Luigi and Giovanna had no intention of handing him over without some quid pro quo.

IN PRISON IN MARSEILLE

King Giannino's case must have started to decline in importance a few days later, when the pope succeeded in coming to terms with the mercenaries holding Pont-Saint-Esprit. Innocent VI managed to get rid of these dangerous neighbors in early May by offering money to the marchese of Monferrato to hire them for his war against the Visconti of Milan. They got 30,000 or 40,000 florins directly from the pope in exchange for serving the marchese, and as Giannino tells the story, left Pont-Saint-Esprit on 2 May. It cost more than 100,000 florins to "rid the place of them."[14]

Finally the companies departed, leaving a trail of death, starvation, and pestilence behind them in Provence. Many crossed the Alps, others headed for Marseille and Nice, wreaking havoc as they went. Two companies remained on the Rhône, "living for a long time by preying on and robbing the inhabitants."[15] And Giannino, witness and indeed contributory cause to some extent of all this harm, was still locked up in prison.

Summer arrived, and with it a terrible pestilence, which carried off many members of the Sacred College, among them some of the cardinals whose backing Giannino had tried to get. The plague also claimed Luca Tolomei, Girolamo Piccolomini and Neri d'Andrea Beccarini, his brother-in-law, and many other friends of Giannino with them; now he was really on his own. Another who died at this time was Francesco of Montefioralle, the innkeeper to whom Giannino had entrusted his seals; the seals went to his brother Sacco, subvicar of Aix, and ended up in the hands of Giovanni di Caramanico.

As soon as the death rate began to tail off, the seneschal Matteo di Gesualdo left for Marseille with his whole household, bringing along his prisoner, with the intention of sailing for Naples. It was 16 July 1361.

Giannino was held in a room in the palazzo of the vicar of Marseille, Caramanico. Matteo di Gesualdo had been replaced in office by his brother-in-law, Filippo di Sangineto, whom Giannino calls the count of Melito. But since the new seneschal of Provence was too ill to face the sea voyage from Naples, Matteo di Gesualdo continued to carry out his functions. He thus found himself obliged to return immediately to Aix-en-Provence, the capital of the county, to deal with a company of Castilians that had penetrated the region and laid siege to Arles.

While the seneschal was away, Giannino learned from the soldier who brought him his food—a certain Antonio from Naples—that the new seneschal was so unwell that he would not arrive for two years and that in the meantime he, Giannino, was to be sent in secret to Aigues-Mortes in the kingdom of France. Knowing what would become of him in the hands of his enemies, Giannino began to plan his escape, promising Antonio 500 florins if he would help and accompany him.

On the night of 13 September 1361, as soon as the palazzo was asleep, Giannino tied his sheets, a blanket, and a towel together and lowered himself from the window. He expected to find Antonio waiting for him, but no one was there. He waited till morning, and then, not knowing what else to do, went down to the port. He asked for passage, but nobody wanted to help him, claiming that a permit was required to leave the port. Giannino left the city and began wandering through the countryside, traversing a landscape completely unfamiliar to him, until the next night.

When it was already dark he came to a church dedicated to Saint Lawrence, but the curate, Messer Fransese, refused to open the doors to him. The vagabond merchant slept nearby. The morning after he once again sought passage, but once again he was told that the practice at Marseille was that no one could leave without written permission from the authorities. Giannino entered the small hotel of a good woman whose name he could no longer recall later.

He announced himself as the king of France, and the woman received him graciously. Meanwhile the hunt for him had started: Giovanni di Caramanico spread a rumor that Giannino was responsible for the arrival of the Castilians and declared him an outlaw and a rebel against the crown, guaranteeing a reward of fifty gold florins for whoever revealed his whereabouts.

But the woman kept him hidden in a cellar, either out of pity or (according to Giannino) hoping to be rewarded on the day the fugitive became king of France. While he was in the cellar he was spotted by a shoemaker, who reported him to get the fifty florins. Giannino was captured and returned amid a buzzing crowd to the palazzo from which he had fled. Giovanni di Caramanico flew into a rage the moment Giannino appeared in his presence, seized his beard and tore it out by the roots. He then took out his knife and began smacking Giannino on the head with the flat of the blade, so hard that the knife broke off from the handle. He then punched the prisoner in the face repeatedly, leaving it swollen and livid. The citizens of Marseille disapproved of the behavior of their vicar, but Caramanico locked Giannino in a dark room with two iron bars on his legs. Later the prisoner recalled their exact weight: fifty-one pounds. His hands were also chained to a bar.

Giannino remained in this state for four months and three days. The iron chafed his flesh, causing it to suppurate. Three times he was fed poison. Only when his jailers brought his meals did his eyes see the light; as soon as he had received some disgusting scraps of food, the lantern was taken away: "And they left him in the dark, and he ate and drank and remained day and night in the dark; and a horde of vermin, lice to be exact, swarmed over him."[16]

By now Giannino, a declared rebel against the crown and a recaptured fugitive, was good only for hanging. But on what charge? According to him the Marseillais took his side, failing to understand why he was being held. In his memoirs Giannino blames his jailer, whom he despised, for what happened next, asserting that Caramanico, for fear of being deprived of his position and losing custody of the prisoner, began to spread appalling rumors about his conduct, saying that he had heard them in Avignon and getting others to say so too. This is worth noting, because it would appear that the royal officials had no intention of executing Giannino solely because he had proclaimed himself king of France. Evidently they feared a popular uprising. So there was a new political player involved, one Giannino had never given any thought to: the common people. But by now it was too late.

Giannino was charged with having "committed fornication in the act of sodomy with cardinals and other prelates, that is, having been with them like a true whore."[17] On top of that Caramanico accused him of counterfeiting at Avignon, showing the Marseillais some false coins which he claimed Giannino was carrying when he was recaptured. Various jailbirds, delinquents, and indigents were found to swear to all this, and Caramanico also arranged to have useful letters of accusation forwarded to him. Sodomy and counterfeiting: all that was missing was a charge of heresy. The Middle Ages regarded sodomy, counterfeiting, and heresy as conceptually very similar to one another because all were seen as acts contrary to nature.[18] But heresy was already entailed in the fact that by professing himself king of France, the merchant was guilty of lèse-majesté.

Within a few days Giannino had turned into a monster of deceit in the eyes of the people, the spawn of the archdeceiver himself, the Devil. (It is no accident that Dante Alighieri puts fraudsters, heretics, forgers, and traitors in the lowest circles of hell.) It is odd that we do not find Giannino charged with forging credentials as well: perhaps he left that part out.

The tried and true expedient of making one's adversary out to be a monster in order to get public support for taking extreme measures worked so well that most of the Marseillais, upon discovering what he had been up to, were ready to see him burned, boiled, dragged by wild horses, and broken on the wheel. They made up lewd songs about him, calling him "Giovanna, queen of France."[19]

Despite being treated as the worst of criminals, Giannino never lost his faith that he was a sovereign descended from Saint Louis. Though he never draws an explicit parallel with the imprisonment of the saint-king in 1240, he appears to allude to it implicitly when he asserts that he bore his burden patiently, thanking God and remaining calm, ready to face martyrdom.[20]

He was a king, certainly, but part of him was always a merchant too. Giovanni di Caramanico showed up unexpectedly one night accompanied by two soldiers carrying naked swords to compel him to confess his crimes: "I want you to confess of your own free will that these things, said and done by you, were all done and commanded precisely by you, and that you did so with malice, and that you had forged seals; and if you refuse to say so, I will cut your hands and feet off, and have you thrown into the sea."[21]

So all of a sudden the seals, which Giannino has mentioned several times with excessive nonchalance, are an issue again. Once more King Jean I tries to defend himself:

> How do you want me to confess what isn't true, what was never even thought of by me? Suppose I do say everything you want; it won't be believed, because it is obvious that the tribune sent for me, and there are those there who saw me speaking with him, and the letters being written, and there are the senators there in Rome who wrote letters, and the citizens of Siena who were assigned to counsel me.[22]

So in his eyes the epiphany of Cola di Rienzo was an overwhelming proof, just like his acceptance by his fellow Sienese. Evidently though it failed to convince Caramanico, who grabbed him by the throat, brandished a knife, and said: "If you don't confess as I tell you, I will put you to death immediately." And poor Giannino, who was a king but also a forger, gave in: "Write out everything you want me to say."[23]

Next morning Caramanico called a council meeting attended by numerous Marseillais and read Giannino's confession to them, declaring that he had made it to unburden his soul. The council resolved that he should be executed, but Giannino, who was locked in the next room, began shouting loudly that it was all false and that the confession had been extorted. The sentence was suspended. His jailers gave him nothing to eat all day, "and if they treated him badly before, they treated him worse now."[24]

IN PRISON IN NAPLES

Not all of Giannino's friends had vanished. While Caramanico wondered how to proceed (increasingly tempted, perhaps, by the notion of handing him over to the French), the Tuscan merchants resident in

Provence, who knew him for an honest and morally upright individual, interceded with the city council of Marseille to request that their fellow merchant be brought before the king to be judged directly by him. And indeed, when the acting seneschal of Provence, Matteo di Gesualdo, set sail for Naples on the evening of Monday, 16 January 1362, Giannino was on board.

The ship's captain, Jean Bourguignon of Toulon, had orders from the Marseillais to convey Giannino safe and sound to the king. Finally his shackles were removed, but he was locked in the dirtiest, darkest, smelliest corner of the galley. The voyage took thirty-three days, during which the prisoner ate nothing except hard tack, vinegar, and Sardinian cheese.[25] He was covered with so many lice that he infested the whole galley with them.

On the evening of 19 February 1362 the seneschal led him into the presence of Luigi I, king of Naples, in Castel Nuovo (known today as the Maschio Angioino).[26] Giannino wore no shirt, his breeches had no bottom, his stockings and shoes were in shreds, and the lice were eating him alive. Luigi of Naples asked him the reason "that had driven him to enter with tall tales and a military force and demand to be lord of the kingdom of France."[27]

Giannino told him the whole story, from the switch in the cradle down to the present moment. The king listened, then gazed at him. He took pity on Giannino and handed him over to his Genoese chatelain, Manuello, commanding him to dress Giannino decently. The merchant-king remained under guard in the king's palace for three days. He was then sent before a judge, Pierre de Charly, who on 22 February transferred him to the prison of the Vicaria, where he was put in with the common prisoners. There irons were once again attached to his feet, legs, and hands, and a heavy chain attached to a pole was fixed around his neck. For eight days he was without bed or clothing. Then the king sent him a comfortable mattress and a fine set of new clothes, and good things to eat and drink.

Giannino's prison regime grew milder. He could receive visits, and various gentlemen came to console him. In the meantime, other things began going his way: Giannino records, with satisfaction and in rich detail, how Matteo di Gesualdo was summoned by the new seneschal to account for the embezzlement and fraud he had committed, how he fled by sea and was eventually caught.

After all his travels, Giannino could now see a few relatives and fellow citizens. Bartolomeo di Francesco Baglioni took care of him, sending him food and drink every day, and something to wear. Toschetto of Siena gave him a heavy cloak. A monk, Don Nicola, came to visit him, and many other Sienese "did him honor."[28] Things were indeed turning up, and Giannino must not have been displeased to watch, from the prison of the Vicaria, as the Galea Rossa, the king's personal ship, was burned on 27 February by Catalan corsairs, going up in flames before the sovereign's own eyes.

Now that he was in better shape and could once again dress properly, eat, and receive visitors, Giannino regained courage and began drafting numerous petitions requesting King Luigi to release him and declaring that he had never done anything against Provence or the kingdom of Naples. He wrote again to King Luigi and to his brothers Roberto d'Acaia and Filippo di Taranto, Queen Giovanna, the archbishop of Naples, and Margherita d'Andria, the king's sister. All of them were asked to intervene to have the jewels, pearls, money, and written documents that had been taken from him returned.

It was during this period that the merchant got the idea of writing down all that had befallen him. Presumably he did so between the end of February and 27 March 1362, for on that date, with all his petitions dispatched, Giannino drew a long breath and wrote: "And here we end, and we shall see what will be, and how things will go, and will continue our writing."[29]

The months that followed were employed by the merchant in recording the events in Naples he was able to learn of. So, for example, he tells us of a general parliament held in Castel Nuovo for eight days, starting on 4 April 1362, and of the liberation of Luigi, duke of Durazzo, whom the king had been holding in Castel dell'Ovo.

He learned, too, of the death of Daniello and the loss of everything he had left in the Jew's custody. The news must have been a shattering blow, but Giannino had not forgotten his mercantile training and immediately set about drawing up an inventory of everything that had been stolen from him.

On 8 April 1362 he received letters from his wife and children, brought by Pasquino, the courier of the commune of Siena. On 13 April, Holy Thursday, the messenger carried his replies. The same day some Sienese in the pay of the king of Naples departed. On 2 May Giannino quarreled with a French knight who did not believe him; on 17 May he entrusted other letters to one Tommè of Casole di Volterra, who took them to Siena to his family and friends. And he wrote and he wrote and he wrote, to his friends in Siena and Provence, recording the date every letter was sent and received, and the names of the addressees and couriers, with minute care.

On 24 May King Luigi I died. Ten days later, on 3 June, Giannino sent yet another petition to the widowed queen, the archbishop of Naples, Roberto d'Acaia and Filippo di Taranto. The queen handed the case over to the two princes, both brothers of her late husband. In June Giannino wrote to numerous Sienese, and recorded the death of the duke of Durazzo, which occurred on 21 June. That same day, the queen decided that Giannino should receive an indemnity of 22 tarì, a coin used in the kingdom of Naples, for the expenses he had incurred since the day the king died and that he should henceforth receive 12 tarì per month. A merchant again, in good shape again, Giannino settled his bill with the innkeeper Bartolomeo of Bergamo, who looked after him and held his funds on deposit: Bartolomeo kept the 28 carlini that Giannino owed him and gave a carlino to the porter, leaving 37 carlini for Giannino (3 carlini = 1 tarì).

On 2 July 1362, Queen Giovanna had him transferred from the prison of the Vicaria to Castel dell'Ovo, with a stipend of 36 carlini per month, which he was paid starting in October 1362. Giannino was bound over into the custody of Torello Falconari, chatelain of Castel dell' Ovo: "And I am chained here inside."[30]

THE KING'S TREASURE
In the month of April 1362, Giannino compiled a detailed inventory of all the objects of value that he had possessed at Avignon and had entrusted to Daniello. It was a real treasure, with a total value of 61,512 florins, but the account contains a few inexactitudes, and no value is

put on the crown. On top of this, there is the value of the money and jewels that Giannino had kept sewn into his jacket: 15,000 florins. The inventory shows clearly how his belief in his own royalty was translated into material symbols and also gives us information about the Sienese merchant's financial resources—he had available a notable sum in Venetian ducats, newly minted—and the logistical organization of his military campaign. But Giannino had only enjoyed possession of this treasure for a few months, from June to December 1360.

The inventory is itemized in a precise order: cash money comes first, even ahead of the crown (perhaps because with it the crown could be purchased), and then expensive clothing, arms, armor, trappings for horses, table services, kitchen implements, and carpets, chests and valises for the military camp. Here it is in its entirety.[31]

Here following will be written down in order all the money and possessions which the said Giovanni lost at Avignon, things that the papal marshal seized, and that the said Daniello had in his keeping, in the month of January 1361.

[1] In the first place, 25,000 gold florins in new ducats *da mezzo quarro*.[32]

[2] also a crown of pure fine gold of 24 carats, weighing 4 pounds and 8 ounces, made with enameled relief figures. These were images of the kings that there have been in France, beginning with Flovus, grandson of Constantine, emperor of Rome, who was the origin of the royal house of France and received the standard that came from heaven, the oriflamme that is, which the angel gave to a holy hermit at Radicofani when the said Flovus fled from Rome. And then all the other renowned kings, who were virtuous, as were kings Pippin and Charlemagne, and Saint Louis who was king, and King Philippe the Fair, and King Louis X, and yet others to the number of twelve. And each on his throne, crowned, and above the head of each king there was a lily of the same fine gold; and the crown was equipped with little hooks so it could be taken off and put on,[33] and it was made so it could be put on over a helmet, or an open helmet,[34] or over

a hood, and then over a silk cap. And this crown was entirely finished, except for the fact that the jewels and pearls, which the aforementioned seneschal had taken, had not been mounted.

THE CLOTHING FOR MY PERSON
(*DI MIO DOSSO*) AND THE ARMOR

[3] First, a suit [*robba*] of three lengths of fine gold fabric, lined with ermine, with large buttons of gilded silver and with a clasp of fine gold on the mantle, with precious stones and large pearls; this suit cost 1200 gold florins.

[4] Also, a suit of three lengths of fine scarlet lined with fine ermine, trimmed with large golden decorations and circles, and between one decoration and the next embroidery of fine pearls with the story of Jason and Hercules when he left Thessaly and went in search of the golden fleece, when he carried off Medea, and the battles of great Troy; and the mantle was made in Neapolitan style, all pleated, with large buttons of gilded silver and fine enamel. This suit cost 2600 gold florins.

[5] Also, a suit of fine blood-red violet [*di sanguigno di viola fino*], of three lengths, lined with grey vair,[35] trimmed with gold ornaments in herringbone pattern with gilded buttons; it cost 120 gold florins.

[6] Also, a suit of three lengths of fine deep violet lined with grey vair, with cloth buttons; the said suit cost 60 gold florins.

[7] Also, four jackets, one of gold fabric with gilded buttons and three of velvet of fine samite,[36] respectively, blue, vermilion, and green, worked with embroidery of gold and pearls, and with buttons of worked silver. In all they cost 450 gold florins.

[8] Also, six pieces of velvet of fine samite, two vermilion, two blue, and two green, and six pieces of fine French cloth, respectively, two of fine scarlet, two of fine violet, and two of fine blood-red rosy violet [*di viola sanguigno rosato fino*], and six pieces of fine tartaresque gold cloth of various colors; in all they cost 1200 gold florins.

[9] Also, three belts, one with pearls and enamel of fine gold, and the other two of gold thread with precious stones, pearls, and gold enamel; in all they cost 2600 gold florins.

[10] Also, three swords with pommels, hilts, and clasps of fine gold, and the scabbards lined with velvet of vermilion, blue, and green samite; and likewise the belts for these swords, with pearls, gold enamel and precious stones, and three daggers for striking made like the swords, and three pairs of fine beautiful gilded spurs. In all, these things cost 2260 gold florins.

[11] Also, three sets of armor for my person, and three covers for the chargers, one of conch-shaped steel plates, the second of coat of mail, the third of marine turtle shells, joined and embellished with silver and gilded brass, and three shields, and three overgarments to be worn over armor for my person, of velvet samite: the first of blue samite embroidered with gold lilies, with a visage in the center made to resemble a sun with twelve rays, and at the tip of each ray a small embroidered star; the second of vermilion samite with gold decorations in a herringbone pattern; the third of green samite with gold decorations disposed vertically. The three shields were made in similar fashion, and moreover three bridles for the chargers, three low saddles for the chargers covered with the same samite, and straps and overstraps, and *posole*,[37] and pectorals, all of silk and velvet of samite with gold decoration and golden lilies in relief; and three large flags, and two pennants of blue sendal[38] with gold lilies and with the sun and the stars at the center, in the manner of the shields and the overgarments; and three open helmets and three helmets for my head; and on top of each helmet, a crest of gilded brass made like a star with twelve rays, with the twelve small stars; and a cover for the charger and an overgarment for my person of fine gold fabric with parrots; and three saddles and three bridles for three palfreys, and straps for pack-saddles, and pectorals like the ones for the chargers, with letters of gilded silver and pearls. All the above-mentioned things cost in total 3200 gold florins, including all the fine work carried out.

THE EQUIPMENT OF GOLD, SILVER,
BRASS, COPPER, AND IRON

[12] First, two cups of 50% gold alloy worked with enamels and fine reliefs; two large plates of the same gold alloy with

enamels; six large plates for slicing food, six soup plates, six little soup plates, six spoons, six forks, all made of the same gold alloy. All these things weighed 42 pounds and cost 50 gold florins per pound; all in all, the cost came to 2100 gold florins.

[13] Also, two gilded silver basins with enamels for hand-washing, which weighed 16 pounds, and two gilded silver jugs with enamels which weighed 4 pounds; twelve beakers of gilded silver which weighed 4 pounds; twelve wine cups [*nappi*] of gilded silver which weighed 12 pounds; two gilded silver sweet boxes which weighed 8 pounds; and all these things were enameled with figures and beautiful work. They cost 12 gold florins per pound, and the total cost amounted to 624 gold florins.

[14] Also, four silver basins for hand-washing, which weighed 32 pounds; eight large silver plates, which weighed 64 pounds; fifty silver plates for cutting food, that weighed 100 pounds, one hundred small silver soup plates that weighed 50 pounds; one hundred silver spoons that weighed 20 pounds; one hundred silver forks that weighed 10 pounds; one hundred silver wine cups with enamel in the middle, that weighed 100 pounds; one hundred silver sweet boxes with enamels that weighed 20 pounds; twelve silver jugs of a capacity of one *mitadella*[39] that weighed 36 pounds; twelve silver jugs of a capacity of one *mezzetta*, that weighed 18 pounds; six jugs of a capacity of one *mezzo quarto*, that weighed 30 pounds; fifty silver candelabras with enamels that weighed 25 pounds; four large silver candelabras to hold as *doppieri*, as torches that is, that weighed 50 pounds; two silver basins for foot-washing that weighed 20 pounds. And all the silverwork was made with large and small enamels as necessary, and with gold where the enamels were; the said objects weighed 625 pounds in all, and cost 8 florins per pound. The total amounted to 5000 gold florins.

[15] Also, twelve large brass basins for keeping in the reception room and the bedroom, that weighed 20 pounds each, with twelve pedestals of iron that weighed 50 pounds each; and twelve small brass basins for hand- and foot-washing, that weighed 10 pounds each; fifty *misciarobbe* for holding water for

hand-washing, that weighed 8 pounds each; one hundred brass chandeliers, finely wrought, for placing on tables, that weighed 100 pounds all together. All the brasswork weighed 940 pounds: at 15 gold florins per 100 pounds, the total cost amounts to 141 gold florins. The iron pedestals for the basins weighed 600 pounds: at 5 gold florins per 100 pounds, the cost amounts to 30 gold florins.

[16] Also, six large pots for cooking meat, twelve pans, twelve copper cauldrons, twelve ladles, twelve copper cooking spoons, that weighed in all 1600 pounds. They cost 8 florins per 100 pounds and the cost amounted to 128 gold florins.

[17] Also six large iron tripods for the pots; twenty iron spits for roasting meat; twelve large iron forks for arranging the fire; twelve andirons for putting wood on the fire; twelve iron grates for roasting fish. This iron weighed in all 1200 pounds: at 5 gold florins per 100 pounds, the cost amounts to 60 gold florins.

[18] Also, a large pavilion, covered on the outside with waxed linen cloth, and on the inside with cotton painted blue with the stars and the golden lilies, furnished with four beds of fine feather, with fine sheets and covers of sendal and velvet of samite lined with vair; ironbound French jewel-cases, eight of which to be carried on horseback; ten field tents [*trabacche*] covered on the outside with *guarnello*[40] and lined on the inside with linen cloth; each tent and the pavilion furnished with ropes and other necessary gear. All these things were made to order in Venice. Shipped to Avignon, they cost in all 8500 gold florins. They were seized by the pope's marshal along with others, when Daniello the Jew was seized.

[19] Also, twelve tablecloths, each 12 *braccia* long, fifty towels, and fifty smaller hand towels, that cost 300 gold florins.

[20] Also, six knife cases, each with two large knives and one small one, for cutting at table, with the sheaths all covered with velvet of vermilion, blue, and green samite, with bindings[41] of gilded and enameled silver, with silk drawstrings, with the following handles: two of ivory with fine intaglios, two of crystal, two of shafts of coral and two of jasper, all with bindings of

gilded and enameled silver, well wrought with beautiful figures. In all they cost 120 gold florins.

[21] Also, a silver container in the form of a little ship with figures in relief, with two fine silver salad bowls and the sideboard. The little ship had wheels like a cart, for putting it on the table, and weighed 25 pounds. The cost, including the work, was 30 gold florins per pound; the total came to 750 gold florins.

All these things, together with the others recorded previously, were taken by the pope's marshal when he seized Daniello the Jew. He also took the things noted on the other page that follows.

[22] Also, fifty Tartaresque carpets that cost 500 gold florins.

[23] Also, twenty ironbound wooden chests for storing the equipment, that cost 60 gold florins.

[24] Also, twenty large leather valises lined on the inside with linen cloth to put equipment in, that cost 150 gold florins.

[25] Also, 3000 gold ducats of mezzo quarro, that I had deposited with the cardinal of Aragon, which the pope seized.

[26] Also, before going to Provence, at Avignon I had left 1500 gold florins with Neri d'Andrea Beccarini of Siena, so he could purchase a bill of exchange and send them to Siena, divided as follows: 1000 florins for my wife and children and 500 florins as a gift for himself, so that he could send them to his home to pay his debts. I do not know if he was able to arrange this bill, or whether the money was seized by the pope's marshal, since Neri died in prison in Avignon in 1361.

THE END OF GIANNINO

Our information about Giannino di Guccio ends in October 1362. In our last glimpse of him, he is a prisoner of Queen Giovanna in Castel dell'Ovo. What became of him? I would like to think he was released, and spent the last years of his life with his family. There was a rumor at Siena, it seems, that Giannino surrendered his claims in exchange for his freedom and an indemnity of a few thousand gold florins.[42] It would be nice to think so—but things in real life are rarely as we would like.

We could also search for him among the various "Johannes Gucii" who dwelt in Europe at that time. One was a canon of the cathedral of Florence in 1363, another was a merchant working for the pope at Barcelona in the same year. Hunting for homonyms gets us no farther than that.[43]

Unfortunately we know nothing. It is likely that his death occurred not too long after the last information we have about him. The only certain thing is that our merchant king was dead by 1369, when his widow, Necca, made her will.[44]

Let us take our leave of him by imagining him busily writing away, telling us the story of his life.

Chapter Six

·◁▷·

Giannino in History, Legend, and Literature

È mai possibile—brontolava
[il re d'Inghilterra] un po' fra sé e sé,
un po' rivolgendosi ai suoi milordi
che ci siano al mondo dei pazzi
che fanno concorrenza ai sovrani?

Is it at all possible—muttered
the king of England, half speaking to himself
half addressing his milords
that there are madmen in the world
trying to compete with sovereigns?

—Guido Edoardo Mottini,
Il romanzo di Giannetto Parigi re di Francia

DID KING GIANNINO REALLY EXIST?
In the first five chapters I have narrated a story in straightforward fashion. I have followed the career of King Giannino as it has been transmitted to us, commenting on the main source—the so-called *Istoria del re Giannino di Francia*—or departing from it only for specific reasons. At various places my reconstruction differs from what Giannino asserts in his memoirs; for example, he never admits to being a forger, even though the evidence that he was comes directly from what he does assert. At this point, the tale has been told, and if you wish you may stop reading here.

But those whose curiosity has been aroused, readers who have been left with unanswered questions as they followed the story, and naturally everyone who likes history for its problems, not just its narrative, are entitled to some further investigation. In Agatha Christie's novels the detective makes a final speech, untangling the strands of a complicated case and proving who the murderer is with stark clarity. That's not what I attempt here; rather the opposite. In this final chapter I intend to show how Giannino's career poses a whole series of problems for history. As I rewind the skein that I teased apart in the narrative, I come back to all the knots and tangles once again.[1]

The first question we have to ask is this: "Did King Giannino exist?" Posed in these apparently blunt terms, the question actually raises a problem of a kind that has teased historians for centuries: that of distinguishing between individuals who once lived and legendary personalities. Sometimes, as in the case of Pope Joan studied by Alain Boureau, it has been demonstrated that a story widely known and accepted as true for centuries is actually a legend.[2] The same question, however, can also be put regarding persons whose existence is not really in doubt. In the second part of his book on Saint Louis, Jacques Le Goff goes so far as to ask "Did Saint Louis exist?" What he means is: how much can we know about the man who lived and how much has the royal myth clinging to Saint Louis made him into an icon and obscured the human being?[3] The question is just as important when it comes to Giannino, and it starts with his very physical existence. Was Giannino di Guccio a historical figure or a literary invention?

Many who have addressed it, including the scholar who wrote the entry on him for the modern Italian biographical dictionary, have expressed serious reservations about his existence.[4] Or rather, they have split him in two, maintaining that the Sienese merchant Giannino Baglioni, who lived in the middle of the fourteenth century, was unconnected with the legendary protagonist of the *Istoria*, "Giannino." They deny that this text has any historical value, regarding it largely or entirely as "the fruit of the imagination of a story writer [*novelliere*], who took a real fact (the existence in Siena of a Baglioni who believed he was the legitimate successor to the French throne and made this claim known in Sienese territory and perhaps beyond) and built a fantastic tale around it, with motifs typical of the fourteenth-century *novella*, like the switched babies."[5]

For my part, I would obviously not have begun this project (or rather, would not have written the historical reconstruction you have just read) if I had not made up my mind at the outset that the character was real and that the principal source, the *Istoria del re Giannino*, has value. So there are two challenges: to explain, first, why it is possible to believe that the man existed and, second, why the *Istoria* can, to some extent, be relied upon. The *Istoria* cannot be used to address the first challenge, since it is provisionally under suspicion itself: to do so would be to engage in circular reasoning. What we have to do is see whether Giannino ever turns up in the guise of claimant to the French throne in other independent sources.

To start with, the European historical background is important: the research on "hidden kings" and impostors carried out by Yves-Marie Bercé and Gilles Lecuppre reveals that there were so many of them in late medieval and early modern Europe that they were virtually a standard way to mount a political challenge.[6] Giannino himself ran into two of them: as he tells it he was "discovered" by Cola, the self-proclaimed son of Emperor Henry VII, and an audience with the king of Hungary was refused him because of the concomitant presence of another phoney pretending to be the king's brother Andrea. Nor were false kings especially characteristic of the fourteenth century: after the French Revolution there were numerous Louis XVIIs about.[7] One thinks as well of all the tsars wandering hither and yon over the Russian plains in the modern period. Celebrated among them is the false Dmitri, alias the monk Gregory, who disputed the crown with Boris Godunov in the guise of the returned son of Tsar Ivan IV the Terrible. The little tsarevitch had been murdered by Boris himself, who had usurped his throne—a story that attracted various authors as early as the seventeenth century, to which Prosper Mérimée later dedicated a historical essay and from which Alexander Pushkin extracted a drama that finally became the celebrated lyric opera of Modest Mussorgsky.[8]

So Giannino's case is not exceptional in itself, since the historical category to which it belongs is well known. But obviously that is not enough to prove his existence—which I can, however, demonstrate, thanks to two documents independent of one another, each rich in detail. We have looked at them already, but they are worth returning to at this stage of the analysis.

The first is the recorded deliberation of the General Council of the commune of Siena, dated 27 October 1359 and still preserved in the State Archive in Siena.[9] With this deliberation, Giannino saw his own election to a place on the board of Twelve quashed and the possibility of his ever holding public office again barred, on the basis that he was claiming royal blood and corroborating the claim with a letter bearing the seal of the king of Hungary, the full text of which was for this reason "read into the record" (as they say in the US Congress). This Sienese archival document confers a patent of authenticity upon the entire story, because it puts on record both Giannino's claims and the (obviously) phoney letter of King Louis the Great. So the attempts of the self-proclaimed sovereign to make contact with the king of Hungary, leading to the "present" of a copy of the secret seal, become believable. The *Istoria* is careful not to mention these proceedings at Siena, which were highly prejudicial to Giannino and his heirs, and powerfully redolent of ridicule. His forgery had brought down disaster on his head.

The letter that Pope Innocent VI wrote to the king and queen of Naples on 16 April 1361 carries even greater weight.[10] This epistle, whose authenticity can no longer be doubted, since the original register containing it has been located, renders a large part of the story credible at one stroke: it affirms that "Johannes Guga," a Sienese, is claiming to be the king of France, that he has been active in Provence, where he has formed a band of robbers and has had "Johannes de Vernayo," an English knight, as his lieutenant. This Englishman has engaged in pillage and has taken the fortress of Codolet. Of Giannino, it is stated further that he has been captured by Mattia (i.e., Matteo) di Gesualdo, that at present he is a prisoner in Provence, and that he is still stoutly professing himself a king. That is a lot of corroboration.

I could rest my case on these two contemporary attestations, which for a minor personality of the fourteenth century like Giannino already amount to ample evidence. There is no need to press matters further by proposing as some have done, for example, that Giannino di Guccio was the same person as Gianni della Guglia, an English condottiere mentioned by Matteo Villani.[11]

Actually there is at least one more trace of Giannino. He must have been a figure of some renown, for Benvenuto of Imola, in the commentary on the *Divine Comedy,* which he composed around 1375, cites Giannino to illustrate the lines in which Dante, speaking through Sapia, calls the Sienese people "vain" for trying to obtain a seaport at Talamone: "And what would our Poet have said about Giannino the Sienese, who not long ago allowed himself to be convinced, as easily as vainly, that he was the king of France? And he was already conferring dignities and promising offices, throwing away his entire patrimony."[12]

Note that Benvenuto emphasizes the ingenuousness of Giannino, the derisory merchant who becomes the archetype of Sienese vanity. What would our commentator have said if he had known that the entire commune of Siena had made him a laughingstock?

Still, there were a few who genuinely believed in Giannino, an unfortunate figure around whom a halo of legend formed. His descendants had the text of his memoirs in their possession, reworking it and ensuring that it has come down to us. His sons, grandsons, and descendants are traceable down to the middle of the sixteenth century and are reported to have had a white cross visible on their right shoulders, a mark of their royalty. The Sienese had a legend that in 1427 a group of bourgeois pallbearers had tried and failed to lift the coffin of Gabriello, a son of King Giannino. Only when a few knights decided to pay him the honor of bearing it instead did it allow itself to be lifted.[13]

So who was Giannino? A merchant, a man deluded himself and deluding others, a confidence man, a forger, a subversive? All of these at once. Did he act in bad faith? I don't believe so. He must certainly have felt a stab of doubt at times, especially when fabricating the truth in order to demonstrate it. Yet it seems impossible that a man would walk away from a comfortable and secure existence and into a nebulous dreamworld lit by the glimmer of a distant golden crown if he did not believe in what he was doing.

With Giannino di Guccio established as a person who really did exist and tried to prove to the world that he was the king of France, let us now try to see whether and to what extent we may credit the *Istoria*.[14] The first thing to note is that the version that has come down to us can be dated to around the middle of the fifteenth century and that it is the work of a certain Bartolomeo di Pietro of Novara, who declares at the commencement of the manuscript that he is executing "the copy of a book, with nothing added or subtracted, which King Giovanni, rightful king of France, wrote in his own hand."[15] This Bartolomeo of Novara, who held positions with the commune of Siena, states further that he is making his own transcript from a copy executed by Salomone di Nicolò di Spinello Piccolomini, who had in turn copied from one executed by Tommaso di Bartolomeo degli Agazzari. These are identifiable individuals, closely related to Giannino's descendants by family ties, milieu, and economic interests.[16]

Information about Bartolomeo of Novara and Salomone is sparse, but I do not believe that Tommaso degli Agazzari, a writer fairly well known around the start of the fifteenth century and likewise a close relative both of Giannino's second wife and the wife of Giannino's son Gabriello, was a mere copyist. On the contrary, I believe he was responsible for transforming the words originally set down by Giannino di Guccio into the *Istoria del re Giannino* we have.[17] Starting as copyist, he perhaps imposed structure on the narrative, presenting events in an ordered sequence beginning with the genealogy of the royal house of France. Likewise he probably knit the text together, adding narrative transitions and temporal indicators, such as: "Now let us leave the said count and his troops, and return to Giovanni, who is in Hungary and is waiting for the king to send back his letters."[18]

The motives of this copyist/rewriter were not too different from those of the original author himself. Tommaso degli Agazzari wished to defend and pass on the memory of King Giannino, in whom it seems certain he himself believed, for he never betrays any doubt about his genuineness. Though some have maintained that Agazzari was the real creator of the *Istoria,* and although the problem of the transmission of this text has enflamed the passions of numerous Italian and French scholars from the sixteenth century to the present, I am firmly of the view that most of the raw drafting was done by Giannino, who wrote down his memoirs while he was in prison in Naples. Thus I believe that much of the content of the *Istoria* originates with him and that Agazzari gave more coherent shape and better narrative flow to a preexisting text. Giannino was indeed his own biographer, I maintain (although today we can no longer determine just how much his work was adapted) and the story he tells is, to a very large extent, "true."[19] My conviction springs from the following observations.

First, the *Istoria* yields information that essentially fits with what we know from other sources. The differences are few, and very often even secondary details coincide. Above all, we see strong convergence between the *Istoria* and the letter of Innocent VI in the dates relating to the Provençal phase. Even if the *Istoria* is the result of literary elaboration, we still have to admit that it recounts the career of an individual who really existed, and thus that it is not pure invention. The small differences between the two sources (Giovanni Vernee captured alternatively by the French or the Provençals; Codolet or alternatively Pont-Saint-Esprit seized by the mercenaries) are immaterial: we know that the two places are only a few kilometers apart and that they were sacked within twenty-four hours of each other, almost certainly by the same bands. Yet these very differences are sufficient to warrant the view that the writer of the *Istoria* did not have the letter of Innocent VI before him: in other words the two sources are independent of one another.

Moreover Giannino's actions are closely correlated, implicitly or explicitly, with the political context in Europe generally, in Italy and Hungary, and above all in France: he reveals himself just when France is in disarray after the battle of Poitiers and the capture of Jean II; his Sienese followers abandon him in May 1357, just when the Dauphin gains the capacity to strike back; Giannino recruits troops after the peace of Brétigny; he is captured after the reconciliation between the kings of Navarre and France. The way the merchant's actions match the timeline of these political developments shows an internal logic, in my view.

Almost all the individuals named in the memoir are part of the historical record, as are their interactions with one another.[20] Anyone setting out to write Giannino's adventures would have needed detailed knowledge of what was going on in many scattered locations at the same time: Siena, Hungary, Avignon, Naples. If it was not Giannino himself, we must still assume, as a subordinate hypothesis, that it was someone very close to him.

Second, some parts of the *Istoria* point to the fact that the writing was done in the last months of Giannino's life. The incipit is a prime example: here it is easy to spot a shift of grammatical tense from the remote past to the present perfect, in precise connection with what from the writer's viewpoint is a terminal date: "This is the manner in which King Giovanni was switched [*fu scambiato*] . . . and how he was raised [*fu allevato*] in Siena . . . and how he was rediscovered [*fu ritrovato*], and what he has done [*quello che à fatto*] down to day 19 of February in the year 1361, when he was brought [*fu menato*], a prisoner, to Naples."[21]

Toward the end, in the account of his imprisonment in Naples and the inventory of his treasure, we observe a shift from the third person, prevalent hitherto, to the first person. From then on, the narrating voice alternates between the first and third persons. Indeed, convinced that he was at a turning point after dispatching several petitions requesting release, Giannino leaves the narrative hanging at the end of March 1362, writing in the first person and present and future tenses: "And here we end, and we shall see what will be, and how things will go, and will continue our writing." The record of events then resumes until the following October, when, once again, the final notation is in the first person and present tense: "And I am chained here inside."[22]

So the final part of the *Istoria* looks like a work in progress. The book's overall profile is that of an account of events in the past that shifts into diary mode in the final months, then abruptly breaks off. This, too, could be a literary artifice, of course, but an artifice of that kind would be unique in the panorama of fifteenth-century literature, the context in which the *Istoria* originates for those who attribute authorship to Tommaso degli Agazzari. As matters stand, therefore, it seems to me more correct to date the compilation of Giannino's memoirs using information found in the text itself. And from that it results that the main body of the work was composed by Giannino himself between the end of February and 27 March 1362 and that a few pages of a different tenor were added between April and October 1362.

Third, the alterations to Giannino's own text, leading to the definitive version of the *Istoria*, were done "in house" by a close relative, Tommaso degli Agazzari. This point is worth noting, because we may interpret it as evidence that the memoirs were preserved in the family, as the *libri di ricordanze* of merchants normally were.[23] Unfortunately, we have no record of any other writings by Giannino, which, if they existed, would enable us to bring him into focus as a working merchant and etch a sharper profile of him. If we possessed such sources, we would also have a better grasp of his cultural universe and would probably be able to assess the degree of re-elaboration imposed on his text by successive copyists.

The *Istoria* we have today is a text that has long since "left home," a story that became the object of erudite curiosity. But it was not always so, and the similarity of Giannino's memoirs to the typical *libri di ricordanze* of Italian merchants can be seen in the function he himself assigned to them. He produced this text primarily as a memorandum, a documentary record of immediate utility to himself; its function was not that of a narrative, either novelistic or historiographical. So it was not, properly speaking, an *istoria*, but a text of a kind not easy to pigeonhole. It is significant that among the last things Giannino chose to register was an itemized list of the objects in his treasure that had been taken from him and the text of the petition he had sent to the archbishop of Naples to try to get them back.

Incarcerated, and stripped of the official documents, genuine and forged, that attested to his dignity, Giannino wrote a composition meant to ensure his own memory, and security. Only after he had set down everything he wished to remember and have remembered about himself, and with nothing more of a personal nature to add, did Giannino decide to fill up a few final sheets with the news about doings in Naples that reached him in prison. In sum, the *Istoria* of Giannino is not in the least a "forgery," the term we would use if it were a work of the imagination pretending to be a historically grounded biography. This is the final paradox: the man who believed he was king was a forger and an impostor, but his story, though regarded as a literary "forgery," is actually authentic and does recount (with however strong a slant) his own life.

Fourth, the *Istoria* is constructed in an interesting way. In the first part, comprising the genealogy of the French royals, the story of the switch in the cradle, the first years of Giannino's life as a merchant, and the revelation of Cola di Rienzo, stylization is more evident, and we can detect narrative elaboration. It is here that we find motifs from folktale and medieval romance; I will come back to these. But as the chronicle of Giannino's rackety divagations throughout Europe progresses, the tone becomes flat and repetitive, even wearisome: "a crude and tedious composition," one seventeenth-century commentator calls it.[24]

The author must have made use of preexisting materials in the first part of his work, but when he begins to narrate directly, he has no intention of trying to give his work a literary polish. On the contrary, in the second part of the *Istoria* the numerous opportunities for narrative heightening are left unexploited. Instead dates, places, and names are simply heaped up. Of course there is an even more obvious literary opportunity that is bypassed completely: Giannino's story could have been told as that of a poor dolt, a Calandrino fooled and mocked by others, as we would expect from an Italian storywriter of the fourteenth and fifteenth centuries, who would have found to hand the material for a lively novella. On the contrary, the writer of Giannino's story (who naturally calls him "Giovanni" throughout, in the third person), believes in him.

Dates are given with increasing precision toward the close of the work. The description of Giannino's sufferings in his various prisons, the least interesting material for a dramatic plot, occupies a considerable amount of space in the *Istoria*. Evidently Giannino writes in greater detail about what he remembers best, since it happened most recently. Girolamo Gigli, a perceptive and original Sienese erudite, made a remark about the way Giannino dwells on his lice that bears repeating:

That which causes many to believe that he who wrote this story was actually not an impostor, is that he recounts more miseries about himself than great deeds. For had he wished to enhance his person, he would have invented favors from women, success in duels, and similar things of which all romances are full; by means of such actions the reader is made to sympathize with the hero of the story.[25]

Finally, it is not just heroic deeds that are missing from Giannino's story: the supernatural is almost completely absent. In an age that, as Marc Bloch said, "loved the miraculous,"[26] when the kings of France, members by definition of a holy lineage, possessed the gift of the curative touch; when their bodies performed prodigious actions; when the myths of the miraculous oil and the oriflamme were being promoted everywhere—poor Giannino is entirely without sacrality and is a far cry indeed from the model of a saintly king. The merchant speaks about his lice and his earthly misadventures. In France they were rewriting the legend of the lilies that appeared on the armor of Clovis to assure him of victory (like a new Constantine), and even comparing Saint Louis to the sun.[27] Giannino states that he decided to include the sun in his own coat of arms simply because he happened to have available a seal of Cola di Rienzo bearing that feature. Nor does he base his claim to the throne on revelatory signs or spiritual faculties: the merchant announces no prophecies, displays no charisma, performs no miracles.

He displays no supernatural virtues at all, and we get the feeling that the institutional power to which he lays claim is missing the aura of the marvelous. What eschatological aspects and "royal messianism" there are in the tale appear to be linked to his "learned" sources, Friar Giordano, Friar Antonio, Friar Bartolomeo, and Cola di Rienzo, much more than they are to him. For example, Giannino never says a word about marks on his own skin which would show that he was of royal blood—the white crosses his descendants supposedly bore—but often emphasizes the mark a seal makes when it is pressed onto parchment. His attempt to reconquer his kingdom is grounded solely on the value he assigns to documents on paper. Giannino, a merchant, has faith in the written document and its publica fides.

Occasionally we come across judgments expressed by others in the *Istoria,* praising and defending him. We do not know if he drafted these himself, or if they were written in by his "copyists." What is of interest is their tenor: Giannino is always said to be wise, of respectable morals, without vices, pious, humble, upright and faithful in exercising civic magistracies, compassionate toward the poor, capable of reading, writing, and dictating in Italian, and pure in his dealings with married women. On one occasion we read this assessment of his economic activity at Siena: "And this trade he engaged in more to supply utility and gain to the poor people, than from desire for gain."[28] Shortly after, he or his rewriter asserts that in the jubilee year 1350, "he chose not to make any profit from business dealings."[29]

What can we deduce from this? It could be seen as a refusal of the stereotype of the merchant thinking only of his own advantage, as a list of moral qualities not entirely remote from sainthood. We might suspect an intent to assimilate the pretender to a holy king, by demonstrating that he behaved like one even before discovering who he really was, simply because he belonged to the *beata stirps* (the blessed lineage) of the Capetians. "He for whom I am looking is descended from him [Saint Louis] and will follow in his footsteps" is the promise made by Friar Antonio to Cola di Rienzo, and through him to Giannino himself.[30] But the result achieved is different, since the *Istoria* attributes a perfectly laic, and I would even say bourgeois, type of piety to Giannino. We are given an honest man, certainly, but a far cry from a *rex iustus;* a man eager to regain his throne, no doubt, but one just as careful not to take the field of battle himself; a man prepared to suffer wrongs at the hands of the wicked, like a patient and suffering saint, but not to the point of embracing death; displeased that Jerusalem is not in Christian hands, probably, but also prepared, when there seems no other way, to cede his own dynastic rights to the infidels. Overall, the figure that emerges from the *Istoria* is that of a king seen in the distorting mirror of a merchant: a "king" from a Tuscan folktale, who can step out onto the balcony of his house and spend time chatting with the king next door.[31]

The possibility that the switch in the cradle really took place and that Giannino's claims were thus well founded, is one I have often pondered. But I have concluded that the initial story was invented, in the first place because the quantity and quality of similar claims by impostors in the late Middle Ages is now well-known, and in the second place because neither of the two redactions that relay the act of substitution is reliable: they are constructed with an abundance of literary *topoi*, to which I shall return, and they crumble when subjected to internal criticism.

We know that the first draft of the two versions was made in the Tuscan language; this is evident from many words and expressions. So we are not dealing with texts composed originally in French and Latin, but two stories composed in Italian. Even the Latin letter of Cola di Rienzo is, in reality, a translation from Italian, as we can tell, for example, from the fact that a few names of French persons and places are given, not in French or Latin, but in Italian or a highly Italianized Latin: "filius regis Philippi dicti *el Bello*," "rex Luygius," "Parigius," "uno castro quod dicebatur *Nefolle del Vecchio* [i.e., Neauphle-le-Vieux]," and so on.[32] This is obviously hard to explain considering that the texts are supposed to depend directly on the confession of the French noblewoman Marie and the letters of Friars Giordano and Antonio, residents of France and certainly not Italians.

If the linguistic form demonstrates an origin outside France, the content also raises doubts. The first version, the naive and fantasizing one I labeled "sentimental," possesses an element of credibility. It relates the action, dangerous and apparently absurd, of a desperate woman who clung wailing to her own dead child, and for love of her husband decided to raise the one left alive as her own, risking the ire of members of the French court, who could have blamed her for killing the son of the king. In the account of this senseless deed, we can perceive the literary elaboration, but also the memory of a fortuitous event that led to a series of unforeseen consequences.

Paradoxically, therefore, the version closest to folktale is also in some respects the most credible. It makes intuitive sense, for example, that lady Marie, having done such a rash thing, kept absolutely quiet about it until the day she died. Likewise, the fact that the only accomplice was the wet nurse Amaloth, with the whole court intrigue left out, would make it possible to account for the otherwise unaccountable fact that the little king was taken away without any control. Yet this version, which Giannino had from Cola di Rienzo but did not include in his own memoirs, contains little that can be checked, and those few glaring mistakes already discussed. It is also generic and could be made to fit into many analogous tales.[33] Moreover, it has a weakness in common with the second version, the one I have called "political": both claim to derive from a deathbed confession. Finally, the sentimental version devotes a lot of space to Friar Giordano's dreams, which feature a prince who is the son of a living king and who cannot therefore be Jean I the Posthumous.

In the "political" version, the one most widely known, Marie de Cressay is a pawn in a court intrigue whose protagonists are the countess of Artois and two French barons. Now it is certain that on 19 November 1316 a baby identified as Jean I of France died at the French court, and it is also probable that his death was deliberately caused. But the legendary version of this deed, while naming Mahaut, countess of Artois, as the author of the homicide, is careful not to name the two barons who made the switch to save the little king's life. This is a huge missing piece, since only their testimony could have made the story credible. Yet nothing is known about these barons: the crime took place before the eyes of the world but had no witnesses. Their conduct is inexplicable, not so much in making the switch beforehand as in keeping silent about it afterward, for they are reported not to have revealed anything, even to the baby's mother, Queen Clémence, thus making it impossible for Jean to reclaim his throne. He supposedly grows up in ignorance, among people equally ignorant, with no surveillance. Moreover, there was an interval of some hours between the public presentation of the infant and his death, which occurred during the following night. The actions taken—or not taken—in that stretch of time are utterly unknown and utterly fundamental.

If the babies had really been switched as a precaution, and if Marie's baby was the one who died swaddled in royal robes, why would the two babies not have been switched back again, restoring things to their proper order, as would logically have been the plan? Giannino would have died and King Jean would have lived. Evidently none of this took place: I believe that it was indeed the royal offspring who died on 19 November 1316, and that nobody had put the merchant's son in his cradle.

The reclining statue of the baby can still be seen at Saint-Denis, lying at the feet of his father Louis X and beside his sister Jeanne of Navarre. The infant has the enigmatic smile familiar on contemporary statuary. He wears no crown because he was never consecrated, but his hair is bound with a circlet adorned with imitation jewels as a sign of his royal standing.[34] Jean I was placed in his tomb without wasting time, the day after his death, with a funeral procession that cost a little less than 112 livres.[35] If the body of a newborn baby of the fourteenth century could have been preserved; if his gravesite had not been despoiled in October 1793 by revolutionaries who exhumed the royal corpses and buried them in two graves outside the basilica;[36] if in the ossuary erected in 1817 it were still possible to identify body parts of the little king and one of his close relatives; and if DNA could be extracted and analyzed from them—then we would be able to draw a firm conclusion. But history cannot be made out of so many "ifs." We must content ourselves with the conclusion that the switch of Jean I for Giannino appears highly improbable.

THE FORMATION OF THE LEGEND

At this point, we would like to know how the legend of the switch in the cradle of the little king for his fellow nursling originated. Unfortunately, the evidence about this is thin, and all we have are hints.

It is worth emphasizing that this story of switched babies must have been widely known around the middle of the fourteenth century. Giannino claims to have heard of it from a French knight in 1350, a few years before Cola di Rienzo "revealed" to him who he really was. Cola himself supposedly heard of it while at Avignon, and Friar Bartolomeo Mini while a student at the University of Paris.

Hence the story might have originated, taken shape, and been diffused in France, in oral form. This hypothesis is perhaps strengthened by the fact that Giannino was aware of two different versions of the same legend. Moreover, when he himself retells the story of the murder committed by Mahaut of Artois, the merchant reports various accounts of the method she used:

> And with the intention to cause his death, she then squeezed the said infant, some say round his waist, others said round his temples; and some said she stuck a pin into his head; and some said, that she put her finger into the back of his throat; and some said, that she bore poison on her fingers and put it on the infant's lips.[37]

In this exposition of the various possibilities, repeatedly punctuated by a set phrase (*chi disse*) referring back to public rumor, it seems to me that we catch an echo of word-of-mouth tales that passed over into the written text.[38]

The passage from the phase of oral diffusion to that of redaction in written form is a critical moment, which requires deeper investigation. For this reason too, it is to be hoped that sooner or later a new critical edition of the *Istoria del re Giannino* will be undertaken. For the moment, since it is evident that the redactions we do have are in Italian, or in a Latin translated from Italian, we may legitimately suspect that both versions of the legend were written down in an Italian setting. At any rate, it does not appear at the moment that there exist any other versions of this legend with a tradition independent of those already discussed. There are, for example, no contemporary chronicles that narrate the event, and the many scholarly citations we encounter in the modern era all show direct dependence on the sources already familiar to us. So the hypothesis is that the legend originated and evolved in France, certainly not Siena, but that in Siena, or at any rate in Italy, it acquired its final form.

Rumors that the little king had been switched in the cradle would have been all the more likely to propagate because they converged with various historical data: Countess Mahaut really did have the reputation of a poisoner; there must have been strong suspicion that Jean I had been murdered; opponents of the crown had an interest in spreading rumors of this kind; subsequently, during the Hundred

Years' War, conditions were so calamitous in the kingdom of France that they would have facilitated the spread of rumors about the return of a king of the pure "race" who would restore order.[39]

It is certain, moreover, that the exchanging of infants and the use of doubles (which is what we have here) on the part of those in power, really did occur. The Florentine chronicler Giovanni Villani, for example, relates such a story concerning Corradino of Swabia as a child. Manfredi wanted to be crowned king of Sicily, but he knew that his nephew Corradino, the heir of his deceased brother Corrado, represented an obstacle. Manfredi told the Sicilian barons that his nephew was very ill and would never be able to govern. So envoys were sent to investigate the state of his health. When they arrived in Swabia, they found that the child's mother was watching over him with care, keeping him together with other children, the sons of nobles, all dressed alike. When the envoys inquired about Corradino, the mother, fearful of Manfredi, pointed to one of these other children. The envoys presented him with rich presents, among them some poisoned sweets. As soon as he ate them, the boy died.

This story, which begins in compellingly similar fashion to ours, also unfolds in the same way: nobody at the Swabian court revealed the trick to the Sicilian barons, who took ship at Venice in galleys hoisting black sails as a sign of mourning. They brought the news of the death to Manfredi, who immediately had himself crowned at Monreale.[40]

This precedent, which dates from 1255, is arresting and could have functioned as a model for the story we know. But it is also a much more acceptable and logical precedent since it attributes the act of concealment to the child's mother and above all because the child, who was not a newborn, was recognizable and was immediately restored to his status. Indeed, he later descended into Italy to claim the throne, although with disastrous results.

Overall, with the information at our disposal today, there is little that we can say about what really happened in Paris in 1316. I take the view that the tale of the murder and the switched babies belongs in the category of rumor and gossip, and the fact that it was received and passed on as authentic is one reason to think so. The legend would have originated in the diffusion of true and presumptive elements—

all of them expressions of political and social dissent, however—and over the course of time, assumed a narrative form close to that of a novella.[41]

That leaves open the problem of how a piece of hearsay, one not unlike the urban legends that haunt our own contemporary imaginary, could have entered into the real life of a man of the fourteenth century and driven him to the most extreme lengths. Where was the moment of fusion between legend and life?

While I do not believe that Giannino invented his own legend for himself, I do think that it was, in a sense, tailored to fit him. The linkage between Giannino and the tale of the switched babies lies in what students of folktale call the initial situation, in which elements already known to the audience are adduced, such as persons who really lived, places that really exist, known historical facts. These serve to introduce the actual tale.[42] In our case, the initial situation can be identified in the village of Cressay and the person of Marie.

What I think is that Marie de Cressay, whom I take it was Giannino's mother, really was the wet nurse of little King Jean of France, or at any rate that Giannino was convinced that the revelation about him was true because he recognized persons and places from his own infancy in the story. The village of Cressay is attested in the Middle Ages and still exists, situated on the banks of the Mauldre a couple of kilometers from the town of Neauphle-le-Vieux in the department of Yvelines in the Île-de-France region. We have records of members of Marie's family, chevaliers of the abbey of Saint-Pierre-de-Neauphle-le-Vieux, which held the domain of Cressay. The squire Pierre de Cressei, called Piquart, appears in 1277 and can be identified with Piccardo di Charsi, the father of the lady Maria in the *Istoria*. A Jean de Cressey is documented in 1286.[43] Thus, there is little reason to doubt that this was the historical and geographical setting of the early childhood of the boy who later became Sienese.

THE DOUBTS THAT REMAIN

We have come to the end of our review and analysis of the evidence: Giannino di Guccio, self-proclaimed king of France, actually lived, and a large part of what we know about his adventure corresponds to events that occurred. Yet the doubts that remain are many, nor do I think they can all be dispelled. Some are relatively trifling, such as the presence of the odd namesake on the scene.[44] But others carry greater weight, and need to be discussed if not resolved, to illustrate the degree to which the story of King Giannino is still an unresolved problem.

The first and perhaps gravest series of questions to which I don't have all the answers concerns the personality of the protagonist. How did Giannino di Guccio manage to convince himself that he was a king? How heartfelt was his belief in the justice of his own cause? How much awareness did he have of the world around him, the political interests he impinged on? What mental picture was he able to form of the context in which he was living and acting?

For Bercé, who offers a psychological analysis of his actions, Giannino's ability to convince himself that he was royalty was a "healing scheme" formed as a reaction to having been called a bastard when he was a boy. "He had discovered, deep inside himself, in his patchy French memories, that he was Jean I, king of France."[45]

If his mother had in fact been at court, what would she have been able to tell him? And how did Giannino process these memories? Taken from his mother's embrace as a child, by a father he barely knew who soon returned to France and died there, and raised by his grandfather in what was at first a foreign city, he would, in this interpretation, have begun to fantasize about his lofty origins, inventing his own revenge on fate and finding external confirmation of it, first in a widespread rumor and then in the revelation of Cola di Rienzo.

Though the documentation is insufficient, and I would not be qualified to interpret it from the psychopathological point of view anyway, I don't think it is too far-fetched to follow Bercé in reading the symptoms of delirium in Giannino's adventure: his ideation had its own internal coherence and logic, but it was cut off from the data of the real world. It is possible that Giannino, lucid and unshakeable in his confidence, the prisoner of his own thought process, was mentally ill. But it must be emphasized that we have no way of adequately assessing the mental balance, or unbalance, of a man of the Middle Ages.[46] Moreover, his manner of proclaiming himself a king is utterly different from that of the stereotypical modern psychiatric inmate who thinks he is Napoleon. Of course, every epoch expresses insanity through fantasies proper to itself, and before the time of Napoleon the asylums did not contain frowning emperors in bicorne hats. But Giannino is different: his putative insanity does not consist of believing that he was once a king and wanting to be one again—believing that he had fought at Crécy or Poitiers, for example, then somehow vanished and subsequently reappeared. On the contrary, what he says is that he is a man who ought to have lived as a king, but who was robbed of his own legitimate existence. From the moment the "evidence" of the switch in the cradle is accepted as probative, this way of thinking appears rational, not pathological.

This cannot be unconnected with another rather striking fact about his place in society: the merchant king was not an indigent vagabond living from hand to mouth, like almost all the other impostors we know of. Others take him seriously, and he enjoys a certain amount of respect: he is rich, he dresses well, he can engage in quite high-level contacts. We can discuss the bizarre claim he advanced endlessly, but there is no doubt that he was a person integrated into his world, capable of conducting himself with dignity and participating in the culture around him. Giannino does not refuse the established order; he believes so strongly in inherited birthright as to make it the principal motive of his actions. A merchant among merchants, he is at home with their way of thinking, writing down his own memoirs with the precision that a libro di ricordanze demands. As fascinated as any other bourgeois by stories about the French royal family, he may have become spellbound to the point of believing them true and basing his whole existence on them.[47]

So I suspect that Giannino, rather than being someone else's invented character, was the victim of such literary inventions himself and that his familiarity with tales set in France may have helped him to delude himself (something which, for that matter, happened with real princes of royal blood).

What had the merchant king read? How many tales similar to "the ancient stories" of Cola di Rienzo had he heard? How many stories of saints' lives and hagiographical literature were part of his daily diet?

How often had a fiery sermon riveted him to the pew?[48] If only we knew. We should perhaps imagine him as a kind of Don Quixote (a literary invention for sure!) enamored of books and heroes. "And he greatly delighted to read and write and dictate in the vulgar tongue," says the *Istoria* about him.[49]

The second set of unresolved problems lies in the fact that the alteration of factual data in the *Istoria* takes place on more than one level and is in large part intentional. Every writer, even the historian, shapes his story by selecting, emphasizing, and omitting, but here it is a prominent factor because we are dealing with the memoirs of a forger. The interface of "truth" and "deceit" is the dominant theme of Giannino's whole adventure, as he tells the story of his life his way. The dividing line is uncertain and beguiling: it is like looking at a sunset reflected in a lake. Thus, there is an apparent paradox at the root of Giannino's quest. Since he believes in the publica fides of written documents, he is disposed to believe as well in the supposed testament of Marie de Cressay, the confession that makes him a king. The frame of mind that makes him trustful of documents is the same one that leads him to forge evidence, creating fresh testimonials on purpose.

When he writes his life, Giannino aims to set down everything that has happened to him, apparently without realizing how many shady characters and conmen had swarmed around him and eaten at his table. He describes facts and situations which he dates with care, he rattles off the names of persons who have had dealings with him (helped him, betrayed him), he lists the objects he possessed, he records the names of his children, their dates of marriage, their dates of burial. But he doesn't always apply the filters we would expect him to and is relatively incapable of carrying out an effective control and selection of what he recalls. Engaged in composing a self-justifying narrative of his own misfortunes, he clues us in without actually saying so to the fact that he was a forger: you would have to be gullible indeed to believe in the authenticity of the letters of Cola di Rienzo and the king of Hungary, knowing that their addressee had received a seal from each of them "as a gift" and observing that in the second case he even goes so far as to mention the price he paid to the faithful chaplain who had procured this "gift" on his behalf.

Are we to conclude that the forger deliberately left these clues? Why would he? I believe that this oddity arises mainly because Giannino is simply expressing his own version of the facts and, secondarily, because writing in this mode enabled him to recall facts and names, modifying the truth just enough (as he saw it) to shield himself against possible accusations. This was an elementary device to ensure that the factual record he was compiling would not be too damaging if it fell into the wrong hands—remember that he was in prison when he wrote it. Thus, in the same way and for the same reasons, the identification of the notary who accompanied him to Rome, Angelo d'Andrea Guidaregli, implies that he had a role, unspecified but decisive, in the production of the forged "clarities" on which the merchant placed so much reliance. In fact, we know from other sources that the notary who traveled to Rome with Giannino at the outset of our story is the same man who recopied the letters of Cola and certified their authenticity. Finally, amid the chiaroscuro of names and facts thronging the page for reasons that aren't always clear, we may note the references casually thrown in to his relations with the princes of Navarre, the enemies of the French crown who were probably his most important allies but also the ones requiring the most discretion. Various other portions of Giannino's narrative may likewise have been modified by discretion and caution. Just as we pass from wakefulness to sleep without knowing it, so in a narration the slide from recounting into inventing is often imperceptible.

In practical terms, the *Istoria* includes the right ingredients, but their dosage is erratic. It is highly probable that all or almost all the individuals named in Giannino's account did have dealings with him, but not necessarily the exact ones he describes. What occurs in his version of the facts is a little like the wonderful device for generating stories that Gianni Rodari, in his book *The Grammar of Fantasy* called the "fantastic binomial" (*binomio fantastico*).[50] Take two words, "man" and "umbrella," for example; you may couple them in the predictable form "the man with the umbrella." But couple them in the form "the man in the umbrella," and the imagination is sparked. That's how it is with Giannino: Cola di Rienzo, the citizens of Siena, the senators of Rome, the king of Hungary, the queen of Naples, the pope, the cardinals, the princes of Navarre and their envoys, the various seneschals, friars, Jewish merchants, soldiers and horsemen, together with a plethora of bit players, all had dealings with Giannino. But in what fashion? "With the umbrella," the way he tells it, or some other way?

The third cluster of queries to which we don't have answers is this: what was the role of those who had dealings with Giannino, and what were they thinking? Who believed him and why?

Take Daniello, the converted Hungarian Jew who seems like a conman at first but appears to get so involved in the intrigue that he winds up dying in prison. What did Daniello have to gain by selling Giannino's "rights" to the Turks and Tartars? What sense did this truly incomprehensible proposal make? Maybe he thought he could profit, but in the end he appears to be just another deluded victim of the twists of fate. Be that as it may, next to Giannino himself Daniello seems like the most singular character in the whole story, and his role is still hard to grasp, leaving us with many questions. How, for example, was this recent convert to Christianity able to maintain such a close relationship with his former coreligionists? How could he claim he was ready to lend the sum of 200,000 florins, far too high to be credible, without the merchant Giannino ever mentioning the payment of any interest or the pledging of any security in his memoirs? Convinced of the good faith of the hidden king, Daniello supposedly put his own wealth and that of the Jewish community, to which he evidently continued to belong, at Giannino's disposal in return for the mere promise of a return of the Jews to the kingdom of France. But if Daniello had really converted, why would he offer to mediate between the king awaiting coronation and the Jewish people awaiting readmission to France? It's clear that something doesn't quite fit here.[51]

In effect, Daniello's function transcends the simple one of moneylender. Even if Giannino doesn't say so in as many words, we may hazard a guess that Daniello, precisely because he is defined as a "converted Jew," actually has a considerable part to play in the concept of the Christian recognition of true royalty that underlies the whole story. In terms of medieval Christian thought, he is a Jew who has made amends for his own doctrinal error: no longer a member of the "deicidal" race of the Jews, cleansed by baptism, he has been illuminated by the revelation that enabled him to recognize the true king, Jesus Christ. And, behind him, the true most Christian king who is our Giannino. For this and other reasons, it might be possible to catch a faint echo of the theories of the friar Jean de Roquetaillade, a contemporary of Giannino who assigned an important role to the Jewish people in the End of Days. But how, and by what channels?[52]

Daniello may be considered emblematic of the fact that many people did believe in the royalty of Giannino and did heed him. Giannino was, of course, surrounded by a swarm of profiteers and spies, shifty political operators who sometimes strung him along, like "the Bishop" who latched onto him in Hungary and the Parisian draper Pierre de La Courneuve. But to suppose that everyone Giannino came across in the course of his long adventure regarded him as a fool to be manipulated, would be superficial and misguided. On the contrary, Giannino's dream was shared by many: a few Sienese at least, a few of his "courtiers," the relatives who followed him on his travels, some of the citizens of Aix-en-Provence, and above all perhaps the band of mercenaries who hoisted his standard and fought in his name for a short while. What was the extent of this collective conviction? How was it possible for the little merchant to win that much trust?

This is one of those problems of social psychology and history of mentalities that were introduced into historiography by Marc Bloch and confronted by Natalie Zemon Davis in her book *The Return of Martin Guerre*. In it the American historian retraces the celebrated story of an impostor of the sixteenth century who lived in a village for several years posing as someone else; he was well accepted by the local people, and even by the wife of the real Martin Guerre, who took him into her house and into her bed for three straight years.[53]

The *Istoria* does not furnish us with a description of Giannino that would enable us to tell whether he bore a physical resemblance to the members of the royal house of France; all we know is that he was short. But it wouldn't have mattered: how many people in the fourteenth century ever got to see the king in person anyway? Neither Giannino nor those with whom he had direct contact (except for the odd cardinal) knew what the members of the royal family looked like. A century later it was thought miraculous that Jeanne d'Arc recognized the Dauphin disguised as a courtier, never having seen him before. And a miracle it was, in an age when the essence of being a prince was to dress like one. For example, in a story by Giovanni Gherardi of Prato, two Florentines fail to recognize King Louis of Hungary when he receives them in a garden: "Look Luca, we would never have believed he was the king, since he neither had, nor has, his crown on his head; we thought it was his priest."[54]

In an age that did not even have realistic portraiture, never mind photographs, fingerprints, and DNA analysis, the problem of recognizing the personal identity of individuals was tricky.[55] People had no choice but to go by such external signs as the lifestyle trappings that individuals displayed and the testimony of others. As regards the first of these, Giannino was no fool. As in the folktale "Puss in Boots," in which the miller's son becomes the marquis of Carabas because his cat succeeds in duping the king by pretending that his master is wealthy, the Sienese merchant displayed trappings at Avignon that enabled him to be convincing: he possessed a crown, sumptuous clothing, several suits of armor, and his table was richly set. Whether he also spoke with "royal eloquence" and delivered inspiring harangues to his followers, we do not know, but we can well imagine his little court calling him "sire" and bowing and scraping.

As for testimony as a guarantee of identity, we find that in the Middle Ages, whenever doubt arises about someone's identity, there is nowhere else to turn except *pubblica fama* (public repute). The common report, tradition, the testimony of elders, a declaration by someone in authority—all of these counted as evidence, both in the popular culture and for jurists. The story of Grasso the woodworker, discussed in chapter four, is based on precisely this factor: since everyone goes along with the joke by changing the way they address the fat woodworker, recognizing him as a citizen called "Matteo," the authors of the beffa succeed in persuading even the victim himself that that is who he is. And since doubt about identity is almost impossible to extirpate, the Sienese statutes from the end of the thirteenth century (still in force in Giannino's youth) made it illegal, in the interests of public order, to cast doubt on the personal identity of citizens. Anyone who denies the "common opinion and report" will be heavily fined, but the victim of such defamation need do no more to prove his own identity than declare it in private before the judge.[56]

Giannino is a king therefore because he is in a position to present convincing testimonials. Who believes him? Those who, unfamiliar with written documents, regard all of them as probative: a will, the letters of Cola di Rienzo, the letters from the king of Hungary, displayed at the right time, cancel all doubt on the part of the soldiers, for example. And who doesn't believe him? On one hand, those who have always known him as "Giannino di Guccio, wool man of Siena," in other words his fellow citizens; on the other, all those alert to the artificiality of the written word and able to spot, in Giannino's "clarities," the conspicuous absence of reliability: for example, the king of Hungary, who tells him he is being manipulated by clerics, and Pope Innocent VI, who considers his arguments "novel and ridiculous."[57]

This brings us to another salient factor, the role that members of religious orders may have played in the whole affair. The Augustinian friars Antonio and Giordano wander through the world looking for a king. The Dominican friar Bartolomeo Mini is the one who makes the solemn gesture of announcing the Sienese merchant's royal nature in public, and he is part of the recorded history of Siena at that time.[58] What was their relationship with Giannino, and what actions did they really take? We do not know at present, but it is possible that further research might bear fruit.[59] Such research will need to focus on the conception of sovereignty, on contemporary political discourse, and on the recorded sermons of friars from the various mendicant orders. One thinks of Egidius Romanus and Ptolemy of Lucca, and perhaps especially of Remigio de' Girolami, well known for his sermons in praise of the Angevin sovereigns.[60] We could hypothesize that the two Augustinian friars, Antonio and Giordano, and especially the Dominican Bartolomeo Mini composed sermons too and that they propagated heterodox theories on the state of the French monarchy in the middle of the fourteenth century; something of the sort seems to transpire from the *Istoria* itself. These very individuals, and perhaps other religious as well, may have reversed the traditional position, declaring that the kingdom of France had been bereft of its legitimate sovereign; asserting that a homicide perpetrated upon an innocent child had thrown the country into disastrous war; maintaining the necessity of restoring the pristine order of things; propagating a "royal messianism" perfectly consonant with the broad stream of late medieval eschatology; and finally encountering a benign, though belated, supporter in Cola di Rienzo. Bartolomeo Mini, the Sienese friar, might have played a bigger part than we can tell at this distance, and it is entirely possible that, behind the merchant, strings were being pulled at a higher cultural level. Perhaps the seeds of Giannino's story were planted under sunny skies, along the roads of Europe frequented by those assiduous travelers, the friars and the merchants, and in the shadowy secrecy of the dreams and tales these voyagers told.

Among all these hypothetical relationships—vessels cruising on the sea of possibilities—the most fascinating, I think, is the one with Cola di Rienzo. The problem is central, because the tribune is presented in the *Istoria* as the Frankenstein who "creates the monster" by revealing his royal birth to a simple merchant. Maybe what we have here is one delusional monomaniac molding another like him before dying. The part Cola plays is so engaging, however, that I took the liberty of retelling it at the start of this book as if every word of the *Istoria* were factually true. But is it? Strong suspicion arises, especially around two aspects: the business about the seal and the tribune's well-known propensity for the dramatic device of anagnorisis—the moment of "recognition" when the hero's real situation and real relationship to other characters are revealed, as when he himself declared that he was the natural son of Emperor Henry VII.

As regards the seal, it seems highly unlikely that a head of government would so lightly donate such a precious object, which was indispensable for certifying his commands. Seals (unless they were stolen) only ever left the chancellery after being defaced or broken to render them useless, or else they followed their masters into the tomb. And although Giannino makes a point of telling us that the seal he received was defective, hence unusable, we can tell from his own words that the design error was minimal: a tiny lily instead of a tiny star. This implies to me that the seal was usable; indeed, it is even possible that this tiny mistake was deliberate, a little secret sign that the chancellery itself would recognize.

If Cola had really wished to let Giannino see and copy his own emblem, he could have given him a wax impression; with that, you could even make a passable forgery. But to make him a gift of the matrix? It stretches belief. Assuming that Giannino really did have those meetings with Cola di Rienzo, we have to assume, I think, that Cola was drunk when he gave him the seal, or else that Giannino pocketed it surreptitiously.

But it is also possible that possession of the seal is the key to solving the whole puzzle, provided we shift our point of view. Giannino could have made up the whole story of his meetings with Cola di Rienzo as a way to explain his possession of certain documents: documents which he had fabricated entirely on his own, once he had got hold of the seal. How did he do so? One possibility is that it came into his hands after the sack of the Capitoline palace that followed Cola's death. Once he had it, he would have constructed his forgeries, being careful to date them to the very last days of the tribune's life. For that matter, we can tell that Giannino was fond of objects of this kind from the fact that he also had a reproduction of the secret seal of the king of Hungary and made a further copy of it for himself. So our first revised scenario goes like this: there never were any meetings between Cola and Giannino, who made them up as a back story to justify his fabricated documents.

The second suspicion, revolving around the fact that Cola had already staged a recognition scene of his own by revealing that he was the son of Henry VII, cuts even deeper. The *Istoria* never mentions this caprice on the part of the tribune, but whoever wrote the book might still have had it in mind. From this perspective, the connection between Cola di Rienzo and Giannino would have been made a posteriori, by a literary artificer drawing an implicit parallel between these two fantasy-world sons of an emperor and a king. There was nobody better suited to such a construct than Cola. And so we have our second revised scenario: Giannino and Cola never had anything to do with one another, and the story that they did was a pure romance concocted in the fifteenth century.

If we exclude Cola di Rienzo in this way, we would have to conjecture a different point of departure for Giannino's adventure, with the revelation arriving from a different source. And yet: having laid out these suspicions fully, I am still inclined to believe that the meeting in Rome between these two extravagant characters really took place. In the irrational act of recognizing King Jean I of France in a Sienese merchant, I detect a way of proceeding utterly typical of Cola di Rienzo, as I argued in chapter one. Consequently, if the story is untrue, whoever wrote it must have been extremely well informed about the tribune's personality. Moreover, the meeting with Cola is recorded not just at the start of the *Istoria* but in the middle of it.[61] Lastly, notwithstanding the charisma he radiated, it is not the case that Cola di Rienzo was considered an authoritative source of legitimation by most contemporaries—certainly not by the pope and the monarchs of Europe. Quite the contrary, many people thought he was crazy. Yet Giannino believed in Cola di Rienzo to the point of basing his own claim for restoration on Cola's warrant.

The initial naïveté of crediting Cola, and more than that, of believing that Cola was credited by others—a naïveté subsequently and clumsily corrected by piling on the further forgery of the letters from Louis of Hungary—leads me to think that there is more than just a core of truth here: it must really have been Cola who sought out Giannino, not Giannino who chose Cola. If he hadn't had dealings with Cola, the merchant would have been able to find some other great lord, authoritative and deceased, and make him declare what needed declaring.

So I hold to the view that it was Cola di Rienzo who launched Giannino on his adventurous career and that we should attribute at least one letter to him, the one containing the sentimental version of the switched babies, even if we have it in a form that cannot be exactly what he wrote, since it is written in the Tuscan language. When the tribune died, Giannino continued to use his seal (and how he got hold of it remains a mystery to me), dating a few further forgeries to the days immediately preceding Cola's death. Having been received on the Capitol and given his first credentials there, he would spend the rest of his life trying to be received by other potentates for the purpose of obtaining further attestations to his royal birth from them.

FOLKTALE, MYTH, AND THE "MATTER OF FRANCE"

Let us now leave the mire of doubt behind and roam in the broad pastures of fantasy. The story of the birth and exchange of Jean I for his fellow nursling has a few links to historical events. Nevertheless, we can detect many points of contact with themes characteristic of folktale and myth. "Reality is never how it is portrayed" would be an appropriate motto for our story. The legend probably persisted because of its closeness to several deep and enthralling motifs that made it possible to experience it and retell it as though it were a folktale (the Italian word for which, incidentally, is *fiaba*, literally "fable").[62]

To convince Giannino, Cola di Rienzo had already "told him about various kings who had been switched at birth."[63] The first part of the *Istoria* chimes with the world of folktale, for we encounter numerous narrative motifs that fit the general pattern of characters who undergo trials, who are victims of deceit, and who experience recognitions.[64] One of the most salient motifs is that of the switching of persons, which often, as in this case, involves two individuals of widely divergent social status: a noble damsel and a young merchant. We encounter this motif in a great many medieval literary works and traditional folktales like the Little Goose Girl, and indeed in modern literary fables such as Mark Twain's *The Prince and the Pauper*.[65] The motif of the babies switched in the cradle is also traditional and widespread, even turning up in the recent children's novel by Bianca Pitzorno, *Polissena del Porcello*.[66]

Other protagonists of the legend of Giannino aside from the little victim of the switch himself have their counterparts in traditional folktale: Mahaut, a princess of the royal blood, is a lot like the baby-killing princess/witch, and variants of one of her killing tools, a long needle, also turn up in the hands of similar maleficent characters: the comb placed on the head of Snow White, the spindle that pricks Sleeping Beauty. The motif of a prince or princess who is taken away from court and hidden, as protection against the wickedness of a close relative, is also a recurrent motif in many a folktale, beginning with Snow White herself, and Sleeping Beauty, and continuing with Perrault's Peau d'âne.

A happy ending to these stories is virtually guaranteed, usually in a moment of anagnorisis in which the hero's or heroine's true identity is recognized; such plots are already frequent in the ancient world. In the case of Giannino, we find all the usual ingredients: the removal of the little prince in peril, a life lived in someone else's place, the recognition at the hands of Cola di Rienzo, who convinces him to try to recover his true kingdom. His "folktale" lacks its happy ending, though, because it is only the beginning of his story that is situated in the realm of fantasy.

If the commencement of the *Istoria* borrows material from the world of folktale, Giannino's whole adventure is pervaded by a dominant theme that belongs to the myth of the return of the hero, or the return of the king (naturally found in folktale as well).[67]

So different from other people, our merchant does bear a close resemblance to the character of the hidden sovereign, exiled from or unacknowledged in his own kingdom. Bercé remarks:

> The myth of the king hidden in infancy was able to join together the virtues of tradition and innovation. It constituted a marvelous utopia, because it combined the power of an ancient legitimacy with the seductive lure of a mysterious renewal lying concealed amid the dense mass of the people, in an impenetrable social opacity.[68]

The story of Giannino resembles that of the babe Jehoash, narrated in the Bible, which perhaps constituted a reference model for the elaboration of the "political" version of the switch of Jean I in the cradle. Jehoash, the son of King Ahaziah, was taken away by his aunt and nurse to prevent him from being killed by his grandmother, and remained hidden for six years. In the seventh year he was revealed to the guardians of the royal palace by the priest Jehoiada, who placed the diadem on his head and anointed him king.[69] And for that matter, Zeus himself was concealed from his father Cronus so that Cronus would not devour him; Xenophon relates that Cyrus the Great was hidden, while still an infant, from his grandfather Astyages, who wanted to feed him to wild beasts, and was taken in by a peasant couple who raised him as their son.[70]

In other respects Giannino is similar to Ulysses, who reaches Ithaca in secret. And he resembles Disney's King Arthur, who grew up believing his name was Wart and that he was the younger son of a country noble. And he resembles Aragorn, who sprang from the imagination, solidly grounded in philology, of J. R. R. Tolkien. This character, who roams through Middle Earth like a wanderer, has even changed his own name, calling himself Strider, but he will become king through his ability, and through birthright, receiving the characteristic sign of French and English sovereigns, the healing touch:

> All that is gold does not glitter
> Not all those who wander are lost
> The old that is strong does not wither
> Deep roots are not reached by the frost
>
> From the ashes a fire shall be woken
> A light from the shadows shall spring
> Renewed shall be blade that was broken
> The crownless again shall be king.[71]

Standing behind all these sovereigns hidden from the eyes of the world and kings asleep under mountains waiting to reawaken (like Arthur or Frederick II), there is a model that, especially for the Middle Ages, is fundamental, although not always explicitly stated: that of Jesus Christ. Giannino is a king without a crown and without an escort, dressed in humble bourgeois clothing and unknown to the world, exactly like the king of kings, whose line passes through David and Solomon, but who is born in a poor manger without clothing or warm fire and lives in the house of the carpenter Joseph. As king of the Jews, Jesus represents a threat to those in power, Herod the Great, Pilate, Herod Antipas. During his crucifixion he suffers the insults of the purple robe, the crown of thorns, and the sign bearing the letters I.N.R.I., *Iehsus Naʒarenus Rex Iudeorum*. As John the Evangelist wrote: "He was in the world that had its being through him, and the world did not know him."[72]

There is no telling how many self-proclaimed sovereigns—often persuaded of their duty to carry out a salvational mission and play a messianic role—modeled themselves on the poor and persecuted king, Jesus Christ, embroiling themselves in an odd species of *imitatio*, in which even apparent failure on earth could represent victory. An example is the sad story of Don Sebastian, "king of Portugal," whose condemnation to the galleys was compared to the passion of Christ.[73] Giannino himself, in the letter he wrote impersonating the king of Hungary, adduces a comparison between him and his "nurse" on one hand and the baby Jesus and Mary on the other, as they fled into Egypt to escape Herod's persecution.

An important point of contact between the adventure of Giannino di Guccio and the world of literature is the vast river of stories about the "royals of France." The adventures, amours, secrets, treacheries, curses, honor, and sanctity of the kings and princes of the blood supplied the raw material for countless romance narratives that have cast their spell over readers from the Middle Ages to today.

There was a legend, propagated in the thirteenth century for purposes of denigration, that Hugues Capet had been the son of a simple citizen, a butcher of Paris. It was known to Dante Alighieri, who places Capet among the greedy and prodigal sinners and gives him these stinging lines as a slam at Charles of Anjou: "The son I was of a butcher of Paris."[74] It was known to François Villon, who asserts in the *Ballade de l'appel* that the founder of the French dynasty "was drawn from butchery."[75] A chanson de geste entitled *Hugues Capet* was composed at exactly the same time Giannino was engaged in his adventure, in which the protagonist is called (with no defamatory intent this time) the son of a knight and a bourgeois woman, the daughter of the main butcher of Paris.[76] Hugues supposedly becomes king by assuming leadership of the bourgeois of Paris and coming to the aid of the widowed Queen Blanchefleur; he is helped by his uncle, the richest bourgeois of the city. This anonymous work, which dates from 1358–1360, reflects in its own way the dynastic crisis, the battle of Poitiers, and the cataclysm of Étienne Marcel's revolt. The poet transposes contemporary events into a distant era, of which he knows nothing. It is a poem of social harmony, about a king whose parents represent two opposed social groups and is therefore capable of uniting the nobility and the bourgeoisie and reasserting monarchical power.

Although this story has no direct connection to ours, the coincidence of dating between the invention of a bourgeois Hugues Capet and the presence of the bourgeois King Giannino on the scene is certainly striking. At just this time King Charles of Navarre, who was promoting his own claim to reign in France, had "bourgeoisie" (non-noble citizenship) conferred on himself at Amiens, supported the merchants of Paris, delivered speeches to crowds, and invited men of low status to dine at his table.[77] Further research may yield interesting insights into the perceived relationship between bourgeois status and regal status in the fourteenth century. From this perspective, Giannino's story has real significance.

There is an even more direct and stringent comparison with a work that appeared a few decades after the death of our protagonist, Andrea da Barberino's *Il Guerrin Meschino*.[78] This chivalric romance narrates the myriad adventures of young Guerrino as he wanders through West and East to discover who he is, living through incredible events and searching out oracles, sibyls, and prophecies. At the end it is revealed that Guerrino is of royal blood, the son of Milone, duke of Durazzo, who is in turn the son of the duke of Burgundy, and that he (Guerrino) had been put on a boat while still an infant by his governess, to save him from death. Set in a fantasy version of the age of Charlemagne, this romance was still very popular in Italy within living memory. Equally beloved was another work of Andrea da Barberino, *I reali di Francia* (The Royals of France), a sort of highly colored genealogy of Charlemagne's family that includes plot lines from chansons de geste of the thirteenth century.[79] The interesting part for our purposes is the episode in which King Pippin marries Berta of Hungary, but a servant is then substituted for her in the nuptial bed. Charlemagne (Carlo Magno in Italian) is born from a secret encounter in a forest between the king and Berta and, while still a youth is forced to flee the court, driven out by his half-brothers, the sons of the servant. Young Carlo takes the name Mainetto (Mainet, i.e., Magnetto, a diminutive of Magno), and must wage a long struggle to regain his throne.

In sum, the popular literature on the court of France is full of hidden princes and characters who have switched places, like the Dauphin whom Jeanne d'Arc recognized. (She herself spun off at least three doubles who roamed France after her death, claiming to be her; and of course one thinks of the dark legend of the "man in the iron mask" from the seventeenth century.)[80] Charlemagne himself went incognito through the forests, and pretended to be a simple soldier.

What is the link between these stories and Giannino? It seems to me certain that the *Istoria del re Giannino*—although it was not, I repeat, originally conceived as a literary tale—does reflect a readerly passion for the "matter of France." The fact that our book has a legendary beginning containing elements in common with these romances and the fact that the protagonist is a little king bent on regaining his birthright have led commentators to the erroneous conclusion that Giannino himself was a creature of fantasy, a species of Guerrin Meschino.

GIANNINO IN LITERATURE

Giannino's story attracted erudite readers but did not have a wide public following, or any literary reworkings, until the republican nineteenth century. Perhaps this silence was due to simple prudence, since the story of Jean the Posthumous, if presented as true, would have been seen as a defamation of the French monarchy. This at any rate was the opinion of Louis de Monmerqué, one of the first historians to study Giannino in a scholarly way, who wrote: "At the conclusion of this discussion, we are pleased to have been led to formulate just one doubt."[81]

His doubt was not insignificant: Monmerqué, a faithful royalist, had to face the disquieting possibility that the French sovereigns subsequent to the infant king had come to the throne thanks to an assassination. For the same reason, the historian issued a warning to whoever might undertake to study Giannino after him:

> In the age in which we live, writers, even illustrious ones, often look to history for nothing except material for their games of imagination: a tiny king of the Middle Ages cast into the position of private citizen through a great crime, may seem to many the ideal hero for a historical romance. For this reason it is all the more important to treat everything that may subsequently be discovered about this singular personage in a serious manner.[82]

The nineteenth-century scholar, whose indignation may have been directed primarily at Alexandre Dumas, was indisputably right: it is important not to get our categories mixed up. The stories of the baby King Jean I the Posthumous and the merchant Giannino have indeed supplied the raw material for several literary works, most of them rather obscure except for the most recent, which is both engaging and well-known. It hardly needs pointing out that the story I have narrated and analyzed here seems ready-made for fictional treatment. You could write a novel or make a film about it tomorrow if you wanted to. Let's leave that prospect aside and briefly see how Giannino has fared in French and Italian works of the imagination, the authors of which became acquainted with him at more or less the same time that historians were growing heated about the topic.[83]

Eugène Muller, a librarian at the Arsenal Library in Paris, printed a small, entertaining comedy of misunderstanding in 1878. It is set in 1365, in a room in an inn at Siena that just happens to be called Auberge des Armes de France. The characters are common folk: the innkeeper Jeannot Baglioni and his neighbor, their two children who wish to marry, and finally two French adventurers who, to pay for their meal, make up the story of the switch in the cradle right there and then. They convince the reluctant neighbor, who is rich and stingy, to permit his son to marry the poor daughter of the innkeeper, who has just turned out to be the daughter of a king.[84]

A year later the writer Eugènie Caroline Saffray, writing under the pseudonym Raoul de Navery, published a long account in a hand-some childrens' book, full of illustrations and featuring women and men who had followed their sense of duty to the point of heroism.[85] The author used the story we know as her framework, elaborating upon and coloring it at will. She assigns important parts to Friar Giordano, the perfidious Queen Giovanna of Naples, and especially to Necca, Giannino's great love, who follows him like a shadow on his wanderings. It is she who, after marrying the dying king in prison, carries his uncompleted autobiography back to Siena.

In 1910 Antonio Palmieri wrote another imaginary tale, included in his book of Sienese stories, *I racconti della lupa,* dedicating "these phantasms from the past to the people of the ancient state of the she-wolf."[86] The author naturally pretends to believe in the switch in the cradle, writing that "the little martyred son of the Sienese merchant was buried in Saint-Denis in the tombs of the kings."[87] The nineteenth century had a predilection for a fantasized Middle Ages reinvented at that time, the "good old days" of Carducci's Madonna Laldomine, and Palmieri's story indulges this taste, with Giannino presented as an unfortunate hero, a double of Aleardo Aleardi's Corradino of Swabia, "who was blond, who was handsome, who was blessed." Tall, blond, and pale, with the aquiline nose of the kings of France, our Giannino becomes an acquiescent victim in this little work, contemplating his unhappy fate with serenity and courage.

In 1936 the screenwriter Vittorio Gonzi published a work under the title *Re Giannino* that amounted to a compendium, in annalistic vein, of the history of France, Italy, and England during the first half of the fourteenth century. The unrecognized King Jean I, who only becomes a full-blooded character in the final pages of the book, is carried along by the general flow of events, with plenty of space given to the kings of France and Cola di Rienzo, and is for the most part based on the Giannino of our *Istoria.* The writer varnishes over the lexical, and especially the logical, difficulties of this text, giving us the portrait of a man without flaws. His book was evidently not a best seller; at any rate the pages of the copy in the National Library of Florence were still uncut in 2004.[88]

Finally, Guccio and Giannino are both characters in the cycle of seven novels, *Les rois maudits,* by Maurice Druon, a member of the Academie Française, the first volume of which appeared in 1955 and which has twice been adapted for the screen, in 1972 and 2005.[89] This vast fresco of the history of France from 1314 to 1360 is woven around a legend, already in existence in the fourteenth century itself, to the effect that the French royal house stained itself with crime by crushing the order of the Templars (or in another version, by causing the death of Pope Boniface VIII) and were cursed in the dying words of Jacques de Molay, grand master of the order; the result was the extinction of the dynasty in the direct Capetian line. Jean I represents one of the main links in this chain of misfortune, and his death did in actual fact lead to one of the great dynastic fractures of history. As the stories of Guccio and Giannino unfold, they continually find themselves mixed up in the dark intrigues of the royal family. Guccio, a courageous and alert young man, appears in the first book, when he runs into Philippe the Fair, who is passing incognito through the streets of Paris, and insults him. This happens on the very day of the execution of Jacques de Molay. The young Sienese and Marie de Cressay share their unhappy love story; and he acts as a reliable messenger in England and Naples, working closely with Queen Clémence.

The story of the exchange of little King Jean for the real Giannino is narrated in book four, *La loi des mâles.* The perpetrator of the infanticide is Countess Mahaut, an outsized figure practiced in the use of poison, who has also murdered Guillaume de Nogaret and Louis X. The countess is so wicked, and the author is so much drawn to her, that he pretends that the mysterious tomb at Saint-Denis known as that of "the unknown queen" is actually Mahaut's.[90]

The countess does not, however, succeed in killing the real infant king, since the guardians of the queen's pregnancy—Hugues, count of Bouville, former grand chamberlain of Philippe the Fair, and none other than the nonagenarian Jean de Joinville, the companion and biographer of Saint Louis—carry out the switch before Mahaut takes the child in her arms. Druon's solution to the problem of why the barons then remain silent functions perfectly: while Joinville is so old and semi-demented that he notices nothing, Bouville and his wife (who also knows the truth) are confounded by the sudden death of the infant, who expires before the eyes of all the great lords gathered to salute him immediately after the regent, who is more or less in cahoots with Mahaut, raises him up and displays him. Those who had made the switch lack the quickness of mind and the courage to declare—in front of the regent who has just become king—that the dead baby is the offspring of the queen's wet nurse, and so "they found themselves caught in their own trap."[91] A minute after, and it is already too late.

Giannino, unaware that he is the legitimate king of France, is raised by Marie de Cressay and subsequently brought to Siena by Guccio. Only Pope John XXII is aware of who he really is, but does not intervene. Our Sienese merchant is the undisputed protagonist of the epilogue of book six, *Le Lis et le Lion*, with which Druon originally intended to bring the cycle to a close. Druon's Giannino tracks the Giannino of the *Istoria* as he travels about trying to regain his crown and ends his days a prisoner in Naples. He is thus the last of the *rois maudits*, destined to share the miserable fate of his blood relations.

In this book I have had a lot to say about falsity and illusion, about facts and legends woven into an intricate and fascinating pattern. Let me end with a phrase of Marc Bloch, who said, in reference to the myths of French royalty, "nothing could be more wrong-headed than to set literature and reality in permanent opposition to one another."[92]

Today the school in the town of Neauphle-le-Vieux is named after a figure from history and literature: Marie de Cressay. I have seen children at play there.

APPENDIX I

·⊂══⊃·

The Direct Capetian Line, the Counts of Valois,
and the Counts of Évreux (Simplified Genealogy)

Louis IX, Saint
(1215–1270)
king of France (1226)

Philippe III the Bold
(1245–1285)
king of France (1270)

Philippe IV the Fair
(1268–1314)
king of Navarre (1284–1305)
king of France (1285)

Charles of Valois
(1270–1325)

Louis of Évreux
(1279–1319)

Louis X the Quarrelsome
(1289–1316)
king of Navarre (1305)
king of France (1314)

Philippe V the Long
(1294–1322)
king of France & Navarre (1316)

Charles IV the Fair
(1294–1328)
king of France & Navarre (1322)

Isabelle
(1292–1357)
m. Edward II of England

Philippe VI the Fortunate
(1293–1350)
king of France (1328)

Philippe III the Wise
(1301–1343)
king of Navarre (1329)
m. Jeanne of Navarre

Jean I the Posthumous
(1316)
king of France & Navarre

Jeanne
(1311–1349)
queen of Navarre (1329)
m. Philippe III of Évreux

Female daughters

Louis
(1316–1317)

Female daughters

Louis
(1324)

Edward III
(1312–1377)
king of England

Jean II the Good
(1319–1364)
king of France (1350)

Marie
(1326–1347)
m. Pedro IV the Ceremonious king of Aragon

Charles II the Bad
(1332–1387)
king of Navarre (1349)

Philippe
(1336–1363)
count of Longueville

Agnès
(1337–1396)
m. Gaston de Foix

·◖━━━◗·

The Angevins of Naples and Hungary (Simplified Genealogy)

Charles II
the Lame
(1254–1309)
king of Sicily (1285)

Charles Martel
(1271–1295)
titular king of Hungary (1290)

Louis of Toulouse
(1274–1297)
Saint

Roberto I
the Wise
(1278–1343)
king of Sicily (1309)

Filippo I
(c. 1278–1331)
prince of Taranto (1294)

Charles Robert
(1288–1342)
king of Hungary (1308)

Clémence
(1293–1328)
m. Louix X, king of France

Carlo
duke of Calabria
(1297–1328)

Luigi I
(1320–1362)
king of Naples (1352)
m. Giovanni I
queen of Naples

Louis I
the Great
(1326–1382)
king of Hungary (1342)
king of Poland (1370)

Andrea
duke of Calabria
(1327–1345)
m. Giovanni I
queen of Naples

Jean I
the Posthumous
(1316)
king of France
and Navarre

Giovanna I
(1326–1382)
queen of Naples (1343–1381)
m. Andrea, duke of Calabria
m. Luigi of Anjou, prince of Taranto

NOTES

·◦⟺◦·

Abbreviations

ASR   Rome, Archivio di Stato
ASS   Siena, Archivio di Stato
BAV   Vatican City, Biblioteca Apostolica Vaticana

Chapter One

1. "Bene sappiamo come voi sete fatto"; *Istoria del re Giannino di Francia,* ed. Latino Maccari (Siena: Tip. C. Nava, 1893), p. 40. Cited hereafter as *Istoria.*

2. Two recent works on Cola are A. Collins, *Greater than Emperor: Cola di Rienzo (ca. 1313–1354) and the World of Fourteenth-Century Rome* (Ann Arbor: University of Michigan Press, 2002), and Tommaso di Carpegna Falconieri, *Cola di Rienzo* (Rome: Salerno Editrice, 2002).

3. "Non che io, ma tutta la Cristianità il dovrebbe fare, perché voi non sete colui, che vi credete essare, e che voi m'avete detto; ancho sete ragionevole e dritto re di Francia, e fuste figliuolo delo re Luigi, et dela reyna Clementia, e fuste scambiato pochi dì doppo la vostra natività"; *Istoria,* p. 41.

4. *Istoria,* pp. 158–66. Another edition of the letter, the one I cite, can be found in *Briefwechsel des Cola di Rienzo,* ed. K. Burdach and P. Piur (Berlin: Weidmann, 1912–29), vol. 4, no. 72, pp. 188–94.

5. "Io me n'andarò ne' miei paesi, et poco starò ch'io tornarò"; *Istoria,* p. 190.

6. "Se Guccio torna de' suoi paesi e trovarà el figliuolo suo morto, non mi vorrà mai bene. E eccho che avarò perduto l'onore e 'l figliolo e 'l marito"; *Istoria,* p. 191.

7. "Fa' che questo fanciullo mi mandi a Parigi"; *Istoria,* p. 192.

8. "Et prima che ella morisse mandò per me frate Giordano romito presso di Charsi, e confessossi da me generalmente e contiommi tutto el detto fatto e imposemi che del fanciullo dovessi invenire, e se io el trovassi vivo, che subito el dovessi dire al papa e al suo Collegio, e al re di Francia che allora fusse. E allora el dovessi insegnare acciò sia restituito ne la sua reale dignità"; *Istoria,* p. 192.

9. "Pensàmi che fusse morto, avendo rispetto che la magior parte de la gente morì nel quarantotto"; *Istoria,* p. 192.

10. "Padre, dammi la tua benedizione, ché io voglio andare a liberare el sipolcro di Cristo"; *Istoria,* p. 192. See R. Manselli, "Il sogno come premonizione, consiglio e predizione nella tradizione medievale," in *I sogni nel medioevo. Seminario internazionale, Roma 2–4 ottobre 1983,* ed. T. Gregory (Rome: Edizioni dell'Ateneo, 1985), pp. 218–44. And see now Jean-Claude Schmitt, *La conversion d'Hermann le Juif. Autobiographie, histoire, et fiction* (Paris: Seuil, 2003), chap. 3, "Le rêve et son interprétation," pp. 89–142.

11. "Mai non finirò se questa insegna non pongo sopra le porti de Gierusalem"; "E fie bisogno che 'l sipolcro di Cristo sia libero e francho e che ogni fedele cristiano el possa sicuramente visitare"; *Briefwechsel des Cola di Rienzo,* vol. 4, pp. 192 ff.

12. "Tu se' vecchio e non fa per te el caminare. Manda in verso Roma di terra in terra, e da' per scripto ordinatamente la confessione de la donna, e la rivelatione che avesti puoi, sì che colui el quale tu mandi ne vada bene informato a' veschovi e a' signori de le terre per invenire s'egli è vivo. E se si trova vivo, fa pregare quello veschovo o signore ne la cui terra egli è, che el debba fare manifesto al papa e a' suoi chardenagli e al re di Francia che oggi reggie, e a' suoi baroni. E se egli non si trova, se' ischusato a Dio, e a loro non ne dire nulla, ché ne potresti ricevere danno d'averlo tanto tempo tenuto segreto"; *Briefwechsel des Cola di Rienzo,* vol. 4, pp. 192 ff.

13. ". . . serà messa pace generale per tutta la Cristianità et raquistata la Terra Santa"; *Briefwechsel des Cola di Rienzo,* vol. 4, pp. 192 ff.

14. ". . . sarà chiamato Giannino di Guccio, credendosi essare figliuolo di Guccio"; *Briefwechsel des Cola di Rienzo,* vol. 4, pp. 192 ff.

15. "Ciò fu el dì di santo Luigi che fu re di Francia, e fece el passaggio più volte. Et costui ch'io vo cercando è de' suoi disciesi, et seguitarà lui"; *Briefwechsel des Cola di Rienzo,* vol. 4, pp. 192 ff.

16. ". . . contò di più re, ch'erano stati scambiati nella loro nativitade, come colui che aveva in pronto tutte le storie antiche . . . e tante parole le disse il trebuno, che esso asentì"; *Istoria,* p. 41.

17. The principal French sources on these events are: *Chronographia regum francorum,* ed. H. Moranvillé (Paris: Société de l'Histoire de France, 3 vols., 1891–97), vol. 1, pp. 233 ff.; *Les Grandes Chroniques de France,* vol. 8, ed. J. Viard (Paris: Société de l'Histoire de France, 1934), pp. 333 ff.; *Chronique latine de Guillaume de Nangis de 1113 à 1300 avec les continuations de cette chronique de 1300 à 1368,* ed. H. Géraud (2 vols. Paris: Société de l'Histoire

de France, 1843), vol. 1, pp. 430 ff. In MS Français 2615 of the Bibliothèque Nationale, Paris, *Les Grandes chroniques de France*, a miniature at fol. 280v (by the Maître de Fauvel, first quarter of the fourteenth century) depicts the coronation of Philippe V the Long. The king is surrounded by ecclesiastics who anoint him and hand him the scepter. At his left we see Saint Louis of Anjou (1274–97; canonized in 1317), with his hand resting on little Jean I, whose great-uncle he was. The babe, clad in royal robes, observes the coronation of his successor from Paradise.

18. "... uno grandissimo fatto scielente [= eccellente], il quale sarebbe utile a tutta la Cristianitade"; *Istoria*, p. 42.

19. "... quello che tiene contra ragione la corona di Francia"; *Istoria*, p. 42.

20. "... del quale il primo re fu romano, et di lui sono discesi tutti i re, e reali che sono stati in Francia"; *Istoria*, p. 43.

21. See in general *La religiosità popolare nel medioevo*, ed. R. Manselli (Bologna: il Mulino, 1983). For southern France, see *Fin du monde et signes des temps. Visionnaires et prophètes en France méridionale (fin XIIIe–début XVe siècle)* (Toulouse: Éditions Privat / Fanjeaux, Centre d'études historiques de Fanjeaux, 1992; Cahiers de Fanjeaux. Collection d'Histoire religieuse du Languedoc au XIIIe et XIVe siècles, no. 27). For recent historiographical trends, see *Ricerche sull'influenza della profezia nel basso medioevo*, ed. P. Donadoni, R. Michetti, and G. Milani, and published as a section in *Bullettino dell'Istituto storico italiano per il medio evo* 104 (2002): 145–208.

22. See *La peste nera: dati di una realtà ed elementi di una interpretazione. Atti del XXX Convegno storico internazionale, Todi 10–13 settembre 1993* (Spoleto: Centro italiano di studi sull'alto medioevo, 1994).

23. A recent outline in A. Curry, *The Hundred Years War* (London: Macmillan, 1993). Readers may find it helpful to refer to the genealogical chart of the Capetians at p. 160 above.

24. Anonimo romano [Anonymous Roman], *Cronica*, ed. G. Porta (Milan: Adelphi, 1979), p. 187.

25. "... un tondo fatto a guisa d'una stella con dodici raggi"; *Istoria*, p. 43.

26. "... soa arma de azule a sole de aoro e stelle de ariento e coll'arma de Roma"; Anonimo romano, *Cronica*, p. 249; *Briefwechsel des Cola di Rienzo*, vol. 3, no. 50, and vol. 5, pp. 324 ff.; see Carpegna Falconieri, *Cola di Rienzo*, pp. 73 and 201.

27. *Briefwechsel des Cola di Rienzo*, vol. 3, no. 50, pp. 201 ff.

28. Carpegna Falconieri, *Cola di Rienzo*, p. 161. For more on the theme of recognition, see P. Boulhol, *Anagnorismos. La scène de reconnaissance dans*

l'hagiographie antique et médiévale (Aix: Publications de l'Université de Provence, 1996).

29. English translations of Molière's play are variously titled *The Self-Made Gentleman*, *The Bourgeois Gentleman*, *The Would-be Gentleman*.

30. See below, chap. 6.

31. On the conception of regality in the Middle Ages, see principally Marc Bloch, *The Royal Touch: Sacred Monarchy and Scrofula in England and France*, trans. J. E. Anderson (Montreal: McGill-Queen's University Press, 1973; original title *Les rois thaumaturges*, 1924); Ernst H. Kantorwicz, *The King's Two Bodies: A Study in Mediaeval Political Theology*, with a new preface by William Chester Jordan (Princeton, NJ: Princeton University Press, 1997; first published 1957). Notable recent studies include Jacques Le Goff, *Saint Louis* (Paris: Gallimard, 1996); G. Klaniczay, *Holy Rulers and Blessed Princesses: Dynastic Cults in Medieval Central Europe* (Cambridge: Cambridge University Press, 2002); S. Kelly, *The New Solomon: Robert of Naples (1309–1343) and Fourteenth-Century Kingship* (Leiden and Boston: Brill, 2003).

32. "Et veramente egli è dritto re di Francia sicondo che a noi pare comprendare sì per la confessione de la donna scritta ne la detta lettera, sì per lo tempo che mostra che debba avere, sì per le parole le quali a noi furo manifestate quando noi eravamo a Vignone appo il nostro missere lo Papa. E certamente sì pare comprendere che esso sia figliuolo del re Luigi, prima nato del re Filippo el Bello"; *Briefwechsel des Cola di Rienzo*, vol. 4, no. 72, p. 196. I take the view that this authenticating conclusion added by Cola di Rienzo to the copy of the letter Friar Antonio had sent him was originally drafted in Latin; see pp. 195 ff.

33. "Dite a Giovanni, che si parta el più tosto che può, et se non si parte potrebbe essare morto col trebuno insieme, perciò che noi siamo più di ducento fanti di Toscana a petizione de' Colonesi per uccidare il trebuno. Et noi aviamo più volte veduto Giovanni intrare, et uscire di Campo Dolio, e stare ale finestre del palazo col trebuno insieme. Et perciò dite a lui che si parta se non vuole essare morto"; *Istoria*, p. 47.

34. "Unde il detto Giovanni sentendo la morte del trebuno fu dolente"; *Istoria*, p. 47.

Chapter Two

1. The information about the early years of Giannino's life comes from *Istoria*, pp. 22 ff. On clandestine marriage, which was not uncommon in the period before the Council of Trent and was recognized as valid in the eyes of God

(mutual consent being the sole basis of matrimony), see B. Gottlieb, "The Meaning of Clandestine Marriage," in *Family and Sexuality in French History*, ed. R. Wheaton and T. K. Hareven (Philadelphia: University of Pennsylvania Press, 1980), pp. 49–83.

2. What the *Istoria* says about Giannino's flourishing business activity and tenure of public office was confirmed by the archival research of Latino Maccari, who continued a long tradition of research by Sienese erudites. On the city of Siena in the Middle Ages, see D. Balestracci and G. Piccinni, *Siena nel Trecento. Assetto urbano e strutture edilizie* (Florence: Edizioni CLSUF, 1977); William M. Bowsky, *A Medieval Italian Commune: Siena under the Nine, 1287–1355* (Berkeley: University of California Press, 1981); *Storia di Siena*, ed. R. Barzanti, G. Catoni, M. De Gregorio, vol. I, *Dalle origini alla fine della Repubblica* (Siena: Asaba, 1995); Odile Redon, *L'espace d'une cité. Sienne et le pays siennois, XIIIe–XIVe siècles* (Rome: École française de Rome, 1994). On the mercantile profession, see F. Cardini et al., *Banchieri e mercanti di Siena*, preface by C. M. Cipolla (Siena: Monte dei Paschi di Siena, 1987); and in general, *I ceti dirigenti della Toscana tardo comunale, atti del terzo convegno del Comitato di studi sulla storia dei ceti dirigenti in Toscana, Firenze 5–7 dicembre 1980* (Florence: F. Papafava, 1983). Finally, on medieval merchants, see Jacques Le Goff, *Your Money or Your Life: Economy and Religion in the Middle Ages*, trans. P. Ranum (New York: Zone Books, 1988); and the bibliography of I. Ait, *Il commercio nel medioevo* (Rome: Jouvence, 2005), pp. 211 ff.

3. On the membership of Mino di Geri Baglioni in the Tolomei company, see *Istoria*, pp. 22n–23n, and William M. Bowsky, *The Finances of the Commune of Siena, 1287–1355* (Oxford: Clarendon Press, 1970), p. 195n. On the Tolomei, see G. Bigwood, "Les Tolomei en France au XIVe siècle," *Revue belge de philologie et d'histoire* 8 (1929); R. Mucciarelli, "Un caso di emigrazione mercantile. I Tolomei di Siena," in *Demografia e società nell'Italia medievale (secoli IX–XIV)*, ed. R. Comba and I. Naso (Cuneo: Società per gli studi storici, archeologici ed artistici della provincia di Cuneo, 1994), pp. 475–92; and R. Mucciarelli, *I Tolomei banchieri di Siena. La parabola di un casato nel XIII e XIV secolo* (Siena: Protagon Editori Toscani, 1995).

4. Books of *ricordanze*, also known as *libri di famiglia* (family books) are a type of documentation found primarily in Tuscany. Evolving from the account books of thirteenth-century merchants, they became genuine depositories of family memory. *Ricordanze* were generally compiled by heads of households, who carefully entered their business dealings and domestic events (primarily births, deaths, and marriages); the intended readership was the immediate

family. Often their descendants continued them, passing the manuscript on from one generation to the next. See especially A. Cicchetti and R. Mordenti, *I libri di famiglia in Italia,* vol. 1, *Filologia e storiografia letteraria* (Rome: Edizioni di Storia e Letteratura, 1985); and the recent collection of articles, *Écritures et mémoire familiale,* published as a section in *Annales. Histoire, Sciences Sociales* 59.4 (2004): 785–858.

5. For a recent study of another Sienese merchant, a trader in woad, see P. Guarducci, *Un tintore senese del Trecento. Landoccio di Cecco d'Orso* (Siena: Protagon Editori Toscani, 1998).

6. On the institutions of Siena at this time, see S. Moscadelli, "Apparato burocratico e finanze del Comune di Siena sotto i Dodici (1355–1368)," *Bullettino senese di storia patria* 89 (1982): 29–118 (with a notice of previous bibliography at p. 60, n. 18); and E. Brizio, "L'elezione degli uffici politici nella Siena del Trecento," *Bullettino senese di storia patria* 98 (1991): 16–62. On the stay of Charles IV in Siena, see Matteo Villani, *Cronica, con la continuazione di Filippo Villani,* critical edition by G. Porta (2 vols., Parma: Guanda, 1995), vol. 1, bk. 4, chaps. 61, 81, 82, and bk. 5, chaps. 14, 15, 20, 29, 35, 36. On the destruction of the political documents and its significance, see A. De Vincentiis, "Memorie bruciate. Conflitti, documenti, oblio nelle città italiane del tardo medioevo," *Bullettino dell'Istituto storico italiano per il medio evo* 106.1 (2004): 167–98, with mention of Siena at pp. 191 ff.

7. Siena, Archivio di Stato (henceforth abbreviated ASS), MS A 61, fol. 163r. (Like "Giannino," "Vannino" is a diminutive of the name "Giovanni.")

8. ASS, *Biccherna, Memoriali* 415 (January–June 1356), fol. 1r: "Al nome di Dio Amen. Questo si è el memoriale dela Bicherna del comune di Siena nel quale libro saranno iscritti partittamente tutti coloro che dovarano dare ed avere dal detto comune al tempo de savii e discreti huomini Giannino di Ghucio Baglioni camerlengo del detto comune . . ." ["In the name of God, Amen. This is the record book of the Biccherna of the commune of Siena, in which book will be noted in detail all those who will have to make payments to, and receive payments from, the said commune during the period of the wise and discreet men Giannino di Guccio Baglioni, chamberlain of the said commune . . ."]. This is the only surviving fiscal record book from his tenure of office. See as well ASS, MS C 13, *Spogli fatti da' libri di Biccherna da Celso Cittadini,* fol. 37r. In ASS, *Biccherna, Entrata e uscita* 235 (July–December 1355), Giannino's name appears at fol. 65r, with the date 31 December, as the successor of the outgoing chamberlain. For an overview of the the Sienese archival situation, see G. Catoni, "La dimensione archivistica della ricerca

storica: il caso di Siena," in *Bullettino senese di storia patria* 84–85 (1977–78): 320–92; and Redon, *L'espace d'une cité*, chap. 1. On Italy in general, see P. Cammarosano, *Italia medievale. Struttura e geografia delle fonti scritte*, 6th ed. (Rome: Carocci, 2000).

9.   ". . . che tutte l'entrate della muneta d'essa ciptà andavano per suo mano, e le spese, e molto era honorato, et amato da tutti 'ciptadini'": *Istoria*, pp. 51 ff.

10. The original text actually uses the term *balii*, confusing, or at any rate blurring the difference between, a *balivo* (French *bailli*, English "bailliff"), meaning a royal agent, and a *balio*, meaning the male individual who in medieval and early modern Italy entered into contracts with parents for their children to be wet-nursed; normally, the *balio* was the husband of the actual wet nurse or *balia*. On this, see Christiane Klapisch-Zuber, "Blood Parents and Milk Parents: Wet-nursing in Florence, 1300–1530," in her *Women, Family, and Ritual in Renaissance Italy*, trans. L. G. Cochrane (Chicago: University of Chicago Press, 1985), pp. 132–64, especially pp. 135 ff. on the placing of the infants with wet nurses, and pp. 146 ff. on infant death during nursing; S. Matthews Grieco and C. A. Corsini, *Historical Perspectives on Breastfeeding* (Florence: UNICEF, 1991); R. Sarti, *Vita di casa: abitare, mangiare, vestire nell'Europa moderna* (3d ed., Rome and Bari: Laterza, 2003), pp. 205–11.

11. Italo Calvino, *Fiabe italiane raccolte dalla tradizione popolare durante gli ultimi cento anni e trascritte in lingua dai vari dialetti* (Milan: Mondadori, 1993), vol. 1, p. lii (originally Turin: Einaudi, 1956). See Italo Calvino, *Italian Fables*, trans. L. Brigante (New York: Orion Press, 1959).

12. The field is vast; see G. Constable, "Forgery and Plagiarism in the Middle Ages," *Archiv für Diplomatik* 29 (1983): 1–41; *Fälschungen im Mittelalter. Internationaler Kongress der Monumenta Germaniae Historica, München 16.–19. September 1986*, 6 vols. (Hannover: Hahnsche Buchhandlung, 1988–90; MGH Schriften, 33). On the intentions of forgers and the concept of *pia fraus* (pious fraud), see E. A. R. Brown, "Falsitas Pia sive Reprehensibilis. Medieval Forgers and Their Intentions," in vol. 1, pp. 101–19. On the absence of a clear boundary between "truth" and "fiction" in the Middle Ages, see Schmitt, *La conversion d'Hermann le Juif*, chap. 1, "Fiction et verité," section "Verités et fictions médiévales," pp. 48–59.

13. I interpret the relationship between the two versions of the switch in the cradle as flowing from deliberate action by Giannino on the basis of several indications: it appears certain that he knew both accounts, and that the first of them could not be of much use to him. But that he intervened directly is a conjecture. There is undoubtedly a relationship between the two texts,

and the first would appear to be earlier than the second. But the relationship might be more complex, and its exact nature remains to be established. See below, chap. 6.

14. *Briefwechsel des Cola di Rienzo*, vol. 4, no. 73, pp. 196–204, 1354 October 4; also published in L.-J.-N. de Monmerqué, *Lettre du Frère Antoine . . . à Nicolas de Rienzi . . . suivie de deux lettres de Rienzi, adressées à Giannino, de Sienne. Appendice de la "Dissertation sur Jean Ier, roi de France et de Navarre"* (Paris: Tabary, 1845); and by Maccari in *Istoria*, pp. 187–95. The document in question is the so-called "Monmerqué Parchment," Monmerqué having asserted that he had found it in a flea market in 1844; see L.-J.-N. de Monmerqué, *Dissertation historique sur Jean Ier, roi de France et de Navarre; par M. Monmerqué, Conseilleur à la Cour royale de Paris, membre de l'Académie royale des Inscriptions et Belles-Lettres; suivie d'une charte par laquelle Nicolas de Rienzi reconnaît Giannino, fils supposé de Guccius, comme roi de France, et d'autres documents relatifs à ce fait singulier* (Paris: Tabary, 1844). The charter, lacking a seal, had been owned by the Piccolomini family, and was reproduced by Monmerqué in a facsimile that does indeed appear to be a copy of a parchment in Italian Gothic writing of the fourteenth century. See Maccari's introduction to the *Istoria*, pp. XXXV ff.

15. The description of a seal is extremely rare, and is only provided when a seal has just been changed or has been stolen, with explicit mention being made of the occurrence. There are other clues that this is a false document. One is the fact that the senator writes in his conclusion "Nos timendo perire primo quam daremus aliquam operam sive ordinem circa recuperationem Regni" (We, fearing to die before we can take any steps or give any orders regarding the recuperation of the kingdom). This is suspect because it too clearly foresees his actual death, which did occur within a few days. As well, Maccari analyzes the language and concludes that it is a translation from Italian to Latin, which means there was not a prior French version, and that it was not drafted by Cola's chancellery; see below, chap. 6. Finally, the Latin is rudimentary, a far cry from that in use in the Roman chancellery.

16. On this, see Charles T. Wood, "Where Is John the Posthumous? Or Mahaut of Artois Settles Her Royal Debts," in *Documenting the Past: Essays in Medieval History Presented to George Peddy Cuttino*, ed. J. S. Hamilton and P. J. Bradley (Wolfeboro, NH: Boydell Press, 1989), pp. 99–117. On the trial of Mahaut, see as well F. Collard, *Le crime de poison au Moyen Âge* (Paris: Presses Universitaires de France, 2003), ad indicem. On the struggles for power within the French royal house, see Charles T. Wood, *The French Apa-*

nages and the Capetian Monarchy, 1224–1328 (Cambridge, MA: Harvard University Press, 1966). On the position of Jean I in the dynasty (he was without any doubt the king of France from the moment of his birth) and the succession of Philippe V the Long, see A. W. Lewis, *Royal Succession in Capetian France: Studies on Familial Order and the State* (Cambridge, MA: Harvard University Press, 1981), pp. 149–54 and ad indicem.

17. "... era bella donna, e giovana, e gentile, e ... 'l latte suo era buono, e tenero, megliore, che di veruna donna che allora trovare si potesse in Parigi"; *Istoria*, pp. 16 ff.

18. "... con lacrime e malvolentieri"; *Istoria*, p. 22.

19. For an account of the battle of Poitiers, also known as the battle of Maupertuis, see J. Froissart, *Chroniques*, vol. 5, ed. S. Luce (Paris: Societé de l'Histoire de France, 1874), pp. 18–61.

20. "Ora si vedrà la ragione, e la verità di Giovanni." *Istoria*, p. 50.

21. The letter, which was located by Sigismondo Tizio in the sixteenth century, is published as an appendix to the *Istoria*, pp. 197–99. See as well, chap. 4, below.

22. See *Les Grandes Chroniques de France*, vol. 9, p. 119. On false indulgences, see A. Rehberg, "'Nuntii, questuarii, falsarii': l'ospedale di S. Spirito in Sassia e la raccolta delle elemosine nel periodo avignonese," *Mélanges de l'École française de Rome—Moyen Âge* 115.1 (2003): 31–132, at 102–19.

23. On the role of the religious, see as well chap. 6, below.

24. See chap. 4, below.

25. This is the so-called Sansedoni Parchment, already known to Sigismondo Tizio in the sixteenth century, originally in the possession of the Tolomei. This charter still existed at the end of the nineteenth century, when Maccari was able to examine it in palazzo Sansedoni (see his introduction to the *Istoria*, pp. xi ff.). But today, as far as I can tell, its whereabouts are not known. It is published in *Briefwechsel des Cola di Rienzo*, vol. 4, no. 72, pp. 188–94, and in *Istoria*, pp. 158–66.

26. See chaps. 3 and 5, below. The list of the letters is in *Istoria*, pp. 149 ff.

Chapter Three

1. There were so many Sienese merchants active in the kingdom of France that the city statute book contained specific provisions regulating their presence there; see *Il Costituto del Comune di Siena volgarizzato nel MCCCIX–MCCCX edito sotto gli auspici del Ministero dell'Interno*, 2 vols. (Siena: R. Archivio di Stato di Siena, 1903); I have been unable to consult the recent critical edition

edited by M. S. Elsheik (Siena: Fondazione Monte dei Paschi, 2002). This statue book remained in force until 1337. See, for example, dist. II, rubr. CV: "Che la podestà faccia mendare el danno a chi l'à patito nel regno di Francia, da colui per cui cagione l'ha sostenuto" [That the podestà should cause one who suffered loss in the kingdom of France to be indemnified by him who caused the loss]; rubr. CXXII: "Che neuno possa impetrare lettere o vero comandamenti contra lo comune di Siena o vero compagnie, o vero alcuno cittadino, da missere lo re di Francia, o vero altro qualunque signore" [That no one may seek to obtain letters or commandments against the commune of Siena, or companies, or any citizen, from the king of France, or any other lord]; rubr. CCLXXVIII: "Di fare pilliare chi si cessasse de le fiere di Francia con avere da alcuno, a petitione de' consoli de la Mercantia" [To have anyone who departs from the fairs in France with the assets of anyone else seized, on the petition of the consuls of the Mercanzia]. On the French side, strict regulations governing the activity of all Italian merchants, referred to generically as *lombards*, were frequently issued.

2. See chap. 4 below.

3. *Istoria*, p. 57.

4. See S. Selzer, *Deutsche Söldner im Italien des Trecento* (Tübingen: Niemeyer, 2001; Bibliothek des Deutschen Historischen Instituts in Rom, 98), pp. 368–70 and 373 ff., respectively. In September Hartmann von Wartstein had joined his own forces with those of Konrad von Landau.

5. In this regard, see K. Fowler, *Medieval Mercenaries*, vol. 1, *The Great Companies* (Malden, MA: Blackwell Publishers, 2001); Selzer, *Deutsche Söldner;* D. Balestracci, *Le armi i cavalli l'oro. Giovanni Acuto e i condottieri nell'Italia del Trecento* (Rome and Bari: Laterza, 2003), pp. 26–93. More generally, see *Pace e guerra nel basso medioevo, atti del Convegno di Todi, 12–15 ottobre 2003* (Todi: Centro italiano di studi sul basso medioevo-Accademia tudertina, 2004); and the bibliography of F. Bargigia and A. Settia, *La guerra nel medioevo* (Rome: Jouvence, 2005). For the case of Siena, see A. Professione, *Siena e le compagnie di ventura nella seconda metà del secolo XIV. Ricerche e appunti con un'appendice di documenti inediti* (Civitanova Marche: Casa editrice Domenico Natalucci, 1898).

6. ". . . d'essare nel servigio suo liberamente, et senza veruno soldo con tutta la gente, che erano più di sei migliaia cavalieri et altrettanti fanti a piei bene armati"; *Istoria*, pp. 59 ff.

7. ". . . contra la nostra fede cristiana, né contra l'usanza deli antichi, e santi re, che sono stati in Francia"; *Istoria*, p. 63. ["Tartar" was the word used in

Europe during the Middle Ages, and for a long time after, for the Turkic eth-
nonym now correctly written "Tatar." WM]

8. On the relationship between Jews and self-proclaimed sovereigns, see Yves-
   Marie Bercé, *Le roi caché. Sauveurs et imposteurs; mythes politiques populaires
   dans l'Europe moderne* (Paris: Fayard, 1990), part 3, chap. 7, sec. "Le possible modèle du messianisme juif," pp. 345–52. On the expulsion of 1394, see
   L'Expulsion des Juifs de France 1394, ed. G. Dahan (Paris: Cerf, 2004). See
   also chap. 6, below.

9. ". . . mi credo oparare con loro, ch'essi compraranno vostra ragione più volon-
   tieri, et meglio che veruni altri signori cristiani, et voi ne sarete più sicuro";
   Istoria, p. 64.

10. The Hungarian-language literature on Italian-Hungarian relations is exten-
    sive. See the summary of M. Jàszay, *Incontri e scontri nella storia dei rapporti
    italo-ungheresi* (Soveria Mannelli: Rubbettino, 2003; originally published
    Budapest: Gondolat, 1982). On fourteenth-century Hungary and its close
    links with Italy, see *Colloquio italo-ungherese sul tema: gli Angioini di Napoli e
    d'Ungheria (Roma, 23–24 maggio 1972) organizzato d'intesa con l'Accademia
    delle Scienze d'Ungheria* (Rome: Accademia Nazionale dei Lincei, 1974;
    Problemi attuali di scienza e cultura, Quaderno 210); L. S. Domonkos, "The
    Influence of the Italian Campaigns of Louis the Great on Hungarian Cul-
    tural Developments," in *Louis the Great, King of Hungary and Poland,* ed.
    S. B. Vàrdy, G. Grosschmid, and L. S. Domonkos (Boulder, CO: East Euro-
    pean Monographs, 1986), pp. 203–20.

11. Niccolò Valori looked after relations between the king of Hungary and Flor-
    ence: we come across him in a Florentine document dated 24 December 1359,
    published in *Monumenta Hungariae Historica. Magyar Diplomacziai Emlékek
    az Anjou Korból* (Acta extera), vol. 2 (1342–69), ed. G. Wenzel (Budapest:
    A.M.T. Akadémia Könyvkiadò-Hivatalàban, 1875), doc. 405, p. 559. Valori
    had brought letters from the king to the commune of Florence, requesting
    two lion cubs. The commune had in turn entrusted Valori with a pregnant
    lioness, to be shipped to the king.

12. The self-proclaimed King Andrea also appears in *Monumenta Hungariae
    Historica,* vol. 2, p. 568. On this, see É. G. Léonard, *Histoire de Jeanne Ière,
    reine de Naples, comtesse de Provence (1343–1382),* vol. 3, *Le règne de Louis de
    Tarente* (Monaco: Imprimerie de Monaco; Paris: Picard, 1936), pp. 437 ff.;
    G. Lecuppre, *L'imposture politique au Moyen Âge. La seconde vie des rois* (Paris:
    Presses Universitaires de France, 2005), pp. 42, 140.

13. Both individuals appear often as participants in the royal administration. The

"gran Conte Nicola" to whom Giannino refers (*Istoria*, p. 67) might also be a "comes Nicola filius Ugrini," "iudex curie domini Ludovici," who appears frequently in Hungarian documents of the period. See, for example, *Codex diplomaticus Hungariae ecclesiasticus ac civilis*, ed. Georg Fejèr, t. 9, vol. 3 [for the period 1359–66] (Budae: typis Typogr. Regiae Universitatis Ungaricae, 1834), doc. 5, p. 40; doc. 8, p. 44; doc. 70, p. 155.

14. The Hungarian court did in fact reside at Visegrád. For the rest, the pursuit of secret meetings and boasts of the favor shown by royalty are recurrent features of the careers of self-proclaimed sovereigns. For example, a false Louis XVII, Jean-Marie Hervagaudt, the son of a Norman tailor, announced in the course of his trial in 1802 that he had been honorably received by the king of England, the queen of Portugal, and the pope. The first two sovereigns are each supposed to have put a ship and crew at his disposal, to assist him in his travels. The pope, it seems, took a different attitude, "treating him with all the regard due his rank," while at the same time urging him to abandon his state. The pope "wished that his identity, of which he appeared convinced, to be guaranteed in such a way that it was beyond dispute. Hence he had two stigmata or signs branded on him with a red-hot iron, one on the right leg depicting the arms of France with the initial letters of his name, and the other on his left arm, composed of the letters making up the words *Vive le roi!*" See *Les imposteurs fameux. Ou histoires extraordinaires et singulières des hommes de néant de toutes les nations qui, depuis les temps les plus reculés jusqu'à ce jour, ont usurpé la qualité d'empereur, de roi et de prince; terminées par celles des deux faux Louis XVII, Hervagaudt et Bruneau* (Paris: Eymery, 1818), pp. 134–48, especially pp. 137 ff. Giannino, too, supplies us with several attestations to the honors that were paid him, recalling the favor shown by Cola di Rienzo, the commune of Siena, the lord of Bologna, and the duke of Austria; and we will see him continuing to try to obtain meetings with those in power.

15. ". . . tutta la redità del mondo procede dalla cherica"; *Istoria*, p. 67.

16. ". . . col suo sugiello pendente dela faccia sua"; *Istoria*, p. 72. Though it does not appear to be the case here, Franciscan friars did have great influence at the court of Louis the Great, whose chaplains they often were. Friar Johannes de Kéty was his official historiographer. See T. Klaniczay, "Attività letteraria dei francescani e domenicani nell'Ungheria angioina," in *Colloquio italo-ungherese*, pp. 27–40, especially p. 30.

17. "Se voi volete avere aiuto, et favore dalo re d'Ongharia, a voi conviene tenere la maniera che si tiene nele corti. . . . In tutte le corti nele quali io so' stato, o che io ò udito, chi vuole gratia da re, o da papa, o da altro signore, sempre si

vuole avere alcuno mezo, il quale sia confidente, e segretario del signore, dal quale l'uomo aspetta d'essere servito, et questo non si può avere senza alcuno dono di muneta o d'altro presente"; *Istoria*, pp. 72 ff.

18. "Ecco, io non so che più bello, e migliore dono io lo possi fare, né più segreto, che di moneta"; *Istoria*, pp. 72 ff.

19. ". . . el quale è il papa de' saracini"; *Istoria*, p. 78.

20. A vivid description of Hungarian horsemen, of whom there were many in Italy around the middle of the fourteenth century, is given by Matteo Villani in his *Cronica, con la continuazione di Filippo Villani*, vol. 1, bk. 6, chap. 54, pp. 773 ff. See as well Jàszay, *Incontri e scontri nella storia dei rapporti italo-ungheresi*, pp. 96. ff. There is an interesting depiction of a chamberlain of the commune of Siena paying a Hungarian archer on a Biccherna tablet held at the Victoria and Albert Museum, London (inv. 415-1892; the cover of the register for July–December 1357), reproduced in *Le Biccherne. Tavole dipinte delle magistrature senesi (secoli XIII–XVIII)*, ed. L. Borgia et al. (Rome: Ministero per i Beni culturali e ambientali, Ufficio centrale per i beni archivistici, 1984), pp. 110 ff.

21. ". . . [un] sugiello d'attone fatto proprio come il . . . sugiello segreto"; *Istoria*, p. 77.

22. This Saracino, "monetiere della corona," of whose identity I was initially dubious, was a real and important person, linked to the king of Hungary. In 1371, while at Visegrád (Giannino's city, and also the normal residence of the court), King Louis is on record as having donated an island in Dalmatia, in return for services rendered, to a master Saraceno, "comes Camere nostre" (i.e., treasurer) of the region of Pécs. See *Codex diplomaticus Hungariae*, t. 9, vol. 4, doc. 187, pp. 337–39. This privilege was corroborated with the secret seal. A silver coin minted from 1358 to 1371 was named "Saracino's Head" after him.

23. *Codex diplomaticus Hungariae*, t. 9, vol. 4, doc. 4; see also docs. 9 and 10.

24. On the Hungarian chancellery at this period, see T. Kardos, "Ideali e problemi dell'Umanesimo in Ungheria nel periodo angioino," in *Colloquio italo-ungherese*, pp. 7–20; Domonkos, "The Influence of the Italian Campaigns," pp. 209 ff.

25. *Monumenta Hungariae Historica*, vol. 2, doc. 396, p. 526.

26. ". . . agli universi e singoli re e principi del mondo"; *Istoria*, pp. 149 ff.

27. ASS, *Consiglio Generale, Elezioni e Cerne* 390, fols. 41 ff., published in *Monumenta Hungariae Historica*, vol. 2, doc. 398, pp. 528–31, and in *Istoria*, pp. 184 ff. The most recent volumes published of Hungarian documents from the Angevin period, *Codex diplomaticus Hungaricus Andegavensis. Anjoukori Okmànytar*,

7 vols. (Budapest: Kiadja a Magyar Tudomànyos Akadémia, 1878–1920), reach 31 March 1359. The collection of Hungarian-language registers of documents from the Angevin period, *Anjou-kori Oklévéltar. Documenta res Hungaricae tempore regum Andegavensium illustrantia (1301–1387)* (Budapest-Szeged: 1990–), does not yet include the volume for 1359. On Giannino's Hungarian adventure, see as well the essay of Antal Pór, "Nagy Lajos magyar király viszonya Giannino di Guccio, Franczia trónkövetelöhöz . . . [The relations of the king of Hungary Louis the Great with Giannino di Guccio, pretender to the throne of France]," in *Értekeẕések a történeti tudományok Köréböl* XV kötet, 9 szám (1892), pp. 1–31 in the offprint. The author displays his conviction (like others before and after him) that the king's letter was authentic. This essay is useful, since it establishes (p. 517) that the seal described does coincide exactly with the secret seal of the king of Hungary. Further bibliography on the seal is cited in É. G. Léonard, "Louis Ier de Hongrie protecteur du 're Giannino,'" *Revue des Études Hongroises* 6 (1928) : 379–84. Léonard here publishes a version of the same letter from a different textual tradition, asserting that he found, "in private archives," a modern and defective copy of an original, dated 12 May, sent by the king to Niccolò Acciaiuoli. In his book *Les Angevins de Naples* (Paris: Presses Universitaires de France, 1954), p. 389, Léonard republishes the document, asserting that this copy is to be found in the archive of the Acciaiuoli family of Florence, whereas in his *Histoire de Jeanne Ière*, vol. 3, p. 441, he declares that he found the original among the parchments of the Archivio Ricasoli in Florence. I have recently located and consulted this document in the Fondo Acciaiuoli of the Archivio Ricasoli at Florence.

28. 2 Maccabees 1:22. The Latin Vulgate text: "Refulsit sol qui prius in nubilo, et accensus est ignis maximus." *The Jerusalem Bible* (New York: Doubleday, 1971) translation: "the sun, which had previously been clouded over, shone out, [and] a great fire flared up."

29. ". . . sì che paresse quelo viso uno sole." *Istoria*, p. 43.

30. "[Sol] insuper occultatus a nubibus fulget gracius expectatus"; *Briefwechsel des Cola di Rienẕo*, vol. 3, p. 250. On this question, see Carpegna Falconieri, *Cola di Rienẕo*, p. 73.

31. Clémence of Hungary died at Paris on 13 October 1328. The inventory of her possessions at the time of her death survives; among them were various images of John the Baptist. See *Nouveau recueil de Comptes de l'argenterie des rois de France*, ed. L. Douët-d'Arcq (Paris: Société de l'Historie de France, 1874), pp. 37–112, at pp. 49 and 51.

32. ". . . robbe honorevoli et reali"; *Istoria*, p. 81.

Chapter Four

1. ASS, *Consiglio generale, Elezioni e Cerne* 390, fol. 6. See *Istoria*, p. 180. On the electoral system, see S. Moscadelli, "Apparato burocratico e finanze del Comune di Siena sotto i Dodici (1355–1368)," pp. 66 ff.; and especially E. Brizio, "L'elezione degli uffici politici nella Siena del Trecento," pp. 22 ff. and 32 ff.

2. ASS, *Consiglio generale, Elezioni e Cerne* 390, fols. 41 ff.; published as an appendix to *Istoria*, pp. 179–85.

3. See *Istoria*, p. 5; the copyist Bartolomeo of Novara, writing well into the fifteenth century, relates that King Giovanni "is called King Giannino by the people in Siena."

4. G. Sermini, *Novelle*, ed. G. Vettori, 2 vols. (Rome: Avanzini e Torraca, 1968), Novella 25; also published in *Novelle del Quattrocento*, ed. G. M. Ferrero and M. L. Doglio (Turin: UTET, 1975), pp. 184–97. See as well Piero Veneziano (the Florentine Piero di Filippo del Nero), *Novella del Bianco Alfani*, in *Novelle del Quattrocento*, pp. 629–52, in which Bianco is made to believe, through a phoney official letter, that he has been elected *capitano del popolo* of the town of Norcia. As a result, he orders banners, buys horses, hires a household of servants with livery, borrows money on disadvantageous terms, and finally arrives at Norcia. There the magistrates recognize his letter as a phoney, and Bianco returns home with his banner rolled up "in a nasty rotten canvas."

5. On this, see A. Rochon et al., *Formes et significations de la "beffa" dans la littérature italienne de la Renaissance*, 2 vols. (Paris: Université de la Sorbonne Nouvelle, 1972–75), especially the essays by A. Fontes-Baratto, "Le thème de la beffa dans le *Décaméron*," vol. 1, pp. 12–44 (p. 27 for the mode of the *beffa collettiva*); and A. Rochon, "Une date importante dans l'histoire de la 'beffa': la *Nouvelle du Grasso legnaiuolo*," vol. 2, pp. 211–376. [In addition to the specific meaning of "elaborate practical joke," the word *beffa*, plural *beffe*, bears the generic meaning of "mockery" or "derision," and Giannino himself uses it that way in a couple of passages quoted in chap. 5, notes 8 and 9 below. WM].

6. "Io non sono più el Grasso di certo, e sono diventato Matteo; che maladetta sia la mia fortuna e la mia disgrazia, ché, se si scopre questo fatto, io sono vituperato, e sarò tenuto pazzo, e correrannomi dietro e fanciulli, e corrocci mille pericoli"; *La Novella del Grasso legnajuolo riscontrata col manoscritto e purgata di molti e gravissimi errori* (Florence: Felice Le Monnier, 1856), p. 47. This novella is also included in *Novelle del Quattrocento*, pp. 583–628.

7. See F. Tamburrini, "La Penitenzieria apostolica durante il papato avignonese," in *Aux origines de l'État moderne. Le fonctionnement administratif de la papauté d'Avignon* (Rome: École française de Rome, 1990), pp. 251–68.

8. On the massive Italian presence in Provence: N. Coulet, "Mutations de l'immigration italienne en Basse Provence Occidentale à la fin du Moyen Âge," in *Strutture familiari, epidemie, migrazioni nell'Italia medievale*, ed. R. Comba, G. Piccinni, and G. Pinto (Naples: Edizioni scientifiche italiane, 1984), pp. 493–510.

9. On him, see E. Meyer, *Charles II roi de Navarre, comte d'Évreux et la Normandie au XIVe siècle* (Paris: Ernest Dumont, 1898). On the kingdom of Navarre, see B. Leroy, *Le Royaume de Navarre à la fin du Moyen Âge* (Aldershot: Variorum, 1990).

10. *Chronographia regum Francorum*, vol. 2, pp. 266–67. On the liberation of the king of Navarre, see Froissart, *Chroniques*, vol. 5, pp. 97–99; and J. D'Avout, *Le meurtre d'Étienne Marcel, 31 juillet 1358* (Paris: Gallimard, 1960), pp. 121 ff.

11. *Les grands traités de la Guerre des Cent Ans*, ed. E. Cosneau (Paris: Alphonse Piccard, 1889): treaty of Brétigny (and Calais), pp. 33–68, in particular art. 22, pp. 55–56.

12. See in general Lecuppre, *L'imposture politique*.

13. On this, see Th.-J. Boudet, comte de Puymaigre, "Un prétendant au trône de France, Giannino Baglioni," *Revue des questions historiques* 57 (April 1895): 1–15 in the offprint. The author is convinced that Giannino was a creature of the king of Navarre; see especially pp. 13 ff., in which he discusses the letter, upholding its authenticity. For the edition of the letter, copied by two notaries, Angelo di Guido and Angelo d'Andrea, see *Istoria*, pp. 197–99.

14. "... per certa confessione, che lui hebbe a rivelare, la quale si dice, che era contra del re"; *Istoria*, p. 198.

15. See G. Mollat, *The Popes at Avignon, 1305–1378*, trans. J. Love (London: Thomas Nelson, 1963), p. 306; B. Guillemain, *La cour pontificale d'Avignon (1309–1376). Étude d'une société* (Rome: École française de Rome, 1966; Bibliothèque des Écoles françaises d'Athène et de Rome, no. 201), pp. 237 ff.

16. On medieval Provence, see in general M. Agulhon and N. Coulet, *Histoire de la Provence*, 4th ed. (Paris: Presses Universitaires de France, 2001). On Giannino's adventure in Provence and his relations with the nobles of that region, with the Angevin sovereigns, and with the English court, see Léonard, *Histoire de Jeanne Ière*, vol. 3, pp. 442 and 444 ff.; and Léonard, *Les Angevins de Naples*, pp. 388 ff.

17. "... grande merchatante, et drappiere, et grande huomo borgese di Parigi, et fu molto fedele, et servitore de lo re di Navarra, e fu de' conpagni del provosto de' merchatanti"; *Istoria*, p. 98.

18. "... scripse tutte sue letare e suoi brivileggi"; *Istoria*, p. 104.

19. "... inglesi, et tedeschi, francieschi, brettoni, guasconi, borgognoni, et d'altri linguaggi"; *Istoria*, p. 90.

20. "Nella concordia presa dalli due re di Francia e d'Inghilterra, della quale atendea certa fine di buona pace, essendo i·rre d'Inghilterra co' figliuoli e coll'oste sua tornato nell'isola, molti cavalieri e arcieri inghilesi usati alle prede e ruberie si rimasono nel paese"; Matteo Villani, *Cronica, con la continuazione di Filippo Villani*, vol. 2, bk. 9, chap. 109, pp. 452 ff. Primary sources for the history of the "great companies" include Matteo Villani, the Anonimo romano, and Jehan Froissart; see Balestracci, *Le armi i cavalli l'oro*, pp. 27–93; Selzer, *Deutsche Söldner*; Fowler, *Medieval Mercenaries*, vol. 1, *The Great Companies*.

21. "Finite le guerre, e fatta la pace tra·lli due re d'Inghilterra e di Francia, tornato i·rre Giovanni in Francia, e intendendo dolcemente a rassettare i·reame, fece gridare per tutto suo reame che tutta mala gente si dovesse partire e sgombrare il suo reame sotto gravi pene; e per tale cagione diverse compagne s'adunarono, li quali l'una dopo l'altra poi trassono a Vignone"; Matteo Villani, *Cronica*, vol. 2, bk. 10, chap. 27, pp. 491 ff.

22. "... tutti coloro i quali avevano tenuti la parte delo re di Navarra, e del provosto di' merchatanti"; *Istoria*, p. 94.

23. Andrew de Beaumont is mentioned by Fowler in *Medieval Mercenaries*, vol. 1, p. 45n.

24. This individual has resisted identification. The pope knew him as "Iohannes de Vernayo, miles anglicus"; see chap. 5, below. See as well *Istoria*, p. 94n: he might also have been Provençal. The underlying name might have been Guerney, Guernay, or Vernay. The last form is also the name of a locality in the territory of Roanne, situated in the modern department of the Loire.

25. "... per privileggio sugiellato di suo sugiello dela faccia sua ... suo luogotenente in atto di guerra per tutto lo Reame di Francia"; *Istoria*, p. 95.

26. D.-F. Secousse, *Recueil de pièces servant de preuves aux Mémoires sur les troubles excités en France par Charles II, dit le Mauvais, roi de Navarre et comte d'Évreux* (Paris: Durand, 1755), pp. 172–85, at pp. 180 and 184, respectively. See D'Avout, *Le meurtre d'Étienne Marcel*, p. 282.

27. The king of Navarre would resume fighting not long after, persisting until his conclusive defeat at Cocherel in 1364.

28. Jehan Froissart and Matteo Villani each relate, with some divergence on points of detail, the events of this period: Froissart, *Chroniques,* vol. 6, pp. 70 ff.; Villani, *Cronica,* vol. 2, bk. 10, chap. 27, pp. 491 ff.: "Come una compagnia creata novellamente prese Santo Spirito." Villani appears better informed, at least on the time frame. For the reconstruction I have adopted, see Fowler, *Medieval Mercenaries,* vol. 1, pp. 30–33.

29. Froissart, *Chroniques,* vol. 6, p. 72.

30. Froissart, *Chroniques,* vol. 6, p. 71.

31. "E stando il detto G[iovanni] al castello di Santo Stefano, misser Giovanni Vernee di sopra nominato con quattro milia huomini da cavallo di buona genti, e sentendo, come il trattato fatto di Lione sopra Rodano era pallegiato, e scoperto per lo tradimento del detto Peron dela Corona, allora prese il Ponte Santo Spirito, e la terra con tutto, il quale Ponte è in sulo Rodano, et è proprio delo Reame di Francia, e presalo venardì a notte adì XXV di dicembre anno 1360"; *Istoria,* p. 105.

Chapter Five

1. "E il nobile ponte sopra i·Rodano di presente accupato fu per quelli della compagna, d'onde aviano libera l'entrata nel Venisì, e potieno a·loro piacere cavalcare fino a Vignone; per tale cagione il papa e ccardinali ebbono gran paura, e·lla città tutta prese l'arme serrate le botteghe, e solo si contendea a·ffare steccati e bertesche sì alla città sì al gran palagio del papa, e a provedersi di vittuaglia; e co·soldati s'atendea a buona guardia, e di dì e di notte. E, oltre a·cquesta provisione il papa bandì la croce sopra la compagna"; Matteo Villani, *Cronica,* vol. 2, bk. 10, chap. 27, pp. 492 ff.

2. Froissart, *Chroniques,* vol. 5, p. 94.

3. ". . . e il ponte aforzavano in forma, che ·lle navi che venieno di Borgogna a Vignone co· vittuaglia non potieno passare, onde la corte sostenne grave carestia"; Matteo Villani, *Cronica,* vol. 2, bk. 10, chap. 27, pp. 493.

4. Rome, Archivio di Stato (henceforth ASR), *Collezione acquisti e doni,* b. 23, fol. Vv.

5. Ibid., fol. VIIr–XVIIIr.

6. ". . . [le scritture] le quali aveva rechate di Saracinia . . ."; *Istoria,* p. 134.

7. ". . . cierti amici di Daniello . . ."; *Istoria,* p. 133.

8. "Se questi che mi vengono a parlare sono gienti da bene, io non mi cielarò punto, ma se fussero gienti vile, e di bassa conditione, non ce li fate venire, perciò che io non voglio far fare beffe di me, né gittare mie parole indarno"; *Istoria,* p. 110 ff. On the notable political influence of the self-governing cities

in Provence, and their give-and-take relationship with the power of the count of Provence as represented by his officials (a give-and-take well exemplified here), see M. Hébert, "Aspects de la culture politique en Provence au XIVe siècle," in *Église et culture en France méridionale (XIIe–XIVe siècle)* (Toulouse: Éditions Privat / Fanjeaux, Centre d'études historiques de Fanjeaux, 2000; Cahiers de Fanjeaux. Collection d'Histoire religieuse du Languedoc au XIIIe et XIVe siècles, no. 35), pp. 475–96.

9. "... non erano genti da bene, et che erano genti da fare più tosto beffe di questi fatti, che altro"; *Istoria*, p. 111.

10. "Signore, a' ciptadini di questa villa è stato detto come voi sete figliuolo delo re Luigi e dela reyna Clementia, et che di ragione v'attiene la Corona di Francia; et per tanto questi, che voi vedete qui rappresentano tutta questa ciptà, et di tutti provenzali per volere sapere da voi, se voi sete quello, che si dicie, che vi piaccia di paleggiarvi, perciò che la intenzione nostra et di tutti provenzali si è che voi non siate pregione, ancho vi sia fatto quello onore, che si richiede come re, però che la madre vostra ebbe singulare amore et divotione nella Provenza, et spetialmente nella ciptà di Chassi. Et pertanto noi voliamo pregare, che vi piaccia di dirne la verità"; *Istoria*, p. 111 ff.

11. "... nel servigio del detto G., et per acquistare per lui lo Reame di Francia sicome dritto, et naturale re di Francia"; *Istoria*, p. 114.

12. ASR, *Collezione acquisti e doni*, b. 23, fol. LXII, ed. by Maccari in the introduction to *Istoria*, pp. XIX ff. [The author supplies an Italian translation of the original Latin document; my English translation is made from the Italian. WM]

13. On the value of this papal letter, see also chap. 6, below.

14. "... per levarlisi d'intorno ..."; Matteo Villani, *Cronica*, vol. 2, bk. 10, chap. 43, p. 511.

15. "... lungamente a vivere di preda e di rapina sopra i paesani"; Villani, *Cronica*, vol. 2, bk. 10, chap. 43, p. 511.

16. "E lassavanlo al buio, e mangiava, e beieva, e stava il dì, e la notte al buio; et tanti vermini, cioè pidocchi, gli abondaro adosso"; *Istoria*, pp. 121 ff.

17. "... commesso fornicatione in atto di sodomia co' cardenali, et con altri prelati, cioè stato con loro come fusse vera meretrice"; *Istoria*, p. 122. Accusations of sodomy among ecclesiastics, especially at Avignon, are a recurring motif in literature; see, for example, Boccaccio's novella "Abram giudeo" (*Decameron*, day 1, novella 2), and the exemplum of Filippo degli Agazzari, "Come 'l diavolo usò con un giovano disonestamente," in degli Agazzari, *Gli Assempri*, edited with an introduction by P. Misciattelli (Siena: Giuntini-Bentivoglio,

1922), pp. 60–62. The Sienese statutes dealt very harshly with sodomites and forgers; see *Il Costituto del Comune di Siena*, dist. V, rubr. CCLXXXVII and CCXCVI. On Provençal anticlericalism, see Hébert, "Aspects de la culture politique en Provence au XIVe siècle," p. 482.

18. See P. Herde, "Römisches und kanonisches Recht bei der Verfolgung des Fälschungsdelikts im Mittelalter," *Traditio* 21 (1965): 291–362.

19. ". . . la reyna di Francia Giovanna . . ."; *Istoria*, p. 124.

20. See Le Goff, *Saint Louis*, part 1, chap. 3, sec. "Le roi prisonnier," pp. 192–93, and part 3, chap. 10, "Le roi souffrant, le roi Christ," especially the section "La souffrance du prisonnier," pp. 873–75.

21. "Io voglio, che tu confessi di tua volontà come tu queste cose, che di te sono dette e fatte, ch'elle sieno tutte fatte, et ordinate da te proprio, e che tu l'abbi fatte malatiosamente, con avere falsati sugielli, et in quanto no' le vogli dire, io ti farò tagliare le mani, e' piei, e farotti gittare in mare"; *Istoria*, p. 125 ff.

22. "Come volete voi ch'io confessi quello che non è vero, et che per me non fu mai pensato? E poniamo ch'io dicha tutto ciò, che voi volete, e' non sarà creduto, perciò che palese è come lo tribuno mandò per me, et ivi sono coloro, che mi viddero parlare con lui, et dare le scripture, et ivi sono i *saracini* di Roma che scrissero le letare, et i ciptadini di Siena, che mi furo dati a consiglio"; *Istoria*, pp. 125 ff. The text of *Istoria* reads *saracini*, but the word intended must have been *senatori*.

23. "Se non confessi ciò, ch'io ti dico, di subbito ti farò morire," and "Scrivete tutto ciò, che vi piace ch'io dica"; *Istoria*, pp. 125 ff.

24. ". . . e se prima lo trattaro male, allora lo trattaro peggio"; *Istoria*, pp. 125 ff.

25. For that matter, this was also the diet consumed by the crew while on board; see Ch.-E. Dufourcq, *La vie quotidienne dans les ports méditerranéens au Moyen Âge (Provence—Languedoc—Catalogne)* (Paris: Hachette, 1975), pp. 75 ff.

26. On the kingdom of Naples in the Middle Ages, see G. Galasso, *Il Regno di Napoli. Il Mezzogiorno angioino e aragonese (1266–1494)*, vol. 15 of the series *Storia d'Italia*, ed. G. Galasso (Turin: UTET, 1992). On contacts between the Regno, as it was often summarily called, and Tuscany, see now F. P. Tocco, *Niccolò Acciaiuoli. Vita e politica in Italia alla metà del XIV secolo* (Rome: Istituto storico italiano per il medio evo, 2001; Nuovi studi storici, no. 52). On Giannino's experience in Naples, see Léonard, *Histoire de Jeanne Ière*, vol. 3, pp. 462 ff.

27. ". . . che l'aveva mosso ad entrare con ciancie, e con genti d'armi, et dimandare d'essare signore delo Reame di Francia"; *Istoria*, p. 128.

28. ". . . gli feciero onore"; *Istoria*, p. 131.

29. "E qui facciamo fine, et vederemo che sarà, et come le cose andaranno, e seguiremo nostro scripto"; *Istoria*, p. 132.

30. "Et ine sto inferriato"; *Istoria*, p. 148. His memoir ends with the title of a petition which Giannino had presented on 3 June: "Questa si è la petizione, che io feci al'arcivescovo di Napoli per aver le letare, che mi tolse misser Mateo de' Giesualdi quando mi prese, poi le dé alo re Luigi in Napoli" (This is the petition which I made to the archbishop of Naples, requesting the return of the letters that Messer Matteo di Gesualdo took from me when he arrested me, then he gave them to King Luigi in Naples). There followed a row of little crosses (reproduced in subsequent copies), meant to indicate the point where Giannino's own autograph manuscript broke off. The text of the petitions presented to the archbishop and the queen was added to Giannino's manuscript later; duly reproduced in the copies, it now forms the conclusion to the entire *Istoria;* see pp. 148–53.

31. The inventory is published in *Il tesoro di un re [saggio della storia del re Giannino]*, ed. C. Mazzi (Rome: Forzani, 1892), and in the *Istoria*, pp. 135–44. [In the text the author supplies a transcription in modernized Italian, on which my English translation is based. WM]

32. The *meço quarro* (written *mezzo quarro* in modern Italian) is a measure of weight attested in the Tuscan sources for the fourteenth century: it designated very small quantities, like the amount of cloves to be used in a recipe. It must have been equivalent to around 3.5 grams, the average weight of the florin and the Venetian ducat. The coins in Giannino's possession were likely the gold ducats coined by the doge Giovanni Dolfin (1356–61).

33. The word used in the text for "little hooks" is *gangaretti,* equivalent to *gangherelli* in modern Italian.

34. The word translated as "open helmet" is *barbuta.* This was a helmet with a T-shaped aperture for the eyes, nose, and mouth.

35. The highly prized fur called "vair" (*vaio*) was made from the winter coat of the Siberian squirrel. In describing the same article of clothing earlier in the *Istoria* (see chap. 3, above), Giannino describes it as being lined with ermine rather than vair.

36. "Samite" (*sciamito* in Italian) was a very expensive type of silk cloth.

37. A *posola* (pl. *posole*) is a piece of harness consisting of strip of leather attaching a breeching-strap (*straccale*) to a saddle or pack-saddle.

38. Sendal (*zendado* in Italian) was a finespun cloth.

39. A measure of capacity equivalent to almost one liter.

40. *Guarnello* was cloth woven from a mixture of cotton and hemp.

41. The word in the text translated as "bindings" is *guere* in the original, equivalent to *ghiere* (sing. *ghiera*) in standard Italian. What is meant, I believe, are circular reinforcements around the sheaths.

42. *Istoria*, p. XIII. See also Biblioteca Apostolica Vaticana (henceforth BAV), MS *Chig.* Q. I. 28, fol. 160.

43. See *Urbain V (1362–1370). Lettres communes analysées d'après les registres dits d'Avignon et du Vatican*, edited by members of the l'École française de Rome and M.-H. Laurent, t. I (Rome: École française de Rome, 1954–58), doc. 2608, pp. 276 ff., Avignon, 7 August 1363: Urban V assigns a post as canon at Forlì to Iohannes Guccii, a Florentine canon, allowing him to retain the one he holds in Paris and revoking the one he holds in Pisa; *Lettres secrètes et curiales du pape Urbain V (1362–1370) se rapportant à la France*, ed. P. Lecacheux and G. Mollat (Paris: E. de Boccard, 1954), doc. 731, p. 101, Avignon, 29 December 1363: Urban V writes to the provost and a canon of the church at Valencia ordering them to pay to the merchant Iohannes Gutii, a partner in the Societas Vicecomitis Lapi, who is in Barcelona at the time, the sum of 10,000 florins on behalf of the Camera apostolica.

44. See Maccari's introduction to the *Istoria*, p. LVn.

Chapter Six

1. The principal question guiding the experiment in writing which the present work constitutes is that of establishing a correct relationship between analysis and narrative, in other words of evaluating the extent to which we are able to confer cognitive value on "historical language." On this, see Carlo Ginzburg, "Proofs and Possibilities," *Yearbook of Comparative and General Literature* 37 (1988): 113–27 [published in Italian as "Prove e possibilità. In margine a *Il ritorno di Martin Guerre* di Natalie Zemon Davis," in N. Zemon Davis, *Il ritorno di Martin Guerre. Un caso di doppia identità nella Francia del Cinquecento* (Turin: Einaudi, 1984), pp. 131–54]; Carlo Ginzburg, *History, Rhetoric, and Proof* (Hanover, NH: University Press of New England, 1999) [Ginzburg's *Rapporti di forza. Storia, retorica, prova* (Milan: Feltrinelli, 2000) is an enlarged version of *History, Rhetoric, and Proof*, containing one extra essay]; P. Burke, "History of Events and the Revival of Narrative," in Burke, ed., *New Perspectives on Historical Writing*, 2d ed. (Cambridge: Polity Press/ Blackwell, 2001), pp. 283–300; and my own *Cola di Rienzo*, pp. 289–94.

2. Alain Boureau, *The Myth of Pope Joan*, trans. L. G. Cochrane (Chicago: University of Chicago Press, 2001; first published in French in 1988).

3. Le Goff, *Saint Louis*. The recent book of Jean-Claude Schmitt, *La conver-*

sion d'Hermann le Juif. Autobiographie, histoire, et fiction, deals with several themes akin to those of the present work. Some interesting suggestions for defining the status of the text can alse be derived from a comparison with the "autobiography of Celestin V," on which see *L'autobiografia di Celestino V,* critical edition with translation by V. Licitra (Campobasso: Istituto molisano di studi e ricerche, 1992).

4.   See G. Prunai, "Baglioni Giovanni (Giannino)," in *Dizionario biografico degli italiani,* vol. 5 (Rome: Istituto della Enciclopedia Italiana, 1963), pp. 220–22, who appears to base his own interpretation principally on the essay of E. Callegari, "Re Giannino (Giovanni Baglioni da Siena): storia o romanzo?" *La Rassegna Nazionale,* anno 27, vol. 149 (1905), pp. 460–92. Latino Maccari's introduction to the *Istoria* supplies a useful review of the complex history of the disparate historical interpretations of the *Istoria* and of Giannino the man, since early in the sixteenth century. For a more complete assessment, see as well G. Catoni, "Archivisti ed eruditi alla corte di re Giannino," in *Studi in onore di Arnaldo d'Addario,* ed. L. Borgia, F. De Luca, P. Viti, and R. M. Zaccaria (Lecce: Conte Editore, 1995), pp. 1119–32. Some of the observations made by L.-J.-N. de Monmerqué in his *Dissertation historique sur Jean Ier* are still of interest. The same is true of two unpublished works by Girolamo Gigli, a preparatory manuscript for an edition of the *Istoria* and a set of explanatory notes on it: *La storia del re Giannino di Francia scritta da lui medesimo, e tolta dagli antichi autorevoli manoscritti della Libraria Barberina, e Chisiana da Girolamo Gigli gentiluomo sanese il quale per la prima volta l'ha messa in pubblico con nuovi documenti, e colle osservazioni tanto sopra la storia, che sopra la lingua volgare sanese. Quest'anno 1717:* BAV, MS *Chig.* Q. I. 28; and *Osservazioni sopra la storia del re Giannino di Francia di Girolamo Gigli gentiluomo sanese:* BAV, MS *Chig.* Q. II. 29.

5.   Prunai, "Baglioni Giovanni," p. 222.

6.   Bercé, *Le roi caché;* Lecuppre, *L'imposture politique.* A few essential guidelines emerge from Lecuppre's work, derived from the analysis of around thirty cases of impostors. This book also contains interesting pages on Giannino: see especially pp. 57–58 and 301–2, on the letter of Innocent VI; pp. 63, 172 and 359, on the use of forgeries and seals; pp. 96 and 201–3, on the letter of the king of Hungary and his relationship to Giannino; p. 121, on the social origins of impostors; pp. 133, 147 ff., 155 ff., on the manipulation of the personalities of impostors and political exploitation of them; p. 136, the personality of Giannino; pp. 149–53, 271, and 365, on the role of Cola di Rienzo and the preparatory phase of Giannino's imposture; pp. 162, 330, and 354 ff., on

the role of ecclesiastics in creating intrigues and spreading legends; p. 168, on Giannino's faith in the written word; p. 169, on the names of Giannino's children; pp. 175–77, on Giannino's money; pp. 189 ff., 288 ff., and passim, on the relation between imposture and politics; p. 230, on the switching of infants; pp. 238–40, analysis of the *Istoria*; p. 243, on the confessions made by impostors when arrested; pp. 271 ff. and 365, on Giannino and royal messianism. A conference on the topic *Royautés imaginaires, XIIe–XVIe siècles* was held at the Centre d'Histoire sociale et culturelle de l'Occident médiéval of the University of Paris X, Nanterre on 26–27 September 2003.

7. See Bercé, *Le roi caché*, ad indicem; and P. Conrad, *Louis XVII, l'énigme du roi perdu* (Paris: Ed. du May, 1988).

8. See Bercé, *Le roi caché*, ad indicem; and C. Durand-Cheynet, *Boris Godunov et le mystère Dimitri* (Paris: Perrin, 1986). See further two small and outdated anthologies (neither of which includes Jean I, however): E.-J. Chaudon, *Les Imposteurs démasqués et les usurpateurs punis, ou l'histoire de plusieurs aventuriers qui ayant pris la qualité d'empereur, de roi, de prince, d'ambassadeur, de tribun, de messie, de prophète, etc., ont fini leur vie dans l'obscurité ou par une mort violente* (Paris: Nyon, 1776); *Les imposteurs fameux* (Paris: Eymery, 1818).

9. The original is preserved in ASS, *Consiglio Generale, Elezioni e Cerne* 390, fols. 41r–42r, and was used by Maccari for the edition in *Istoria*, pp. 179–85.

10. The letter is found in the register of Innocent VI for year nine of his pontificate; the original is preserved in ASR, *Collezione acquisti e doni*, b. 23, vol. 4, at fol. LXIIr–v. An older edition of this letter can be found in E. Martène and U. Durand, *Thesaurus Novus Anecdotorum*, vol. 2 (Paris: sumptibus Florentini Delaulne, 1718), coll. 924 ff. It is taken from a manuscript copy of the pontifical register held at Dijon in the eighteenth century, which, unless it is the same one that subsequently came to ASR, is apparently lost. Maccari republishes the edition of Martène and Durand in *Istoria*, pp. XIX–XX. Already in 1717 Girolamo Gigli rightly viewed this papal letter as "the most authoritative document supporting this *Istoria*" (BAV, MS *Chig.* Q. II. 29, fol. 102). On it, see further Lecuppre, *L'imposture politique*, pp. 57–58 and 301–2.

11. Matteo Villani, *Cronica*, vol. 2, bk. 9, chap. 37, p. 337: "Di una compagnia criata d'inghilesi in Francia." Monmerqué, in *Dissertation historique sur Jean Ier*, maintained that Giovanni della Guglia was none other than Giannino di Guccio (see on this, Maccari's introduction to the *Istoria*, p. XXXVII). This cannot be right, though, for we may assume that Villani, a Florentine citizen, would have emphasized the Sienese origin of the person in question if they were the same; instead he identifies Giovanni della Guglia as an En-

glish tailor, active with his band in southern France in the summer of 1361, where he took the city of Pau and alarmed the papal court but then returned to obedience to the English king, to whom he handed over most of his booty. Likewise to be excluded is the identification of Giovanni della Guglia with the then young, later celebrated, condottiere John Hawkwood (known as Giovanni Acuto in Italian; see Balestracci, *Le armi i cavalli l'oro*, pp. 15 ff.).

12. "Sed quid dixisset Poëta noster, non est diu, Zaninum Senensem, qui permisit sibi persuaderi tam facile, quam vane, quod erat rex Franciae? Et iam dabat dignitates, et promittebat officia, dimissa propria hereditate"; Benvenutus de Rambaldis de Imola, *Comentum super Dantis Aldigheris Comoediam*, ed. G. F. Lacaita, vol. 3 (Florence: G. Barbèra, 1887), p. 372; see Maccari, introduction to the *Istoria*, p. VIII. Benvenuto's comment refers to Dante, *Purgatorio*, canto 13, lines 152–55: "Tu li vedrai tra quella gente vana / che spera in Talamone, e perderagli / più di speranza che a trovar la Diana; / ma più vi perderanno gli ammiragli."

13. On this Sienese tradition, see Maccari, *Istoria*, pp. XIV ff. and pp. 171 ff., supplying a detailed review of Italian and French erudite historiography. On Giannino's descendants, see pp. LIVn–LVn. The first to write about this was Sigismondo Tizio, author of the work *Historiae Senenses*, begun in 1506, who knew the last of Giannino's descendants, copied the *Istoria*, and added other information to it. On him, see the introduction to S. Tizio, *Historiae Senenses*, vol. 1, t. 1, ed. M. Doni Garfagnini (Rome: Istituto storico italiano per l'età moderna e contemporanea, 1992; Rerum italicarum scriptores recentiores, 6), and vol. 1, t. 2, part 1, ed. G. Tomasi Stussi (Rome: Istituto storico italiano per l'età moderna e contemporanea, 1995; Rerum italicarum scriptores recentiores, 10). The part of the *Historiae* that includes the life of Giannino and the notice of his descendants has not yet been published. The autograph MS is in BAV, *Chig*. G. I. 32; a later copy is in Siena, Biblioteca comunale degli Intronati, MS B. III. 7.

14. Maccari's edition of the *Istoria* constitutes the critical text of the main source for the life of Giannino di Guccio. His introduction, pp. LVIII–LX, succinctly describes the tradition of the manuscripts, of which the principal one is the fifteenth-century *Barb. lat.* 3958 in the BAV, a codex donated to cardinal Barberini by Giulio Piccolomini; other late redactions are present in BAV (*Chig*. G. I. 32, *Chig*. Q. I. 27, *Chig*. Q. I. 28), in Siena (Biblioteca comunale degli Intronati, MS A. III. 27; MS B. III. 7; MS C. IV. 16), in Florence (Biblioteca nazionale, cod. *Capponiano* 289) and in Paris (Bibliothèque Nationale, MS *Italien* 393). *Barb. lat.* 3958 does not include the notes at the

end, assembled in the sixteenth century by Sigismondo Tizio, about Giannino's descendants, which the other copies do contain. Maccari's edition of the *Istoria* was given a negative review by C. Mazzi—apparently out of resentment—in *Giornale storico della letteratura italiana* 12 (1894): 251–56; nevertheless it is a solid piece of work. However, the deliberation of the Consiglio della Campana (ASS, *Consiglio generale, Elezioni e Cerne* 390, fols. 41r–42r) edited by Maccari at pp. 179–85, does require a new edition. On the general topic, see C. Mazzi, "Mercanti senesi nei secoli XIII e XIV," *Bullettino senese di storia patria* 30 (1923): 217–30 (this article was originally written as chapter 5 of the preface to a work entitled *Storia di re Giannino*, which Mazzi intended to publish). A recent analysis of this source can be found in Lecuppre, *L'imposture politique*, pp. 238–40.

15. ". . . la copia d'uno li‹b›ro niente agionto o minuito, il quale scripse di sua propia mano lo re Giovanni ragionevole re di Francia"; *Istoria*, p. 3; BAV, MS *Barb. lat.* 3958, on the verso of the front flyleaf.

16. See *Istoria*, pp. XLV and 3n–5n.

17. The title *Istoria del re Giannino di Francia* does not appear in the oldest manuscript, since it was given to the text later. About Tommaso degli Agazzari (or della Gazzaia) see his *Praticha di geometria e tutte le misure di terre: dal ms. C. III. 23 della Biblioteca comunale di Siena*, transcription by C. Nanni, introduction by G. Arrighi (Siena: Servizio editoriale dell'Università, 1982), which supplies some information about the author, who is included in neither the *Dizionario biografico degli italiani* nor the *Repertorium fontium medii aevi*.

18. "Ora lassiamo stare il detto conte con sua gente, e torniamo a Giovanni, il quale è in Ongharia, et attende che lo re gli mandi sue letare"; *Istoria*, pp. 70 ff.; and see C. Lavinio, *La magia della fiaba: tra oralità e scrittura* (Scandicci: La Nuova Italia, 1993), pp. 54, 57 ff.

19. On this theme, see *L'Autobiografia nel medioevo, atti del XXXIV convegno storico internazionale, Todi, 12–15 ottobre 1997* (Spoleto: Centro italiano di studi sull'alto medioevo, 1998); and Schmitt, *La conversion d'Hermann le Juif*, chap. 2, "L'autobiographie médiévale," pp. 63–88.

20. After having checked on all the named individuals of note and verified that the historical details given about them are correct, the only incongruence I can report is the mention of Bernard de Bosquet as archbishop of Naples: in 1362 he had not yet achieved this dignity, which came his way only in 1365 (*Istoria*, p. 146). This error (noted as well by Maccari in his note), which might justify the suspicion that the *Istoria* was composed a few years after the death of Giannino, arises in my view from a lacuna in the text, erroneously filled in later.

21. "Questo sì è il modo, come fu scambiato lo re Giovanni . . . et come fu allevato in Siena . . . et come fu ritrovato, et quello che à fatto fino adì 19 di Ferraio anno 1361 che esso fu menato pregione a Napoli . . ."; *Istoria*, p. 7. The date should be understood as "1362" in our reckoning, since Giannino was using the reckoning "from the Incarnation" in use in Siena, in which the first day of the new year is Annunciation day, 25 March. Hence any date falling in the period 1 January–24 March lags one year behind our reckoning.

22. *Istoria*, pp. 132 and 148. We see an analogous shift when Giannino is accused of sodomy, since the *Istoria*, which down to that point has been narrated entirely in the remote past, shifts for a moment into the present: "Et questo è quello peccato, il quale spiace più al detto G[iovanni], che veruno altro del mondo" (And this is the sin that displeases the said Giovanni more than any other in the world), p. 122. The occasion spurs Giannino to employ a notable stylistic *variatio*. On the way that verb forms "manifest the ideological function of the narrator," see Lavinio, *La magia della fiaba*, p. 54. For É. G. Léonard the pages of the *Istoria* that record contemporary events in Naples constitute valuable first-hand testimony; see Léonard, *Les Angevins de Naples*, especially p. 398: while locked up in the jail of the Vicaria, Giannino is supposed to have enjoyed "sufficient liberty to make this part of his memoirs a true chronicle of Neapolitan events of this period." See as well Léonard, *Histoire de Jeanne Ière*, vol. 3, p. 440, in which he summarizes "the three essential characteristics of the memoirs, so rich and virtually unutilized, of the pretender: minute exactness about the raw facts of which he has direct knowledge; a tendency to relate everything to his own concerns; an extreme credulity which leads him to accept everything he is told."

23. See chap. 2, n. 4 above.

24. BAV, MS *Barb. lat.* 5026, fol. 62, "Lettera relativa al manoscritto della vita del re Giannino, al sig. Francesco Piccolomini."

25. BAV, MS *Chig.* Q. II. 29, fols. 104v–105r. On Gigli (1660–1722) see L. Spera, "Gigli Girolamo," in *Dizionario biografico degli italiani*, 54 (Rome: Istituto della Enciclopedia Italiana, 2000), pp. 676–79.

26. Bloch, *The Royal Touch*, bk. 2, chap. 3, sec. 3, p. 132.

27. See Le Goff, *Saint Louis*, part 2, chap. 2, sec. "Guillaume de Chartres," p. 336, for the praise of Saint Louis as "an ideal Christian king, a model king for other kings, a sun-king."

28. "Et questa arte fece fare per dare utile e guadagno a la povara gente più che per volontà di guadagnare"; *Istoria*, p. 30. The laudatory passages are concentrated at pp. 30–33.

29. ". . . non volse fare nullo guadagno in acto di merchanthia"; *Istoria*, p. 33.

30. "Costui ch'io vo cercando è de'... disciesi [of Saint Louis], et seguitarà lui"; *Briefwechsel des Cola di Rienzo*, vol. 4, p. 194; see chap. 1, above. See, further, A. Vauchez, "'Beata stirps.' Sainteté et lignage en Occident aux XIIIe et XIVe siècles," in *Famille et parenté dans l'Occident médiéval*, ed. G. Duby and J. Le Goff (Rome: École française de Rome, 1977), pp. 337–99; Le Goff, *Saint Louis;* Klaniczay, *Holy Rulers and Blessed Princesses;* Kelly, *The New Solomon,* especially pp. 119 ff.

31. Calvino, *Fiabe italiane*, vol. 1, p. LII; see. chap. 2, above. On the prescribed forms of proper behavior for merchants, see especially Paolo da Certaldo, *Il Libro di buoni costumi*, in *Mercanti scrittori. Ricordi nella Firenze tra Medioevo e Rinascimento*, ed. V. Branca (Milan: Rusconi, 1986), pp. 1–99. The author of this work, who was the same age as Giannino and had exactly the same cultural orientation, gathered 388 precepts teaching "many good examples and good customs and good proverbs and good admonishments" (p. 3). Among the most recent studies on Siena and the relationship between religiosity and the mercantile profession, see M. Pellegrini, "Attorno all' 'economia della salvezza.' Note su restituzione d'usura, pratica pastorale ed esercizio della carità, in una vicenda senese del primo Duecento," *Cristianesimo nella storia* 25.1 (2004): 59–102. On laic sanctity, see the bibliography of U. Longo, *La santità medievale* (Rome: Jouvence, 2005), ad indicem. Finally, for an examination of this topic in greater depth, see T. di Carpegna Falconieri, "Il carisma nel medioevo: una considerazione e due casi di studio (Cola di Rienzo e 're Giannino')," in *Carisma e istituzioni nel secolo XI, atti del Convegno, Fonte Avellana, 29–30 agosto 2005* (Negarine di San Pietro in Cariano: Il Segno dei Gabrielli Editori, 2006), pp. 219–42.

32. See Maccari's introduction to the *Istoria*, pp. XLVI ff.

33. See chap. 2, above.

34. There was another statue of Jean I, located in the great hall of the royal palace on the Île de la Cité. The babe was shown with his father, who was holding his hand. The statue was destroyed with all the others in the fire of 1618; see Monmerqué, *Dissertation historique sur Jean Ier*, p. 18.

35. *Comptes de l'argenterie des rois de France au XIVe siècle*, ed. L. Douët-d'Arcq (Paris: Société de l'Historie de France, 1851), pp. 18 ff.

36. On the exhumation of the royal corpses, which took place between 12 and 25 October 1793, see A. Boureau, *Le simple corps du roi. L'impossibile sacralité des souverains français, XVe–XVIIIe siècles* (Paris: Les Éditions de Paris, 1988), pp. 7 ff. The author republishes the *Rapport sur l'exhumation des corps royaux à Saint-Denis en 1793*, by dom Germain Poirier (pp. 71–91). The tomb

of Jean I is mentioned at p. 74; the exhumation of his corpse on 18 October is registered at p. 85: "the little king Jean, his posthumous son, lay beside his father [Louis X], in a little tomb or trough of stone lined with lead, having lived no more than four days."

37. "Et per intentione di farlo morire, allora istrense il detto fanciullo chi dicie ne' fianchi, et chi disse nele tempie, et chi disse, che gli ficchò uno spillo sulo capo, et chi disse, ch'ella vi misse il dito nella fontanella della gola, et chi disse, ch'ella portò veleno ne le dita, et ponesselo ale labra dello fanciullo"; *Istoria*, pp. 17 ff.

38. Lavinio, *La magia della fiaba*, pp. 19 ff. See in general L. Passerini, *Storia e soggettività: le fonti orali, la memoria* (Florence: La Nuova Italia, 1988); "Cultura orale e cultura scritta," in *Lo spazio letterario del medioevo*, 2, *Il medioevo volgare*, vol. I/1: *La produzione del testo* (Rome: Salerno Editrice, 1992), pp. 117–80; G. Barone, "Oralità e scrittura," in *La società medievale*, ed. S. Collodo and G. Pinto (Bologna: Monduzzi Editore, 1999), pp. 553–59.

39. On "expectancy" among the people, see Bercé, *Le roi caché*, part 3, chap. 7, "Des interprétations psychologiques; attentes et impostures," pp. 311–77.

40. Giovanni Villani, *Nuova Cronica*, critical edition by G. Porta, 2 vols. (Parma: Guanda, 1990–91), vol. 1, bk. 7, chap. 45, pp. 357 ff.

41. See S. Benvenuto, *Dicerie e pettegolezzi* (Bologna: il Mulino, 2000); J. H. Brunvand, *Encyclopedia of Urban Legends* (Santa Barbara, CA: ABC-CLIO, 2001).

42. A. Milillo, *La vita e il suo racconto: tra favola e memoria storica* (Rome and Reggio Calabria: Casa del Libro, 1983), p. 83; Lavinio, *La magia della fiaba*, pp. 103 ff.

43. See H. Brame, "Historique de l'abbaye de Saint-Pierre de Neauphle-le-Vieux," *Revue Mabillon*, ser. II, XXII, 46 (April–June 1931), pp. 62, 125 and ad indicem. For the medieval documentation on the abbey of Neauphle, see now *Guide des archives des Yvelines et de l'ancien Département de Seine-et-Oise*, t. I, *Séries anciennes*, ed. A. Bezaud (Versailles: Conseil Général des Yvelines, 2002), pp. 945–47 (with bibliography). There is, however, no record of the existence of an Augustinian convent at Cressay.

44. See chaps. 2 and 5, above.

45. Bercé, *Le roi caché*, p. 343; see in general the section from which this passage comes: part 3, chap. 7, sec. "Les délires d'identité," pp. 339–45 (on Giannino specifically: pp. 343–44).

46. See in general the new complete English translation of Michel Foucault's *Histoire de la folie à l'âge classique* (1961): Michel Foucault, *History of Mad-*

ness, ed. J. Khalfa, trans. J. Khalfa and J. Murphy (London and New York: Routledge, 2006).

47. The Sienese merchant had a literary notion, derived from medieval romance, of French royalty, as we see, for example, in the fact that on two occasions he reveals his belief that the first king of France was a Roman: *Istoria,* pp. 43 and 135. Giannino was actually referring to Fiovo or Flovus, a legendary son of the emperor Constantine. Those who later pored over and reworked his adventure appear to have derived some information from the romance *I reali di Francia,* by Andrea da Barberino, since in a few Sienese manuscripts recording the sons and descendants of Giannino, it is stated that they bore the mark of royalty. This refers to the royal cross, one of the most enduring medieval superstitions deriving from a virtually universal theme traceable to antiquity, which appears in French and German romances of adventure in the course of the thirteenth century. The little cross might be red, or as in this case, white, and it normally appeared on the body of the designated individual above the right shoulder. Charlemagne too was supposedly born with this mark, "a proof of royal blood, a certain pledge of future accession to the throne" (Bloch, *The Royal Touch,* bk. 2, chap. 3, sect. 4, p. 142). Thus, the mark that Giannino himself never claimed to bear—and how advantageous it would have been for him to do so!—obviously worked its way into his legend. Not that it did his descendants much good though, for the family line died out in poverty.

48. See, for example, Filippo degli Agazzari, *Gli Assempri,* pp. 60–62; and *Racconti esemplari di predicatori del Due e Trecento,* ed. G. Varanini and G. Baldassarri (Rome: Salerno Editrice, 1993), 3 vols.

49. "Et molto si dilectò di leggiere, e di scrivere, et di dettare volgalmente [*sic*]"; *Istoria,* p. 32. On another occasion, he cites the *libri da leggere storiali* (historical books for reading) that were stolen from him when he was arrested (p. 131). On the general theme: M. Mancini, "Lettori e lettrici di romanzi," in *Lo spazio letterario del medioevo,* 2, *Il medioevo volgare,* vol. 3, *La ricezione del testo* (Rome: Salerno Editrice, 2003), pp. 155–76, especially sec. 2, "Libro e desiderio mimetico," pp. 159–62, and sec. 3, "Sogni ed eroismi," pp. 162–68, which discuss the widespread tendency of readers to identify with literary characters.

50. Gianni Rodari, *The Grammar of Fantasy: An Introduction to the Art of Inventing Stories,* translated with an introduction by Jack Zipes (New York: Teachers and Writers Collaborative, 1996), pp. 12–15 (In the original Italian: Gianni Rodari, *Grammatica della fantasia* [Turin: Einaudi, 1973, pp. 17–22.)

[Professor Zipes informs me that "fantastic binomial" is now his preferred translation for *binomio fantastico*, although he adopted the translation "fantastic binominal" in *The Grammar of Fantasy* (personal communication, 2007). WM]

51. On Jewish converts to Christianity, see Schmitt, *La conversion d'Hermann le Juif,* passim, with bibliography.

52. Jean de Roquetaillade (aka Johannes de Rupescissa) was aware of some of the events in the life of Cola di Rienzo; and he was a prisoner at Avignon during the time that Giannino resided there. See *Fin du monde et signes des temps;* R. E. Lerner, "Millénarisme litteral et vocation des juifs chez Jean de Roquetaillade," and J.-Cl. Maire Vigueur, "Cola di Rienzo et Jean de Roquetaillade ou la rencontre de l'imaginaire," Mélanges de l'École française de Rome— Moyen Âge 102.2 (1990): 311–15 and 381–89; R. E. Lerner, *The Feast of Saint Abraham: Medieval Millenarians and the Jews* (Philadelphia: University of Pennsylvania Press, 2001), especially pp. 73–88. On the concept—derived from scripture—of "Jews befriended by kings" (which is another potential avenue of research), see Schmitt, *La conversion d'Hermann le Juif,* chap. 3, "Juifs et chrétiens rêvaient-ils différement?" at pp. 93–95.

53. Bloch, *The Royal Touch;* and especially his *Memoirs of War, 1914–15,* translated and with an introduction by Carole Fink (Ithaca, NY: Cornell University Press, 1980), and "Réflexions d'un historien sur les fausses nouvelles de la guerre," *Revue de synthèse historique,* n.s., 7 (1921): 13–35; and Natalie Zemon Davis, *The Return of Martin Guerre* (Cambridge, MA: Harvard University Press, 1983), chap. 5, "The Invented Marriage," pp. 42 ff. See as well Boureau's introduction to *The Myth of Pope Joan.*

54. "Vedi Luca, noi no ·llo aremo mai creduto che fosse stato il re, imperò che non avea, né ha la corona in capo, ma noi ci pensavamo che fosse il prete suo"; Giovanni Gherardi da Prato, *Il Paradiso degli Alberti,* ed. A. Lanza (Rome: Salerno Editrice, 1975), p. 234.

55. *Documenting Individual Identity,* ed. J. Caplan and J. Torpey (Princeton: Princeton University Press, 2001).

56. *Il Costituto del Comune di Siena,* dist. II, rubr. CCI: "De la pena di chi negasse alcuno essere o vero essere essuto padre, o vero fratello, o vero marito" (On the penalty for anyone who denies that someone else is, or was, a father, or brother, or husband). It was also forbidden to assert that someone was alive, it if was known to public opinion that he was dead, or to assert that he had not held public offices when the public voice affirmed the contrary. See as well Agazzari, *Gli Assempri,* no. 54, p. 212: "E sia certo che non è nessun

luogo dove 'l diavolo si diletti tanto di stare et abitare, quanto in su la lengua del mormoratore, e detrattore" (And know for certain that there is no place where the devil so delights in staying and residing, as on the tongue of the murmurer and detractor).

57. See chap. 5, above.

58. Bartolomeo Mini was a renowned preacher, as we discover in the eulogy of him in the *Libro dei morti di San Domenico di Siena*, a eulogy transcribed by G. Gigli (BAV, MS *Chig.* Q. II. 29, fol. 64r–v): "Venerandus frater Barto-lomeus Mini, qui fuit homo magni consilij, clarae litteraturae saecularibus mirabiliter gratiosus, qui in Romana Provincia habuit plures promotiones, tam quoad studia, quam ad praelationes; fuit prior in multis conventibus, ac etiam definitor, et praedicator generalis Ordinis, et sui conventus zelator praecipuus; diem clausit extremum in hospitali sancti Chirici in Hosenna die ultima junij, et /64v/ corpus suum Senis delatum est, et humatum in loco communi fratrum defunctorum die prima iulij cum magna totius civitatis desolatione de absentia tanti patris" (The venerable friar Bartolomeo Mini, who was a man of great counsel, famed for learning, most agreeable to the laity, who had various promotions in the Roman province, in the domains of both study and prelacies; he was prior in many convents, and also definitor and general preacher of the Order, and an outstanding defender of his con-vent; he ended his days in the hospital of San Quirico d'Orcia on the last day of June, and his body was brought to Siena, and buried in the common place for deceased friars on the first day of July, with great desolation of the whole city for the loss of such a father). Gigli also declares that Friar Bartolomeo "was reputed a great servant of God by the blessed Giovanni Colombino," citing a book by Isidoro Ugurgieri Azzolini, *Le pompe sanesi o vero relazione delli huomini, e donne illustri di Siena e suo Stato*, 2 vols. (Pistoia: nella Stam-peria di Pier Antonio Fortunati, 1649), vol. 1, p. 277. But there is no such statement in this book, and Gigli may have confused Bartolomeo Mini with Francesco di Mino Vincenti, one of the first companions of the blessed Gio-vanni Colombini.

59. See, in general, Roberto Rusconi, *Predicazione e vita religiosa nella società italiana da Carlo Magno alla Controriforma* (Turin: Loescher, 1981); Rusconi, "La predicazione: parole in chiesa, parole in piazza," in *Lo spazio letterario del medioevo*, 1, *Il medioevo latino*, vol. 2: *La circolazione del testo* (Rome: Salerno Editrice, 1994), pp. 571–603. Bartolomeo Mini is not recorded in *Repertorium der lateinischen Sermones des Mittelalters: für die Zeit von 1150–1350*, ed. J. B. Schneyer, 9 vols. (Münster: Aschendorff, 1969–80). I have not been able to

consult *Repertorium der lateinischen Sermones des Mittelalters: für die Zeit von 1350–1500*, ed. L. Hödl and W. Knoch, CD-ROM (Münster: Aschendorff, 2001).

60. See Bloch, pp. 75–78 in *The Royal Touch*, bk. 2, chap. 1, sec. 4; on the mendicant orders and their construction of the memory of Saint Louis, see Le Goff, *Saint Louis*, part 2, chap. 2, "Le roi des hagiographes mendiants: un saint roi du Christianisme rénové," pp. 328–44; on Remigio de' Girolami, see J.-P. Boyer, "Florence et l'idée monarchique. La prédication de Remigio dei Girolami sur les Angevins de Naples," in *La Toscane et les Toscans autour de la Renaissance. Cadres de vie, sociétés, croyances. Mélanges offerts à Charles M. de La Roncière* (Aix-en-Provence: Publications de l'Université de Provence, 1999), pp. 263–76; see as well Kelly, *The New Solomon*, pp. 243 ff.; and A. De Vincentiis, "Origini, memoria e identità a Firenze nel XIV secolo. La rifondazione di Carlomagno," *Mélanges de l'École française de Rome— Moyen Âge* 115.1 (2003): 385–443, especially 403–6 and 434 ff.

61. *Istoria*, p. 126.

62. On this, see Lavinio, *La magia della fiaba*, especially pp. 97, and 101–9.

63. ". . . [gli] contò di più re, che erano stati scanbiati nella loro nativitade"; *Istoria*, p. 41.

64. See Stith Thompson, *Motif-index of Folk-literature. A classification of narrative elements in folktales, ballads, myths, fables, mediaeval romances, exempla, fabliaux, jest-books, and local legends*, rev. ed., 6 vols. (Bloomington: Indiana University Press; Copenhagen, Rosenkilde and Bagger, 1955–58; originally published Helsinki: 1932–36). The most relevant motifs are H (Tests) and K (Deceptions). In general, see Stith Thompson, *The Folktale* (Berkeley: University of California Press, 1977; a reprint of the Dryden Press edition, New York: 1946, 1951).

65. A recent edition is Mark Twain, *The Prince and the Pauper*, introduction by Jerry Griswold (New York: Penguin Books, 1997). For narrative motifs common to the *Istoria* and and folklore, see in particular Thompson, *Motif-index of Folk-literature*, motif K1920, "switched babies" (vol. 3, pp. 454 ff.), with variants K1921.1 (p. 455), in which the switch takes place between the son of a blacksmith and the son of a king, and K1921.3, in which the baby is switched by a wet nurse. This last motif also appears in a Spanish *novella* (see D. P. Rotunda, *Motif-Index of the Italian Novella in Prose* [Bloomington: Indiana University, 1942], p. 129). I note in general that the Italian *novella* tradition abounds in motifs that occur in our story, for example, that of the king or prince who goes incognito, often disguised as a merchant (Rotunda, *Motif-*

Index, pp. 122–23; for the switching of babies, pp. 119, 127 ff.); still, there is no single *novella* that parallels it really closely.

66. Bianca Pitzorno, *Polissena del Porcello* (Milan: Mondadori, 1993).

67. See Thompson, *Motif-index of Folk-literature,* A580 (vol. I, pp. 125 ff.).

68. Bercé, *Le roi caché,* p. 318; from part 3, chap. 7, sec. "La découverte d'un prince caché, Valence, 1522," pp. 317–23. On the functions of myths of this type, see part 2, chap. 4, "Le roi sacrificiel," pp. 189–229.

69. 2 Kings 11:1–12.

70. A recent English translation of the *Cyropaedia* is Xenophon, *The Education of Cyrus,* translated and annotated by Wayne Ambler (Ithaca, NY and London: Cornell University Press, 2001).

71. J. R. R. Tolkien, *The Lord of the Rings* (Boston: Houghton Mifflin, 1994), pp. 167, 241 (both in *The Fellowship of the Ring*).

72. John, 1, 10 (English translation from the Jerusalem Bible). See in general J. Leclercq, *L'idée de la royauté du Christ au Moyen Âge* (Paris: Cerf, 1959).

73. Cited in Bercé, *Le roi caché,* Annexes, Pièces justificatives, 1: "Le roi caché sur les traces du Christ," pp. 417–18.

74. "Figliuol fu' io d'un beccaio di Parigi"; Dante, *Purgatorio* 20, 52.

75. ". . . fuit extrait de la boucherie" ; François Villon, *Ballade de l'appel,* ll. 9–10.

76. *Hugues Capet. Chanson de geste du XIVe siècle,* ed. N. Laborderie (Paris: Champion, 1997).

77. D'Avout, *Le meurtre d'Étienne Marcel,* pp. 121 ff.

78. Andrea da Barberino, *Il Guerrin Meschino,* ed. Mauro Cursietti (Padua: Antenore, 2005).

79. Andrea da Barberino, *I reali di Francia,* introduction by A. Roncaglia, notes by F. Beggiato (Rome: G. Casini, 1967).

80. Chaudon, *Les Imposteurs démasqués,* pp. 209–11.

81. Monmerqué, *Dissertation sur Jean Ier,* p. 32.

82. Ibid., p. 33.

83. L. Bréhaut, "Giannino Baglioni roi de France; épisode de l'histoire du XIVe siècle," *Revue contemporaine,* ser. 2, XVII, 52 (1860); E. Tavernier, "Le roi Giannino: étude historique," *Mémoires de l'Académie des sciences, arts et belles lettres d'Aix* 11–12 (1882); F. Gabotto, "Re Giannino. Saggio storico," *Nuova rivista* 2 (1883): 2–16; G. Rondoni, *Tradizioni popolari e leggende di un comune medievale e del suo contado* (Florence: Uffizio della rassegna nazionale, 1886), pp. 65–74; *Il tesoro di un re;* Pór, "Nagy Lajos magyar király viszonya Giannino di Guccio"; *Istoria;* Boudet, "Un prétendant au trône de France, Gian-

nino Baglioni"; Callegari, "Re Giannino" (1905). To this list should be added many other historians who, beginning with Papencordt, have studied the life of Cola di Rienzo; on these, see Carpegna Falconieri, *Cola di Rienzo*, pp. 235 ff.

84. E. Muller, *Jean Posthume*, comédie en un acte (Paris: G. Decaux, 1878).

85. R. de Navery, "Giannino roi de France," in Navery, *Coeurs vaillants. Nouvelles historiques* (Paris: E. Plon, 1879), pp. 59–154.

86. A. Palmieri, "La storia del re Giannino," in Palmieri, *I racconti della lupa* (Milan: Treves, 1910), pp. 3–100. A she-wolf suckling twin boys was a symbol of the city of Siena as well as of ancient Rome.

87. Palmieri, "La storia del re Giannino," p. 9.

88. V. Gonzi, *Re Giannino* (Roma: P. Maglione, 1936).

89. Maurice Druon, *Les Rois Maudits*, 3 vols. (Paris: Plon/Del Duca, 2005), is a reprint issued to coincide with the release of the new version for television directed by Josée Dayan and starring Jeanne Moreau as Countess Mahaut of Artois. All seven novels are in print individually in compact format (Paris: Livre de Poche, 1970). A recent book on Druon's novel sequence is É. Le Nabour, *Les rois maudits. L'enquête historique* (Paris: Perrin, 2005), which is, however, of no use for scholarly research.

90. The sinister "reine inconnue" is the only reclining figure in Saint-Denis entirely sculpted in black rather than white stone; in addition, the woman rests her feet on two dragons instead of two dogs.

91. "Ils se trouvaient piégés à leur propre trappe"; *La loi des mâles* (*Les Rois Maudits*, vol. 4; Paris: Livre de Poche, 1970) from the beginning of part 3, chap. 5, "Un Lombard à Saint-Denis," p. 220. It is worth noting that in the original story, the baby dies during the night after the public presentation; thus there would have been time to switch the real royal baby back where he belonged and subsequently announce that the son of the wet nurse had died.

92. Bloch, *The Royal Touch*, bk. 2, chap. 3, sec. 4, p. 148.

BIBLIOGRAPHY

·◁▭▷·

Manuscript Sources
Florence, Biblioteca Nazionale
Cod. *Capponiano* 289
Paris, Bibliothèque Nationale de France
Ms *Français* 2615
Ms *Français* 2643
Ms *Italien* 393
Ms *Latin* 4975
Rome, Archivio di Stato
Collezione acquisti e doni, b. 23, vol. 4
Siena, Archivio di Stato
Biccherna, Entrata e uscita 235
Biccherna, Memoriali 415
Consiglio Generale, Elezioni e Cerne 390
Ms A 61
Ms C 13
Siena, Biblioteca comunale degli Intronati
Ms A. III. 27
Ms B. III. 7
Ms C. IV. 16
Vatican City, Biblioteca Apostolica Vaticana
Barb. lat. 3958
Barb. lat. 5026
Chig. G. I. 32
Chig. Q. I. 27
Chig. Q. I. 28
Chig. Q. II. 29

Printed Primary and Secondary Sources
Agazzari, Filippo degli. *Gli Assempri*. Ed., with an introduction by Piero Misciattelli. Siena: Giuntini-Bentivoglio & C., 1922.
Agazzari, Tommaso degli (Tommaso della Gazzaia). *Praticha di geometria e tutte
le misure di terre: dal ms. C. III. 23 della Biblioteca comunale di Siena*. Tran-

scription by Cinzia Nanni, introduction by Gino Arrighi. Siena: Servizio editoriale dell'Università, 1982.

Agulhon, Maurice, and Noël Coulet. *Histoire de la Provence*. 4th ed. Paris: Presses Universitaires de France, 2001.

Ait, Ivana. *Il commercio nel medioevo*. Rome: Jouvence, 2005.

Andrea da Barberino. *I reali di Francia*. Introduction by Aurelio Roncaglia, notes by Fabrizio Beggiato. Rome: G. Casini, 1967.

————. *Il Guerrin Meschino*. Ed. Mauro Cursietti. Padua: Antenore, 2005.

Anjou-kori Oklévéltar. Documenta res Hungaricae tempore regum Andegavensium illustrantia (1301–1387). Budapest and Szeged: 1990–.

Anonimo romano. *Cronica*. Ed. Giuseppe Porta. Milan: Adelphi, 1979.

L'Autobiografia di Celestino V. Critical edition, with trans. Vincenzo Licitra. Campobasso: Istituto molisano di studi e ricerche, 1992.

L'Autobiografia nel medioevo, atti del XXXIV convegno storico internazionale, Todi, 12–15 ottobre 1997. Spoleto: Centro italiano di studi sull'alto medioevo, 1998.

Balestracci, Duccio. *Le armi i cavalli l'oro. Giovanni Acuto e i condottieri nell'Italia del Trecento*. Rome and Bari: Laterza, 2003.

Balestracci, Duccio, and Gabriella Piccinni. *Siena nel Trecento. Assetto urbano e strutture edilizie*. Florence: Edizioni CLSUF, 1977.

Bargigia, Fabio, and Aldo A. Settia, *La guerra nel medioevo*. Rome: Jouvence, 2005.

Barone, Giulia. "Oralità e scrittura" in *La società medievale*, pp. 553–59. Ed. S. Collodo and G. Pinto. Bologna: Monduzzi Editore, 1999.

Benvenuto, Sergio. *Dicerie e pettegolezzi*. Bologna: Il Mulino, 2000.

Benvenutus de Rambaldis de Imola. *Comentum super Dantis Aldigheris Comoediam*. Ed. Giacomo Filippo Lacaita, vol. 3. Florence: G. Barbèra, 1887.

Bercé, Yves-Marie. *Le roi caché. Sauveurs et imposteurs; mythes politiques populaires dans l'Europe moderne*. Paris: Fayard, 1990.

Le Biccherne. Tavole dipinte delle magistrature senesi (secoli XIII–XVIII). Ed. Luigi Borgia et al. Rome: Ministero per i Beni culturali e ambientali, Ufficio centrale per i beni archivistici, 1984.

Bigwood, Georges. "Les Tolomei en France au XIVe siècle." *Revue belge de philologie et d'histoire* 8 (1929).

Bloch, Marc. "Réflexions d'un historien sur les fausses nouvelles de la guerre." *Revue de synthèse historique*, n.s., 7 (1921): 13–35.

————. *Memoirs of War, 1914–15*. Trans., with an introduction by Carole Fink. Ithaca, N.Y: Cornell University Press, 1980.

————. *The Royal Touch: Sacred Monarchy and Scrofula in England and France*. Trans. J. E. Anderson. Montreal: McGill-Queen's University Press, 1973. Original title: *Les rois thaumaturges*, 1924.

Boulhol, Pascal. *Anagnorismos. La scène de reconnaissance dans l'hagiographie antique et médiévale.* Aix-en-Provence: Publications de l'Université de Provence, 1996.

Boureau, Alain. *Le simple corps du roi. L'impossibile sacralité des souverains français, XVe–XVIIIe siècles.* Paris: Les Éditions de Paris, 1988.

———. *The Myth of Pope Joan.* Trans. Lydia G. Cochrane. Chicago: University of Chicago Press, 2001.

Bowsky, William M. *A Medieval Italian Commune: Siena under the Nine, 1287–1355.* Berkeley: University of California Press, 1981.

———. *The Finances of the Commune of Siena, 1287–1355.* Oxford: Clarendon Press, 1970.

Boyer, Jean-Paul. "Florence et l'idée monarchique. La prédication de Remigio dei Girolami sur les Angevins de Naples." In *La Toscane et les Toscans autour de la Reinaissance. Cadres de vie, sociétés, croyances. Mélanges offerts à Charles M. de La Roncière,* pp. 263–76. Aix-en-Provence: Publications de l'Université de Provence, 1999.

Brame, Henri. "Historique de l'abbaye de Saint-Pierre de Neauphle-le-Vieux." *Revue Mabillon,* s. II, XXII, 46 (April–June 1931).

Bréhaut, Louis. "Giannino Baglioni roi de France; épisode de l'histoire du XIVe siècle." *Revue contemporaine,* ser. 2, XVII, 52 (1860).

Briefwechsel des Cola di Rienzo. Ed. Konrad Burdach and Paul Piur. Berlin: Weidmann, 1912–29. (Vom Mittelalter zur Reformation. Forschungen zur Geschichte deutschen Bildung, II, 1–5).

Brizio, Elena. "L'elezione degli uffici politici nella Siena del Trecento." *Bullettino senese di storia patria* 98 (1991): 16–62.

Brown, Elizabeth A. R. "Falsitas Pia sive Reprehensibilis. Medieval Forgers and Their Intentions." *Fälschungen im Mittelalter,* vol. 1, pp. 101–19. Internationaler Kongress der Monumenta Germaniae Historica, München 16.–19. September 1986, 6 vols. (Hannover: Hahnsche Buchhandlung, 1988–90; MGH Schriften, 33.

Brunvand, Jan Harold. *Encyclopedia of Urban Legends.* Santa Barbara, CA: ABC-CLIO, 2001.

Burke, Peter. "History of Events and the Revival of Narrative." In P. Burke, ed., *New Perspectives on Historical Writing,* pp. 283 300. 2d ed. Cambridge: Polity Press/Blackwell, 2001.

Callegari, Ettore. "'Re Giannino' (Giovanni Baglioni da Siena): storia o romanzo?" *La Rassegna Nazionale,* anno 27, vol. 149 (1905), pp. 460–492.

Calvino, Italo. *Fiabe italiane raccolte dalla tradizione popolare durante gli ultimi cento anni e trascritte in lingua dai vari dialetti.* Milan: Mondadori, 1993.

————. *Italian Fables.* Trans. Louis Brigante. New York: Orion Press, 1959.

Cammarosano, Paolo. *Italia medievale. Struttura e geografia delle fonti scritte.* 6th ed. Rome: Carocci, 2000.

Cardini, Franco, et al. *Banchieri e mercanti di Siena.* Preface by C. M. Cipolla. Siena: Monte dei Paschi di Siena, 1987.

Carpegna Falconieri, Tommaso di. "Il carisma nel medioevo: una considerazione e due casi di studio (Cola di Rienzo e 're Giannino')." In *Carisma e istituzioni nel secolo XI, atti del Convegno, Fonte Avellana, 29–30 agosto 2005,* pp. 219–42. Negarine di San Pietro in Cariano: Il Segno dei Gabrielli Editori, 2006.

————. *Cola di Rienzo.* Rome: Salerno Editrice, 2002.

Catoni, Giuliano. "Archivisti ed eruditi alla corte di re Giannino." In *Studi in onore di Arnaldo d'Addario,* pp. 1119–32. Ed. L. Borgia, F. De Luca, P. Viti, and R. M. Zaccaria. Lecce: Conte Editore, 1995.

————. "La dimensione archivistica della ricerca storica: il caso di Siena." *Bullettino senese di storia patria* 84–85 (1977–78): 320–92.

I ceti dirigenti della Toscana tardo comunale, atti del terzo convegno del Comitato di studi sulla storia dei ceti dirigenti in Toscana, Firenze 5–7 dicembre 1980. Florence: F. Papafava, 1983.

Chaudon, Esprit-Joseph. *Les Imposteurs démasqués et les usurpateurs punis, ou l'histoire de plusieurs aventuriers qui ayant pris la qualité d'empereur, de roi, de prince, d'ambassadeur, de tribun, de messie, de prophète, etc., ont fini leur vie dans l'obscurité ou par une mort violente.* Paris: Nyon, 1776.

Chronique latine de Guillaume de Nangis de 1113 à 1300 avec les continuations de cette chronique de 1300 à 1368. Ed. Hércule Géraud. Paris: Société de l'Histoire de France, 2 vols., 1843.

Chronographia regum Francorum. Ed. Henri Moranvillé. Paris: Société de l'Histoire de France, 3 vols., 1891–1897.

Cicchetti, Angelo, and Raul Mordenti. *I libri di famiglia in Italia,* vol. 1, *Filologia e storiografia letteraria.* Rome: Edizioni di Storia e Letteratura, 1985.

Codex diplomaticus Hungariae ecclesiasticus ac civilis. Ed. Georg Fejér, t. 9, vol. 3 (1359–1366); t. 10, vol. 4 (1367–1374). Budae: Typis Typogr. Regiae Universitatis Ungaricae, 1834.

Codex diplomaticus Hungaricus Andegavensis. Anjoukori Okmànytar, 7 vols. Budapest: Kiadja a Magyar Tudomànyos Akadémia, 1878–1920.

Collard, Franck. *Le crime de poison au Moyen Âge.* Paris: Presses Universitaires de France, 2003.

Collins, Amanda. *Greater than Emperor: Cola di Rienzo (ca. 1313–1354) and the World of Fourteenth-Century Rome.* Ann Arbor: University of Michigan Press, 2002.

Colloquio italo-ungherese sul tema: gli Angioini di Napoli e d'Ungheria (Roma, 23–24 maggio 1972) organizzato d'intesa con l'Accademia delle Scienze d'Ungheria. Rome: Accademia Nazionale dei Lincei, 1974; Problemi attuali di scienza e cultura, Quaderno 210.

Comptes de l'argenterie des rois de France au XIVe siècle. Ed. Louis Douët-d'Arcq. Paris: Société de l'Historie de France, 1851.

Conrad, Philippe. *Louis XVII, l'énigme du roi perdu.* Paris: Ed. du May, 1988.

Constable, Giles. "Forgery and Plagiarism in the Middle Ages." *Archiv für Diplomatik* 29 (1983): 1–41.

Il Costituto del Comune di Siena volgarizzato nel MCCCIX–MCCCX edito sotto gli auspici del Ministero dell'Interno, 2 vols. Siena: R. Archivio di Stato di Siena, 1903. New edition, ed. Mahmoud Salem Elsheik, Siena: Fondazione Monte dei Paschi, 2003. 2 vols.

Coulet, Noël. "Mutations de l'immigration italienne en Basse Provence Occidentale à la fin du moyen âge." In *Strutture familiari, epidemie, migrazioni nell'Italia medievale,* pp. 493–510. Ed. R. Comba, G. Piccinni, and G. Pinto. Naples: Edizioni scientifiche italiane, 1984.

"Cultura orale e cultura scritta." In *Lo spazio letterario del medioevo, 2, Il medioevo volgare,* vol. I/1: *La produzione del testo,* pp. 117–80. Rome: Salerno Editrice, 1992.

Curry, Anne. *The Hundred Years War.* London: Macmillan, 1993.

D'Avout, Jacques. *Le meurtre d'Étienne Marcel, 31 juillet 1358.* Paris: Gallimard, 1960.

Davis, Natalie Zemon. *The Return of Martin Guerre.* Cambridge, MA: Harvard University Press, 1983.

De Vincentiis, Amedeo. "Memorie bruciate. Conflitti, documenti, oblio nelle città italiane del tardo medioevo." *Bullettino dell'Istituto storico italiano per il medio evo* 106.1 (2004): 167–98.

———. "Origini, memoria e identità a Firenze nel XIV secolo. La rifondazione di Carlomagno." *Mélanges de l'École française de Rome – Moyen Âge* 115.1 (2003): 385–443.

Documenting Indivual Identity. Ed. Jane Caplan and John Torpey. Princeton: Princeton University Press, 2001.

Domonkos, Leslie S. "The Influence of the Italian Campaigns of Louis the Great on Hungarian Cultural Developments." In *Louis the Great, King of Hungary and Poland,* pp. 203–20. Ed. S. B. Vàrdy, G. Grosschmid, and L. S. Domonkos. Boulder, CO: East European Monographs, 1986.

Druon, Maurice. *Les Rois Maudits,* 3 vols. Paris: Plon/Del Duca, 2005; and 7 vols. Paris: Livre de Poche, 1970.

Dufourcq, Charles-Emmanuel. *La vie quotidienne dans les ports mediterranéens au Moyen Âge (Provence—Languedoc—Catalogne)*. Paris: Hachette, 1975.

Durand-Cheynet, Catherine. *Boris Godunov et le mystère Dimitri*. Paris: Perrin, 1986.

Écritures et mémoire familiale. Annales. Histoire, Sciences Sociales 59.4 (2004): 785–858.

Ernoul le Viel. *Crescens incredulitas/go*. In *Lais et chansons d'Ernoul de Gastinais*. Ed. Jean Maillard. American Institute of Musicology, 1964.

L'Expulsion des Juifs de France 1394. Ed. Gilbert Dahan. Paris: Cerf, 2004.

Fälschungen im Mittelalter. Internationaler Kongress der Monumenta Germaniae Historica, München 16.–19. September 1986, 6 vols. Hannover: Hahnsche Buchhandlung, 1988–90; MGH Schriften, 33.

Fin du monde et signes des temps. Visionnaires et prophètes en France méridionale (fin XIIIe–début XVe siècle). Toulouse: Éditions Privat; Fanjeaux : Centre d'études historiques de Fanjeaux, 1992; Cahiers de Fanjeaux. Collection d'Histoire religieuse du Languedoc au XIIIe et XIVe siècles, no. 27.

Fontes-Baratto, Anna. "Le thème de la beffa dans le *Décaméron*." In A. Rochon et al., *Formes et significations de la "beffa" dans la littérature italienne de la Renaissance*, vol. 1, pp. 12–44. Paris: Université de la Sorbonne Nouvelle, 1972–1975.

Foucault, Michel. *History of Madness*. Ed. Jean Khalfa, trans. Jean Khalfa and Jonathan Murphy. London and New York: Routledge, 2006.

Fowler, Kenneth. *Medieval Mercenaries*, vol. 1, *The Great Companies*. Malden, MA: Blackwell Publishers, 2001.

Froissart, Jehan. *Chroniques*. 12 vols. Paris: Societé de l'Histoire de France, 1869–1975. Vol. 5 (1356–1360), ed. Siméon Luce, 1874. Vol. 6 (1360–1366), ed. Siméon Luce, 1876.

Gabotto, Ferdinando. "Re Giannino. Saggio storico." *Nuova rivista* 2 (1883): 2–16.

Galasso, Giuseppe. *Il Regno di Napoli. Il Mezzogiorno angioino e aragonese (1266–1494)*. *Storia d'Italia*, ed. G. Galasso, vol. 15. Turin: UTET, 1992.

Gherardi, Giovanni da Prato. *Il Paradiso degli Alberti*. Ed. Antonio Lanza. Rome: Salerno Editrice, 1975.

Ginzburg, Carlo. "Proofs and Possibilities." *Yearbook of Comparative and General Literature* 37 (1988): 113–27.

———. *History, Rhetoric, and Proof*. Hanover, NH: University Press of New England, 1999.

———. *Rapporti di forza. Storia, retorica, prova*. Milan: Feltrinelli, 2000. (An enlarged version of Ginzburg's *History, Rhetoric, and Proof*, containing one extra essay.)

Gonzi, V. *Re Giannino*. Rome: P. Maglione, 1936.

Gottlieb, Beatrice. "The Meaning of Clandestine Marriage." In *Family and Sexuality in French History*, pp. 49–83. Ed. Robert Wheaton and Tamara K. Hareven. Philadelphia: University of Pennsylvania Press, 1980.

Les grandes chroniques de France. 10 vols. Ed. Jules Viard. Paris: Société de l'Histoire de France, 1920–1953. Vol. 8, 1934. Vol. 9, 1937.

Les grands traités de la Guerre des Cent Ans. Ed. Edmond Cosneau. Paris: Alphonse Piccard, 1889.

Grieco, Sara Matthews, and Carlo A. Corsini. *Historical Perspectives on Breastfeeding*. Florence: UNICEF, 1991.

Guarducci, Piero. *Un tintore senese del Trecento. Landoccio di Cecco d'Orso*. Siena: Protagon Editori Toscani, 1998.

Guide des archives des Yvelines et de l'ancien Département de Seine-et-Oise, t. I, *Séries anciennes*. Ed. A. Bezaud. Versailles: Conseil Général des Yvelines, 2002.

Guillemain, Bernard. *La cour pontificale d'Avignon (1309–1376). Étude d'une société*, 2d ed. Rome: École française de Rome, 1966; Bibliothèque des Écoles françaises d'Athène et de Rome, no. 201.

Hébert, Michel. "Aspects de la culture politique en Provence au XIVe siècle." In *Église et culture en France méridionale (XIIe–XIVe siècle)*. Toulouse: Éditions Privat; Fanjeaux : Centre d'études historiques de Fanjeaux, 2000; Cahiers de Fanjeaux. Collection d'Histoire religieuse du Languedoc au XIIIe et XIVe siècles, no. 35.

Herde, Peter. "Römisches und kanonisches Recht bei der Verfolgung des Fälschungsdelikts im Mittelalter." *Traditio* 21 (1965): 291–362.

Hugues Capet. Chanson de geste du XIVe siècle. Ed. Noëlle Laborderie. Paris: Champion, 1997.

Les imposteurs fameux. Ou histoires extraordinaires et singulières des hommes de néant de toutes les nations qui, depuis le temps les plus reculés jusqu'à ce jour, ont usurpé la qualité d'empereur, de roi et de prince; terminées par celles des deux faux Louis XVII, Hervagaudt et Bruneau. Paris: Eymery, 1818.

Istoria del re Giannino di Francia. Ed. Latino Maccari. Siena: Tip. C. Nava, 1893.

Jàszay, Magda. *Incontri e scontri nella storia dei rapporti italo-ungheresi*. Soveria Mannelli: Rubbettino, 2003.

The Jerusalem Bible. Reader's Edition. New York: Doubleday, 1971.

Kantorwicz, Ernest H. *The King's Two Bodies: A Study in Mediaeval Political Theology*. With a new preface by William Chester Jordan. Princeton, NJ: Princeton University Press, 1997; first published 1957.

Kardos, Tibor. "Ideali e problemi dell'Umanesimo in Ungheria nel periodo angioino" In *Colloquio italo-ungherese*, pp. 7–20. Rome: Accademia Nazionale dei
Lincei, 1974; Problemi attuali di scienza e cultura, Quaderno 210.

Kelly, Samantha. *The New Solomon: Robert of Naples (1309–1343) and
Fourteenth-Century Kingship*. Leiden and Boston: Brill, 2003.

Klaniczay, Gábor. *Holy Rulers and Blessed Princesses: Dynastic Cults in Medieval
Central Europe*. Cambridge: Cambridge University Press, 2002.

Klaniczay, Tibor. "Attività letteraria dei francescani e domenicani nell'Ungheria
angioina." In *Colloquio italo-ungherese*, pp. 27–40. Rome: Accademia Nazionale dei Lincei, 1974; Problemi attuali di scienza e cultura, Quaderno 210.

Klapisch-Zuber, Christiane. "Blood Parents and Milk Parents: Wet-nursing
in Florence, 1300–1530." *Women, Family, and Ritual in Renaissance Italy*,
pp. 132–64. Trans. Lydia G. Cochrane. Chicago: University of Chicago
Press, 1985.

Lavinio, Cristina. *La magia della fiaba: tra oralità e scrittura*. Scandicci: La Nuova
Italia, 1993.

Le Goff, Jacques. *Saint Louis*. Paris: Gallimard, 1996.

———. *Your Money or Your Life: Economy and Religion in the Middle Ages*.
Trans. Patricia Ranum. New York: Zone Books, 1988; *La bourse et la vie.
Économie et religion au Moyen Âge*. 2d ed. Paris: Hachette, 1997.

Le Nabour, Éric. *Les rois maudits. L'enquête historique*. Paris: Perrin, 2005.

Leclercq, Jean. *L'idée de la royauté du Christ au Moyen Âge*. Paris: Cerf, 1959.

Lecuppre, Gilles. *L'imposture politique au Moyen Âge. La seconde vie des rois*. Paris:
Presses Universitaires de France, 2005.

Léonard, Émile G. "Louis Ier de Hongrie protecteur du 're Giannino.'" *Revue des
Études Hongroises* 6 (1928): 379–84.

———. *Histoire de Jeanne Ière, reine de Naples, comtesse de Provence (1343–1382)*,
vol. 3, *Le règne de Louis de Tarente*. Monaco: Imprimerie de Monaco; Paris:
Picard, 1936.

———. *Les Angevins de Naples*. Paris: Presses Universitaires de France, 1954.

Lerner, Robert E. "Millénarisme litteral et vocation des juifs chez Jean de Roquetaillade." *Mélanges de l'École française de Rome—Moyen Âge* 102.2 (1990):
311–15.

———. *The Feast of Saint Abraham: Medieval Millenarians and the Jews*. Philadelphia: University of Pennsylvania Press, 2001.

Leroy, Béatrice. *Le Royaume de Navarre à la fin du Moyen Âge*. Aldershot: Variorum, 1990.

Lewis, Andrew W. *Royal Succession in Capetian France: Studies on Familial Order
and the State*. Cambridge, MA: Harvard University Press, 1981.

Longo, Umberto. *La santità medievale*. With an introductory essay by Giulia Barone. Rome: Jouvence, 2005.

Maire Vigueur, Jean-Claude. "Cola di Rienzo et Jean de Roquetaillade ou la rencontre de l'imaginaire." *Mélanges de l'École française de Rome—Moyen Âge* 102.2 (1990): 381–89.

Mancini, Mario. "Lettori e lettrici di romanzi." In *Lo spazio letterario del medioevo*, 2, *Il medioevo volgare*, vol. 3, *La ricezione del testo*, pp. 155–76. Rome: Salerno Editrice, 2003.

Manselli, Raoul. "Il sogno come premonizione, consiglio e predizione nella tradizione medievale." In *I sogni nel medioevo, Seminario internazionale, Roma 2–4 ottobre 1983*, pp. 218–44. Ed. T. Gregory. Rome: Edizioni dell'Ateneo, 1985.

Martène, Edmond, and Ursin Durand. *Thesaurus Novus Anecdotorum*, vol. 2. Paris: Sumptibus Florentini Delaulne, 1718.

Mazzi, Curzio. "Mercanti senesi nei secoli XIII e XIV." *Bullettino senese di storia patria* 30 (1923): 217–30.

———. Review of *Istoria del re Giannino di Francia*, ed. Maccari, in *Giornale storico della letteratura italiana* 12 (1894): 251–56.

Meyer, Edmond. *Charles II roi de Navarre, comte d'Évreux et la Normandie au XIVe siècle*. Paris: Ernest Dumont, 1898.

Milillo, Aurora. *La vita e il suo racconto: tra favola e memoria storica*. Rome and Reggio Calabria: Casa del Libro, 1983.

Mollat, Guillaume. *The Popes at Avignon, 1305–1378*. Trans. Janet Love from the French edition of 1949. London: Thomas Nelson, 1963.

Monmerqué, Louis-Jean-Nicholas de. *Lettre du Frère Antoine . . . à Nicolas de Rienzi . . . suivie de deux lettres de Rienzi, adressées à Giannino, de Sienne. Appendice de la "Dissertation sur Jean Ier, roi de France et de Navarre."* Paris: Tabary, 1845.

———. *Dissertation historique sur Jean Ier, roi de France et de Navarre; par M. Monmerqué, Conseilleur à la Cour royale de Paris, membre de l'Académie royale des Inscriptions et Belles-Lettres; suivie d'une charte par laquelle Nicolas de Rienzi reconnaît Giannino, fils supposé de Guccius, comme roi de France, et d'autres documents relatifs à ce fait singulier*. Paris: Tabary, 1844.

Monumenta Hungariae Historica. Magyar Diplomacziai Emlékek az Anjou Korból (Acta extera), vol. 2 (1342–69). Ed. Gustàv Wenzel. Budapest: A.M.T. Akadémia Könyvkiadò-Hivatalàban, 1875.

Moscadelli, Stefano. "Apparato burocratico e finanze del Comune di Siena sotto i Dodici (1355–1368)." *Bullettino senese di storia patria* 89 (1982): 29–118.

Mottini, Guido Edoardo. *Il romanzo di Giannetto Parigi re di Francia*. Milano:

Alpes, 1928; Torino: Unione Tipografico-Editrice, 1935, 1941, 1942, 1958, 1973 (La scala d'oro, series 4, no. 7).

Mucciarelli, Roberta. "Un caso di emigrazione mercantile. I Tolomei di Siena." In *Demografia e società nell'Italia medievale (secoli IX–XIV)*, pp. 475–92. Ed. R. Comba and I. Naso. Cuneo: Società per gli studi storici, archeologici ed artistici della provincia di Cuneo, 1994.

———. *I Tolomei banchieri di Siena. La parabola di un casato nel XIII e XIV secolo*. Siena: Protagon Editori Toscani, 1995.

Muller, E. *Jean Posthume*, comédie en un acte. Paris: G. Decaux, 1878.

Navery, R. de. "Giannino roi de France." In Navery, *Coeurs vaillants. Nouvelles historiques*. Paris: E. Plon, 1879, pp. 59–154.

Nouveau recueil de Comptes de l'argenterie des rois de France. Ed. Louis Douët-d'Arcq. Paris: Société de l'Historie de France, 1874.

La Novella del Grasso legnajuolo riscontrata col manoscritto e purgata di molti e gravissimi errori. Florence: Felice Le Monnier, 1856.

Novelle del Quattrocento. Ed. Giuseppe Maria Ferrero and Maria Luisa Doglio. Turin: UTET, 1975.

Pace e guerra nel basso medioevo, atti del Convegno di Todi, 12–15 ottobre 2003. Todi: Centro italiano di studi sul basso medioevo-Accademia tudertina, in course of publication, 2004.

Palmieri, Antonio. "La storia del re Giannino." In *I racconti della lupa*. Milan: Treves, 1910, pp. 3–100.

Paolo da Certaldo. *Il libro dei buoni costumi*. In *Mercanti scrittori. Ricordi nella Firenze tra Medioevo e Rinascimento*. Ed. Vittore Branca. Milan: Rusconi, 1986.

Passerini, Luisa. *Storia e soggettività: le fonti orali, la memoria*. Florence: La Nuova Italia, 1988.

Pellegrini, Michele. "Attorno all' 'economia della salvezza.' Note su restituzione d'usura, pratica pastorale ed esercizio della carità, in una vicenda senese del primo Duecento." *Cristianesimo nella storia* 25.1 (2004): 59–102.

La peste nera: dati di una realtà ed elementi di una interpretazione. Atti del XXX Convegno storico internazionale, Todi 10–13 settembre 1993. Spoleto: Centro italiano di studi sull'alto medioevo, 1994.

Piero Veneziano. *La novella del Bianco Alfani*. In *Novelle del Quattrocento*, pp. 629–52.

Pitzorno, Bianca. *Polissena del Porcello*. Milan: Mondadori, 1993.

Pór, Antal. "Nagy Lajos magyar király viszonya Giannino di Guccio, Franczia trónkövetelöhöz . . .[The relations of the king of Hungary Louis the Great with Giannino di Guccio, pretender to the throne of France]." *Értekezések a történeti tudományok Köréböl* XV kötet, 9 szám (1892).

Professione, Alfonso. *Siena e le compagnie di ventura nella seconda metà del secolo XIV. Ricerche e appunti con un'appendice di documenti inediti.* Civitanova Marche: Casa editrice Domenico Natalucci, 1898.

Prunai, Giulio. "Baglioni Giovanni (Giannino)." *Dizionario biografico degli italiani*, vol. 5, pp. 220–22. Rome: Istituto della Enciclopedia Italiana, 1963.

Puymaigre, Théodore-Joseph Boudet, comte de. "Un prétendant au trône de France, Giannino Baglioni." *Revue des questions historiques* 57 (April 1895).

Racconti esemplari di predicatori del Due e Trecento. Ed. Giorgio Varanini and Guido Baldassarri. 3 vols. Rome: Salerno Editrice, 1993.

La religiosità popolare nel medioevo. Ed. Raoul Manselli. Bologna: Il Mulino, 1983.

Ricerche sull'influenza della profezia nel basso medioevo, atti dell'incontro di studio Roma 11 dicembre 2000. Ed. P. Donadoni, R. Michetti, and G. Milani. *Bullettino dell'Istituto storico italiano per il medio evo* 104 (2002): 145–208.

Redon, Odile. *L'espace d'une cité. Sienne et le pays siennois, XIIIe–XIVe siècles.* Rome: École française de Rome, 1994.

Rehberg, Andreas. "'Nuntii, questuarii, falsarii': l'ospedale di S. Spirito in Sassia e la raccolta delle elemosine nel periodo avignonese." *Mélanges de l'École française de Rome—Moyen Âge* 115.1 (2003): 31–132.

Repertorium der lateinischen Sermones des Mittelalters: für die Zeit von 1150–1350. Ed. Johannes Baptist Schneyer. 9 vols. Münster: Aschendorff, 1969–80.

Repertorium der lateinischen Sermones des Mittelalters: für die Zeit von 1350–1500. Ed. Ludwig Hödl and Wendelin Knoch. Münster: Aschendorff, 2001.

Rochon, André. "Une date importante dans l'histoire de la 'beffa': la *Nouvelle du Grasso legnaiuolo.*" In André Rochon et al., *Formes et significations de la "beffa" dans la littérature italienne de la Renaissance*, vol. 2, pp. 211–376. Paris: Université de la Sorbonne Nouvelle, 1972–75.

Rochon, André, et al. *Formes et significations de la "beffa" dans la littérature italienne de la Renaissance*, 2 vols. Paris: Université de la Sorbonne Nouvelle, 1972–75.

Rodari, Gianni. *The Grammar of Fantasy: An Introduction to the Art of Inventing Stories.* Trans., with an introduction by Jack Zipes. New York: Teachers and Writers Collaborative, 1996.

Rondoni, Giuseppe. *Tradizioni popolari e leggende di un comune medievale e del suo contado.* Florence: Uffizio della rassegna nazionale, 1886.

Rotunda, Dominic Peter. *Motif-Index of the Italian Novella in Prose.* Bloomington: Indiana University, 1942.

Rusconi, Roberto. "La predicazione: parole in chiesa, parole in piazza." In *Lo spazio letterario del medioevo*, 1, *Il medioevo latino*, vol. 2: *La circolazione del testo*, pp. 571–603. Rome: Salerno Editrice, 1994.

———. *Predicazione e vita religiosa nella società italiana da Carlo Magno alla Controriforma*. Turin: Loescher, 1981.

Sarti, Raffaella. *Vita di casa: abitare, mangiare, vestire nell'Europa moderna*. 3d ed. Rome and Bari: Laterza, 2003.

Schmitt, Jean-Claude. *La conversion d'Hermann le Juif. Autobiographie, histoire, et fiction*. Paris: Seuil, 2003.

Secousse, Denis-François. *Recueil de pièces servant de preuves aux Mémoires sur les troubles excités en France par Charles II, dit le Mauvais, roi de Navarre et comte d'Évreux*. Paris: Durand, 1755.

Lo spazio letterario del medioevo, 2, *Il medioevo volgare*. 5 vols. Rome: Salerno Editrice, 1992–2005.

Selzer, Stephan. *Deutsche Söldner im Italien des Trecento*. Tübingen: Niemeyer, 2001; Bibliothek des Deutschen Historischen Instituts in Rom, 98.

Sermini, Gentile. *Novelle*. Ed. Giuseppe Vettori. 2 vols. Rome: Avanzini e Torraca, 1968.

Spera, Lucinda. "Gigli Girolamo." *Dizionario biografico degli italiani*, vol. 54, pp. 676–79. Rome: Istituto della Enciclopedia Italiana, 2000.

Storia di Siena. Ed. Roberto Barzanti, Giuliano Catoni, and Mario De Gregorio. Vol. I, *Dalle origini alla fine della Repubblica*. Siena: Asaba, 1995.

Tamburrini, Filippo. "La Penitenzieria apostolica durante il papato avignonese." In *Aux origines de l'État moderne. Le fonctionnement administratif de la papauté d'Avignon*, pp. 251–68. Rome: École française de Rome, 1990.

Tavernier, Eugène. "Le roi Giannino: étude historique." *Memoires de l'Académie des sciences, arts et belles lettres d'Aix* 11–12 (1882).

Il tesoro di un re [saggio della storia del re Giannino]. Ed. C. Mazzi. Rome: Forzani e C. tipografi del Senato, 1892.

Thompson, Stith. *Motif-index of Folk-literature. A classification of narrative elements in folktales, ballads, myths, fables, mediaeval romances, exempla, fabliaux, jest-books, and local legends*. Rev. ed., 6 vols. Bloomington: Indiana University Press; Copenhagen: Rosenkilde and Bagger, 1955–58.

———. *The Folktale*. Berkeley: University of California Press, 1977 (a reprint of the Dryden Press edition, New York, 1946, 1951).

Tizio, Sigismondo. *Historiae Senenses*, vol. 1, t. 1. Ed. Manuela Doni Garfagnini. Rome: Istituto storico italiano per l'età moderna e contemporanea, 1992; Rerum italicarum scriptores recentiores, 6.

———. *Historiae Senenses*, vol. 1, t. 2, part 1, ed. Grazia Tomasi Stussi Rome:

Istituto storico italiano per l'età moderna e contemporanea, 1995; Rerum italicarum scriptores recentiores, 10.

Tocco, Francesco Paolo. *Niccolò Acciaiuoli. Vita e politica in Italia alla metà del XIV secolo.* Rome: Istituto storico italiano per il medio evo, 2001; Nuovi studi storici, no. 52.

Ugurgieri Azzolini, Isidoro, *Le pompe sanesi o vero relazione delli huomini, e donne illustri di Siena e suo Stato* (Pistoia: Nella Stamperia di Pier Antonio Fortunati, 1649), 2 vols.

Urban V, Pope. *Lettres secrètes et curiales du pape Urbain V (1362–1370) se rapportant à la France.* Ed. Paul Lecacheux and Guillaume Mollat. Paris: E. de Boccard, 1954.

———. *Urbain V (1362–1370). Lettres communes analysées d'après les registres dits d'Avignon et du Vatican.* Ed. members of the l'École française de Rome and Marie-Hyacinthe Laurent, t. I. Rome: École française de Rome, 1954–58.

Vauchez, André. "'Beata stirps.' Sainteté et lignage en Occident aux XIIIe et XIVe siècles." In *Famille et parenté dans l'Occident médiéval,* pp. 337–99. Ed. Georges Duby and Jacques Le Goff. Rome: École française de Rome, 1977.

Villani, Giovanni. *Nuova Cronica.* Critical edition by Giuseppe Porta. 2 vols. Parma: Guanda, 1990–91.

Villani, Matteo. *Cronica, con la continuazione di Filippo Villani.* Critical edition by Giuseppe Porta. 2 vols. Parma: Guanda, 1995.

Wood, Charles T. "Where Is John the Posthumous? Or Mahaut of Artois Settles Her Royal Debts." In *Documenting the Past: Essays in Medieval History Presented to George Peddy Cuttino,* pp. 99–117. Ed. J. S. Hamilton and P. J. Bradley. Wolfeboro, NH: Boydell Press, 1989.

———. *The French Apanages and the Capetian Monarchy, 1224–1328.* Cambridge, MA: Harvard University Press, 1966.

INDEX

·◁▭▷·

Colombiers, Cardinal Pierre Bertrand de, 79
Colonna, Pietro di Giordano, 46
Colonna family, 23
Comtat Venaissin, 72, 82, 93
Corradino of Swabia, 135, 155
Count Lando: see Konrad von Landau
Courneuve, Pierre de La, 80, 87, 91, 142
Court, Cardinal Guillaume (the "White Cardinal"), 79, 85
Crécy, battle of, 40, 138
Cressay, 6, 8, 25, 36–37, 43, 136, 191
Cressay, Dame Éliabel de, 6, 34
Cressay, Dame Marie de, 6–8, 11, 22, 25–26, 30, 32–36, 38–40, 78, 131–32, 136–37, 139, 157
Cressay, Pierre and Jeannot de, 6, 8, 33–34, 40
Cressay, Sieur Piquart de, 6, 33–34, 136
Cronos, 150
cross (bodily mark of royalty), 123–29, 192
Cyrus the Great, 150

Daniello, 52–53, 57, 64, 81, 84, 88, 95, 109–11, 115–16, 141–42
Dauphin, the (= Charles, duke of Normandy, Dauphin of Viennois), 45, 49, 60, 72, 74, 76, 79, 88, 96, 125
Dauphiné, 89, 94
Davis, Natalie Zemon, 142
derision: see beffa
Després, Cardinal Pierre, 74, 86
Disney Studios, 150
Druon, Maurice, 156, 197
Dumas, Alexandre, 154

Edward, the Black Prince, 43, 49
Edward III, king of England, 16, 18, 49, 74–75, 84, 86
Egidius Romanus, 144
Elizabeth of Poland, 60
emblems (including coats of arms, standards, and flags; see also seals), 18–19, 61, 91, 111, 129
Évreux, county of (and house of), 75, 77

Falconari, Torello, 110
Filippo di Taranto, 109, 110
Flammini, Michele, abbot of Vallombrosa, 80
Florence, cardinal of: see Atti, Cardinal Francesco degli
Flovus (legendary founder of French monarchy), 13, 111, 192
folktale (including motifs, oral transmission, popular myth), 31, 128–29, 131, 133–35, 138–39, 148–49, 195
forgery, 32, 46–47, 59, 60–61, 76, 106, 119, 123, 127–28, 147, 169, 182; see also Louis of Hungary
Fortiguerra, Agnolo di Pietro, 44
Foucault, Michel, 191
fourteenth-century crisis, 14–18
France, royals of (in legend, literature, and the popular imaginary), 124, 128–30, 138, 151–53, 192
Francesco di Mino di Buonconte dal Cotone, alias "the Bishop," 55–60, 80, 139, 142
Francesco of Montefioralle, 99, 103
Francis of Assisi, 14
Franciscans, 5, 174

Jeanne of Artois, 33
Jehoash, 149
Jehoiada, 149
Jerusalem (including Holy Land and
    sepulcher of Christ), 9, 11, 15,
    17–18, 37, 43, 53, 130
Jesus Christ, 62, 141–42, 150–51
Jewish community, 52–53, 57, 141–42,
    173, 193
Joachim of Fiore, 14
John the Baptist, 14, 33
John the Evangelist, 151
John XXII, pope, 157
Joinville, Jean de, 156
jubilee year of 1350, 11, 27, 44, 130

Konrad von Landau ("Count Lando"),
    50–52, 55, 64
Konth, Nicholas, 55–56, 59

Lancaster, duke of, 79, 84
Landi, Pietro, 28
languages (Tuscan, Latin, French), 6,
    26, 32, 131, 134, 166, 170, 189
Le Goff, Jacques, 120
Lecuppre, Gilles, 121, 185–86
Léonard, É. G., 176, 189
Louis, saint, of Anjou, 165
Louis IX, king of France and saint, 10,
    12, 17, 25, 106, 111, 120, 129–30,
    189–90
Louis X the Quarrelsome ("le Hutin"),
    king of France, 6, 9, 12, 22, 25,
    30, 32, 39, 61, 68, 75, 77, 98, 111,
    133, 156
Louis the Great of Anjou, king of
    Hungary, 47, 49–52, 54–55, 58,
    121, 143–44, 174–75; the letter pur-

portedly from him in the Sienese
    archives, 61–63, 67–69, 139–40
Luchetto of Pistoia, 85
Luigi, duke of Durazzo, 109
Luigi I of Taranto, king of Naples, 58,
    71, 80, 96, 98, 100–103, 108–10,
    122
Lyon, 84–86, 91

Maccari, Latino, 167, 171, 181, 185–88
Mahaut, Countess of Artois, 33–35,
    39, 62, 132, 134, 148, 156–57, 170,
    197
Maiella Mountains, 5
Malavolti, Vanni, 44
Manfredi of Sicily, 135
Marcel, Étienne, 45, 76, 80, 86, 152
Marguerite, queen of Burgundy, 30, 39
Marie of Navarre, 79
marriage, clandestine, 6, 166
Marseille, 103, 105–8
Martelli, Giovanni di Bartalo, 78
Mattano da Siena: see Gentile Sermini
Matteo, seneschal of Provence: see
    Gesualdo, Matteo
Mazzi, Curzio, 188
mercenaries, 65, 81–84, 88–91, 93–94,
    100, 103, 142, 172, 175, 179
merchants, 167, 190
Michele di ser Monaldo, 44
Mini, Friar Bartolomeo, 29, 43, 46, 129,
    133, 144–45, 194
Mino di Geri Baglioni, 25–26, 28, 71,
    137, 167
Molay, Jacques de, 156
Monferrato, marchese of, 51, 64, 103
Monmerqué, Louis de, 153–54, 170,
    185, 186

solar imagery, 18–19, 61, 91, 129, 176
Swabia, 135

Talleyrand, cardinal Élias de, 87
Tartars and Turks, 52–53, 57, 81, 141,
    172–73
Templars, 156
Thomas, archbishop of Kalocsa,
    55–56
Tizio, Sigismondo, 171, 187–88
Tolkien, J. R. R., 150
Tolomei, Luca, 74, 103
Tolomei, Spinello (and Tolomei com-
    pany of Siena), 6, 10–11, 15, 26,
    33, 44, 167
Tommaso of Montella, 72
Tora, Monna, 88, 96, 98
Turks: *see* Tartars and Turks
Twain, Mark, 148

Ubaldini, Federico degli, 80, 94
Ugolini, Bonaventura, 26, 27
Ulysses, 150
Urban V, pope, 184

Valori, Niccolò di Taldo, 54, 59
Vannino di Guccio di Baglione, 29
Venice, 52–53
Vernee, Giovanni (or: Johannes de
    Vernayo), 84, 86, 88, 91, 99–101,
    122, 125, 179
Villani, Giovanni, 135
Villani, Matteo, 82, 89–90, 93, 123, 180,
    186
Villeneuve (modern name: Villeneuve
    lez Avignon), 72, 84, 89
Villon, François, 151
Visconti, Giovanni, of Oleggio, lord
    of Bologna, 51, 64
Visegrád, 55

wet nursing, 30, 31, 169
White Cardinal: *see* Court, Cardinal
    Guillaume
wool trade, 26, 28, 67–68

Xenophon, 150

Zeus, 150